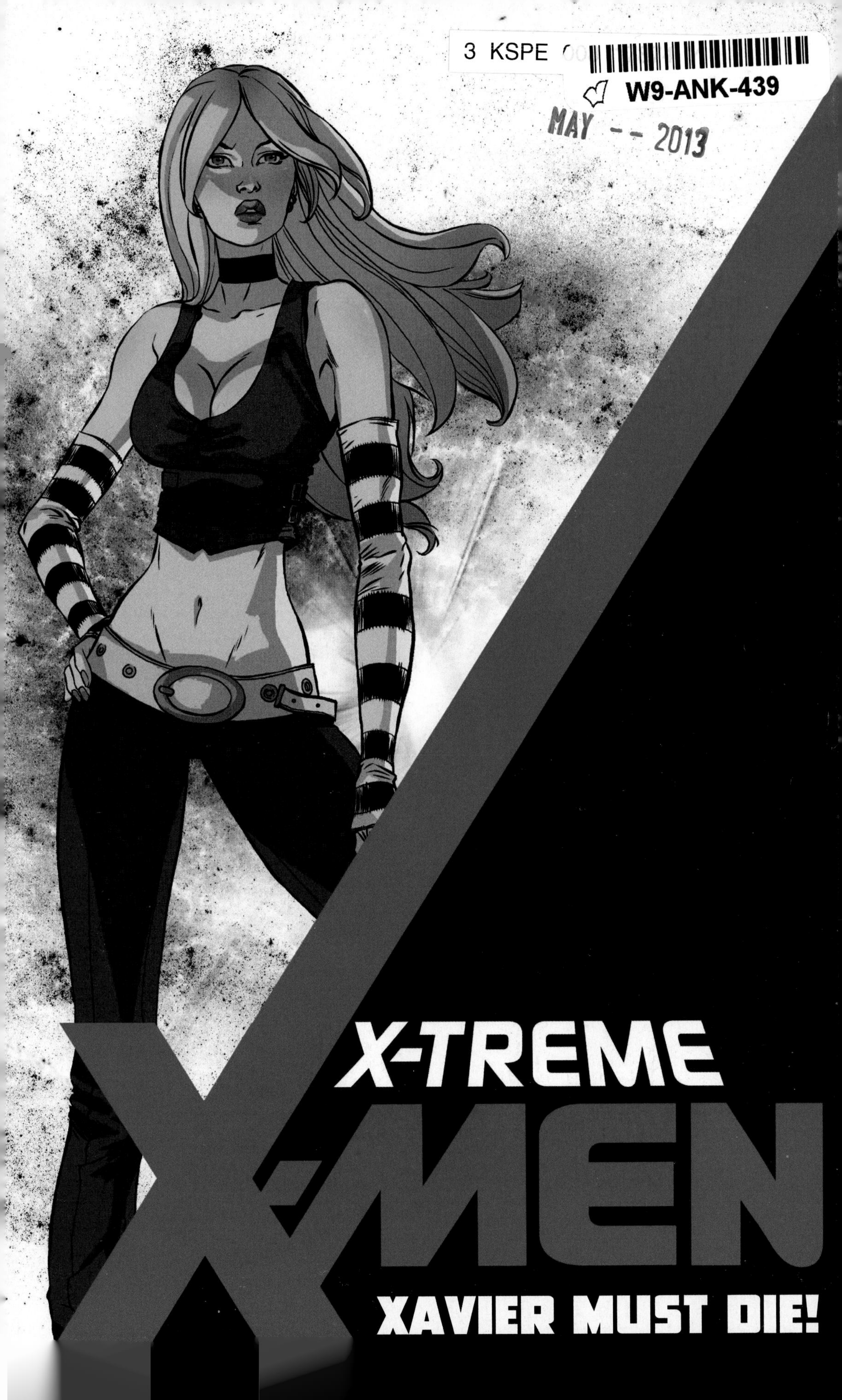
X-TREME
X-MEN
XAVIER MUST DIE!

X-TREME X-MEN VOL. 1: XAVIER MUST DIE! Contains material originally published in magazine form as X-TREME X-MEN #1-5. First printing 2013. ISBN# 978-0-7851-6564-4. Published by MARVEL WORLDWIDE, INC., a subsidiary of MARVEL ENTERTAINMENT, LLC. OFFICE OF PUBLICATION: 135 West 50th Street, New York, NY 10020. Copyright © 2012 and 2013 Marvel Characters, Inc. All rights reserved. All characters featured in this issue and the distinctive names and likenesses thereof, and all related indicia are trademarks of Marvel Characters, Inc. No similarity between any of the names, characters, persons, and/or institutions in this magazine with those of any living or dead person or institution is intended, and any such similarity which may exist is purely coincidental. **Printed in the U.S.A.** ALAN FINE, EVP - Office of the President, Marvel Worldwide, Inc. and EVP & CMO Marvel Characters B.V.; DAN BUCKLEY, Publisher & President - Print, Animation & Digital Divisions; JOE QUESADA, Chief Creative Officer; TOM BREVOORT, SVP of Publishing; DAVID BOGART, SVP of Operations & Procurement, Publishing; RUWAN JAYATILLEKE, SVP & Associate Publisher, Publishing; C.B. CEBULSKI, SVP of Creator & Content Development; DAVID GABRIEL, SVP of Print & Digital Publishing Sales; JIM O'KEEFE, VP of Operations & Logistics; DAN CARR, Executive Director of Publishing Technology; SUSAN CRESPI, Editorial Operations Manager; ALEX MORALES, Publishing Operations Manager; STAN LEE, Chairman Emeritus. For information regarding advertising in Marvel Comics or on Marvel.com, please contact Niza Disla, Director of Marvel Partnerships, at ndisla@marvel.com. For Marvel subscription inquiries, please call 800-217-9158. **Manufactured between 1/10/2013 and 2/12/2013 by QUAD/GRAPHICS, DUBUQUE, IA, USA.**

10987654321

X-TREME X-MEN
XAVIER MUST DIE!

WRITER: **GREG PAK**

PENCILERS: **STEPHEN SEGOVIA** (#1-3) & **PACO DIAZ** (#3-5)

INKERS:
DENNIS CRISOSTOMO
(#1-3) & **PACO DIAZ** (#3-5)
WITH **WALDEN WONG** (#2)
& **JASON PAZ** (#2)

COLORIST: **JESSICA KHOLINNE** (#1-5) WITH **SOTOCOLOR**
(#2-3), **BENY MAULANA** (#3), **CHRIS SOTOMAYOR** (#4-5)
& **JIM CHARALAMPIDIS** (#5)

LETTERER: **VC'S JOE SABINO**

COVER ART: **JULIAN TOTINO TEDESCO** (#1) & **KALMAN ANDRASOFSZKY** (#2-5)

ASSISTANT EDITOR:
JENNIFER M. SMITH

EDITOR:
JEANINE SCHAEFER

X-MEN GROUP EDITOR:
NICK LOWE

COLLECTION EDITOR:
JENNIFER GRÜNWALD

ASSISTANT EDITORS:
ALEX STARBUCK &
NELSON RIBEIRO

EDITOR,
SPECIAL PROJECTS:
MARK D. BEAZLEY

SENIOR EDITOR,
SPECIAL PROJECTS:
JEFF YOUNGQUIST

SENIOR VICE
PRESIDENT OF SALES:
DAVID GABRIEL

BOOK DESIGNER:
RODOLFO MURAGUCHI

EDITOR IN CHIEF:
AXEL ALONSO

CHIEF CREATIVE OFFICER:
JOE QUESADA

PUBLISHER:
DAN BUCKLEY

EXECUTIVE PRODUCER:
ALAN FINE

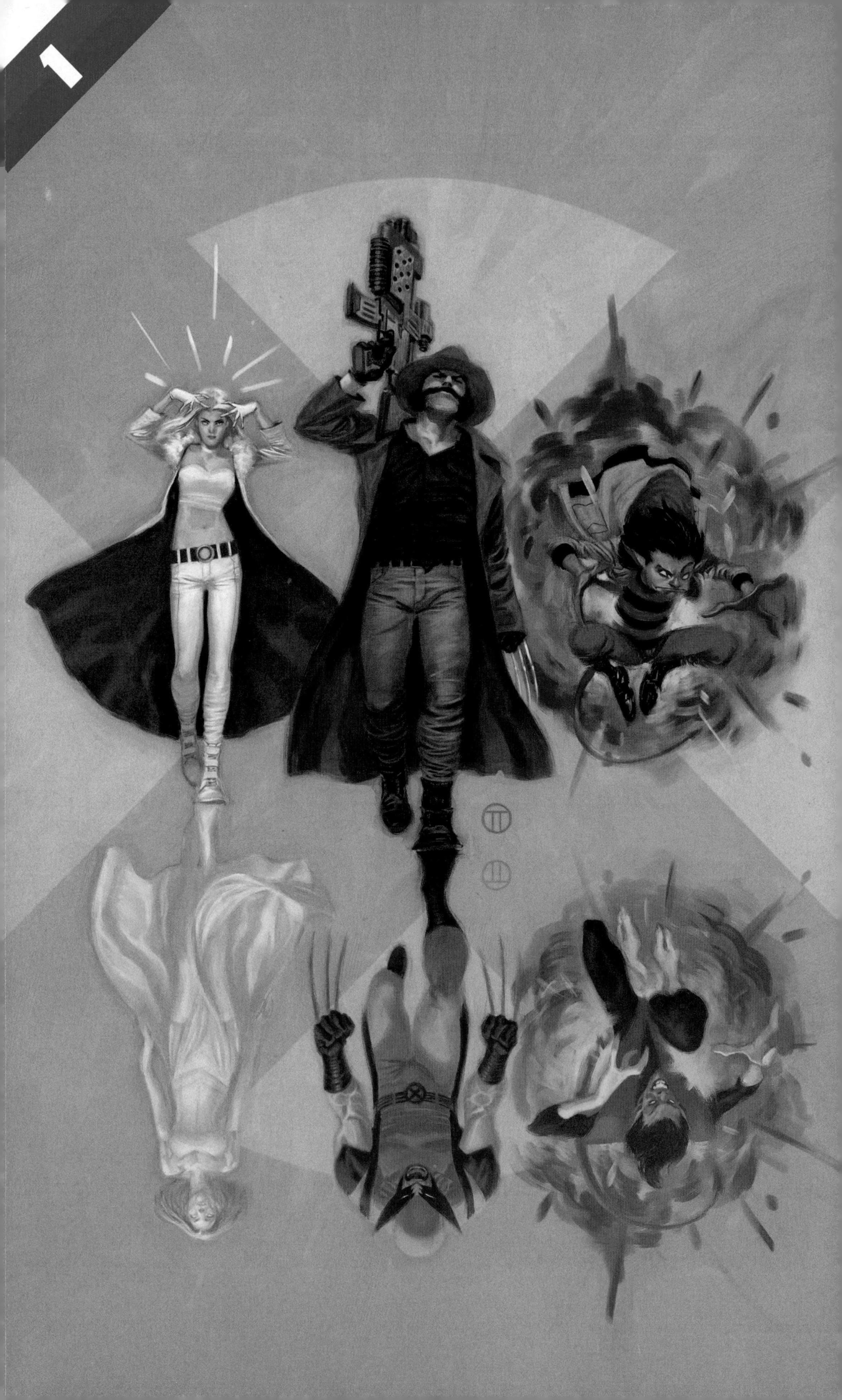
1

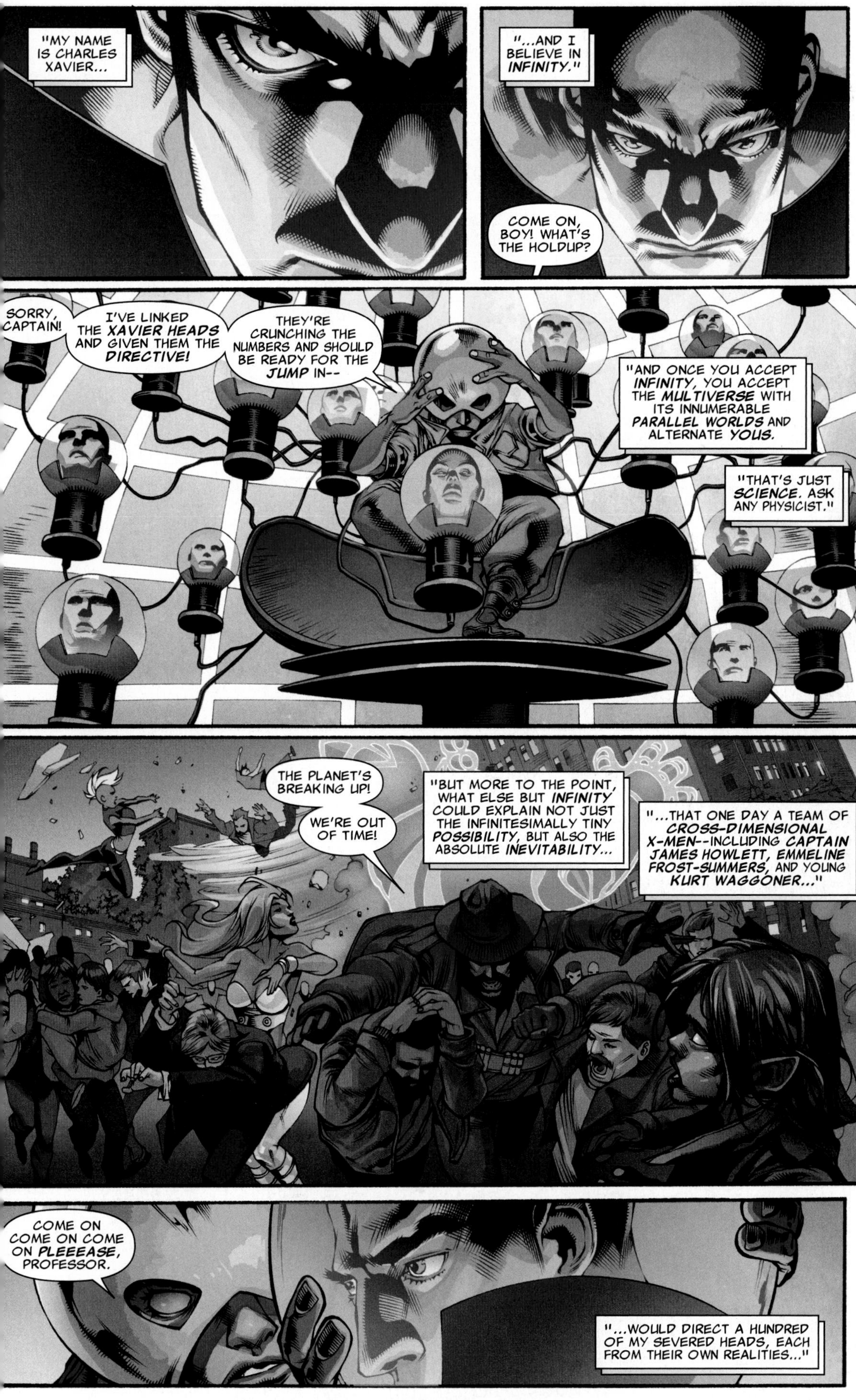
"MY NAME IS CHARLES XAVIER...
"...AND I BELIEVE IN INFINITY."
COME ON, BOY! WHAT'S THE HOLDUP?
SORRY, CAPTAIN!
I'VE LINKED THE XAVIER HEADS AND GIVEN THEM THE DIRECTIVE!
THEY'RE CRUNCHING THE NUMBERS AND SHOULD BE READY FOR THE JUMP IN--
"AND ONCE YOU ACCEPT INFINITY, YOU ACCEPT THE MULTIVERSE WITH ITS INNUMERABLE PARALLEL WORLDS AND ALTERNATE YOUS.
"THAT'S JUST SCIENCE. ASK ANY PHYSICIST."
THE PLANET'S BREAKING UP!
WE'RE OUT OF TIME!
"BUT MORE TO THE POINT, WHAT ELSE BUT INFINITY COULD EXPLAIN NOT JUST THE INFINITESIMALLY TINY POSSIBILITY, BUT ALSO THE ABSOLUTE INEVITABILITY...
"...THAT ONE DAY A TEAM OF CROSS-DIMENSIONAL X-MEN--INCLUDING CAPTAIN JAMES HOWLETT, EMMELINE FROST-SUMMERS, AND YOUNG KURT WAGGONER..."
COME ON COME ON COME ON PLEEEASE, PROFESSOR.
"...WOULD DIRECT A HUNDRED OF MY SEVERED HEADS, EACH FROM THEIR OWN REALITIES..."

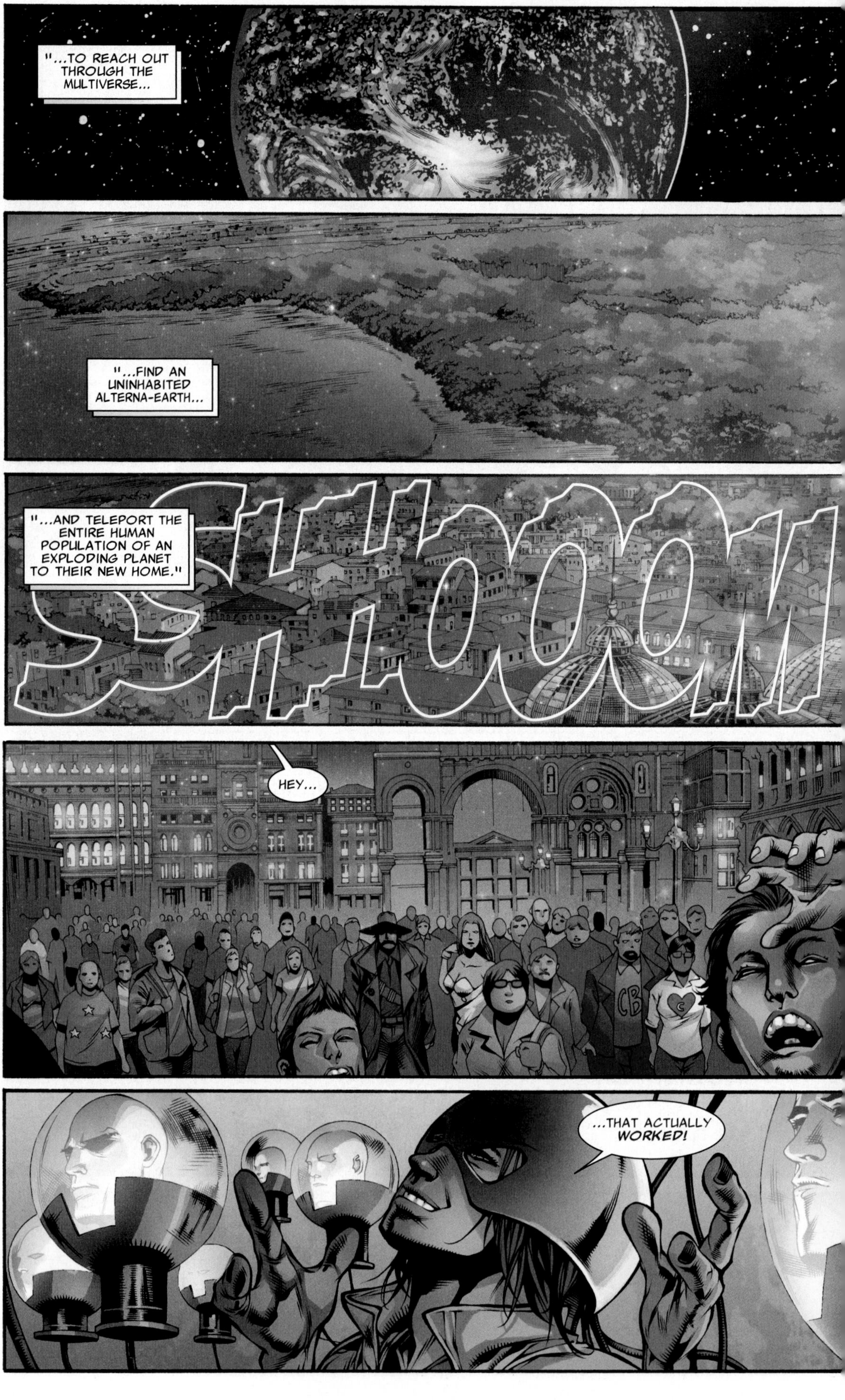
"...TO REACH OUT THROUGH THE MULTIVERSE...
"...FIND AN UNINHABITED ALTERNA-EARTH...
"...AND TELEPORT THE ENTIRE HUMAN POPULATION OF AN EXPLODING PLANET TO THEIR NEW HOME."
SHHOOOM
HEY...
...THAT ACTUALLY WORKED!

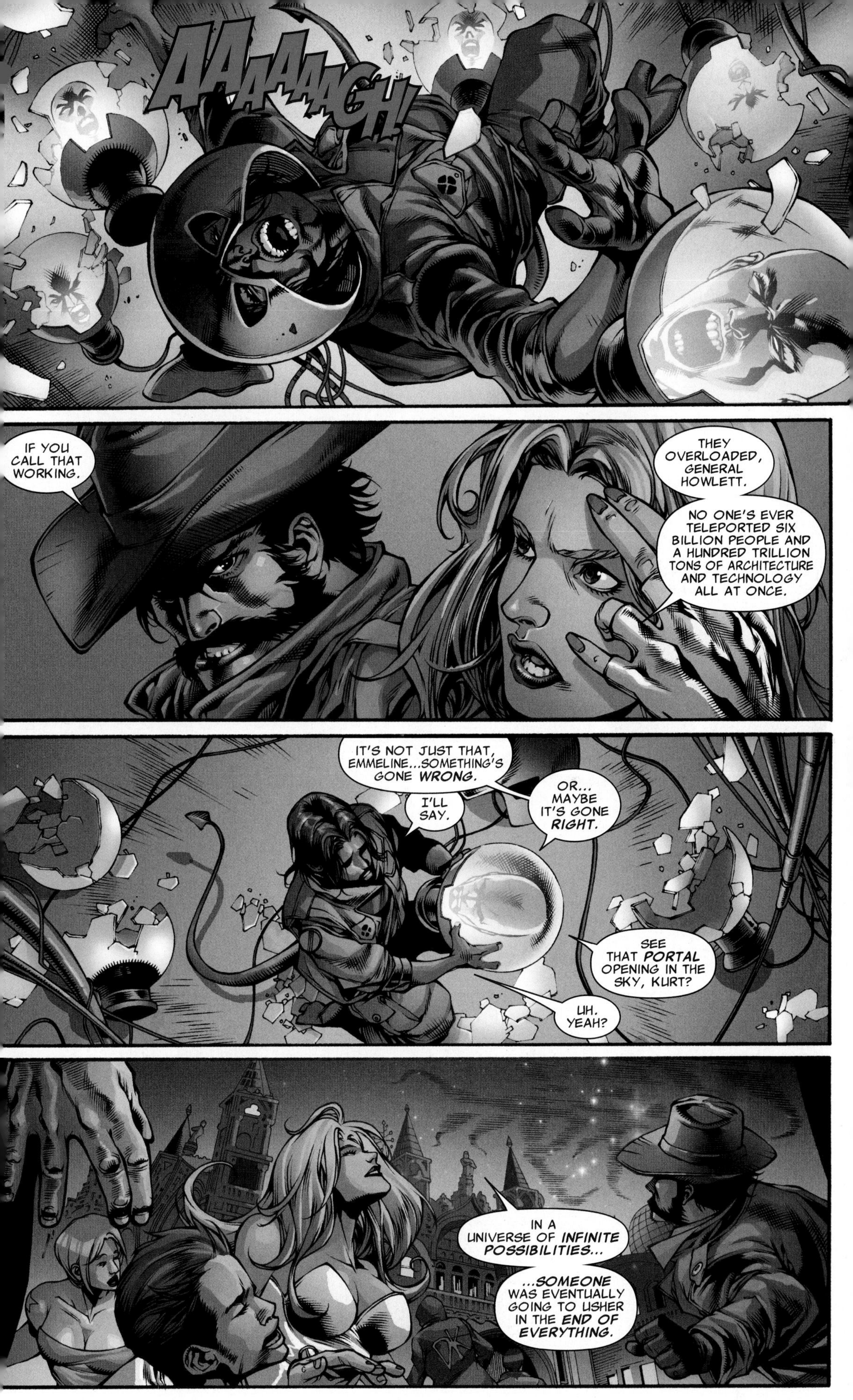
AAAAAAGH!
IF YOU CALL THAT WORKING.
THEY OVERLOADED, GENERAL HOWLETT.
NO ONE'S EVER TELEPORTED SIX BILLION PEOPLE AND A HUNDRED TRILLION TONS OF ARCHITECTURE AND TECHNOLOGY ALL AT ONCE.
IT'S NOT JUST THAT, EMMELINE...SOMETHING'S GONE **WRONG**.
I'LL SAY.
OR... MAYBE IT'S GONE **RIGHT**.
SEE THAT **PORTAL** OPENING IN THE SKY, KURT?
UH. YEAH?
IN A UNIVERSE OF ***INFINITE POSSIBILITIES***...
...***SOMEONE*** WAS EVENTUALLY GOING TO USHER IN THE ***END OF EVERYTHING***.

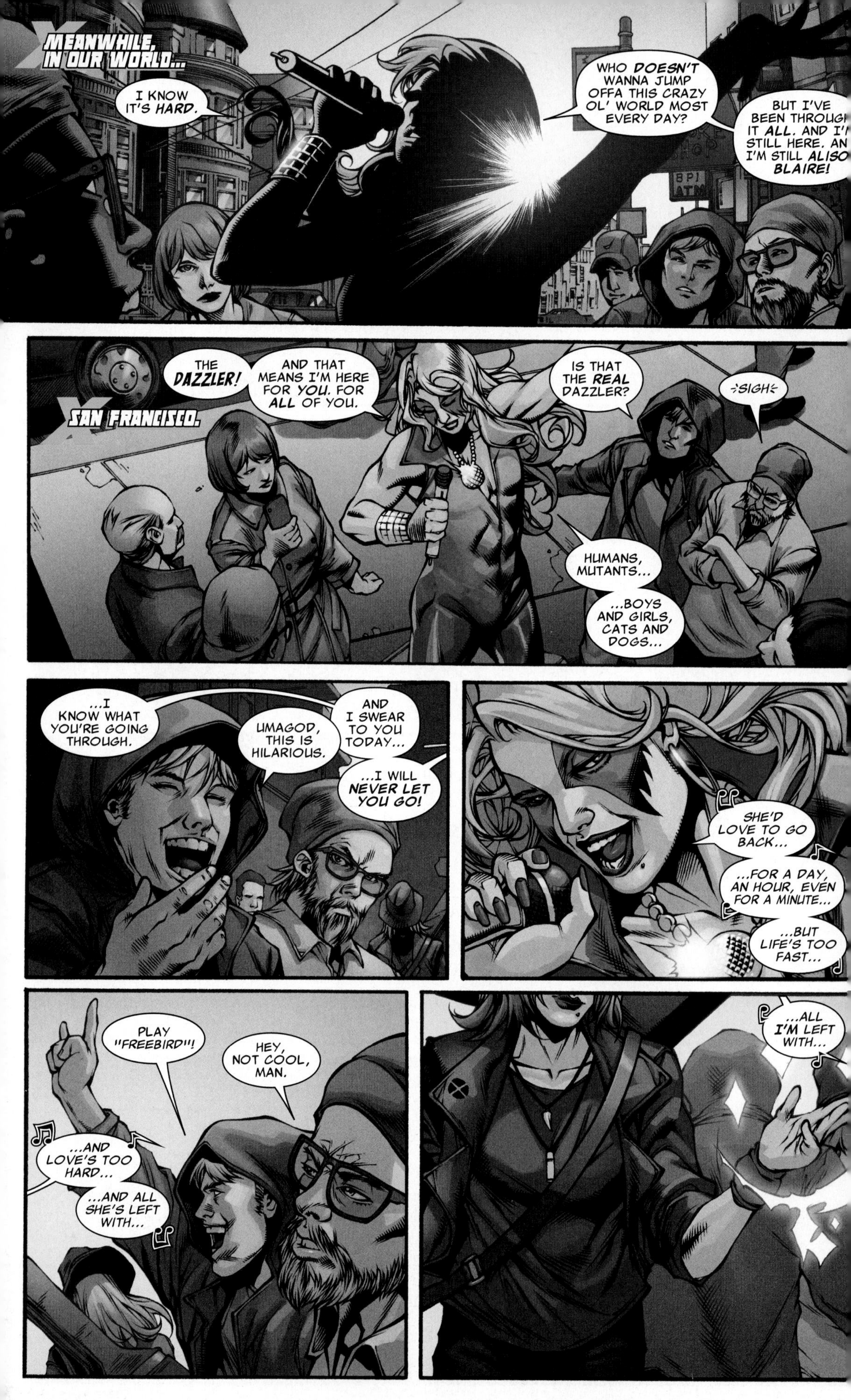

MEANWHILE, IN OUR WORLD...
I KNOW IT'S HARD.
WHO DOESN'T WANNA JUMP OFFA THIS CRAZY OL' WORLD MOST EVERY DAY?
BUT I'VE BEEN THROUG IT ALL. AND I' STILL HERE. AN I'M STILL ALISO BLAIRE!
SAN FRANCISCO.
THE DAZZLER!
AND THAT MEANS I'M HERE FOR YOU. FOR ALL OF YOU.
IS THAT THE REAL DAZZLER?
SIGH
HUMANS, MUTANTS...
...BOYS AND GIRLS, CATS AND DOGS...
...I KNOW WHAT YOU'RE GOING THROUGH.
UMAGOD, THIS IS HILARIOUS.
AND I SWEAR TO YOU TODAY...
...I WILL NEVER LET YOU GO!
SHE'D LOVE TO GO BACK...
...FOR A DAY, AN HOUR, EVEN FOR A MINUTE...
...BUT LIFE'S TOO FAST...
PLAY "FREEBIRD"!
HEY, NOT COOL, MAN.
...AND LOVE'S TOO HARD...
...AND ALL SHE'S LEFT WITH...
...ALL I'M LEFT WITH...

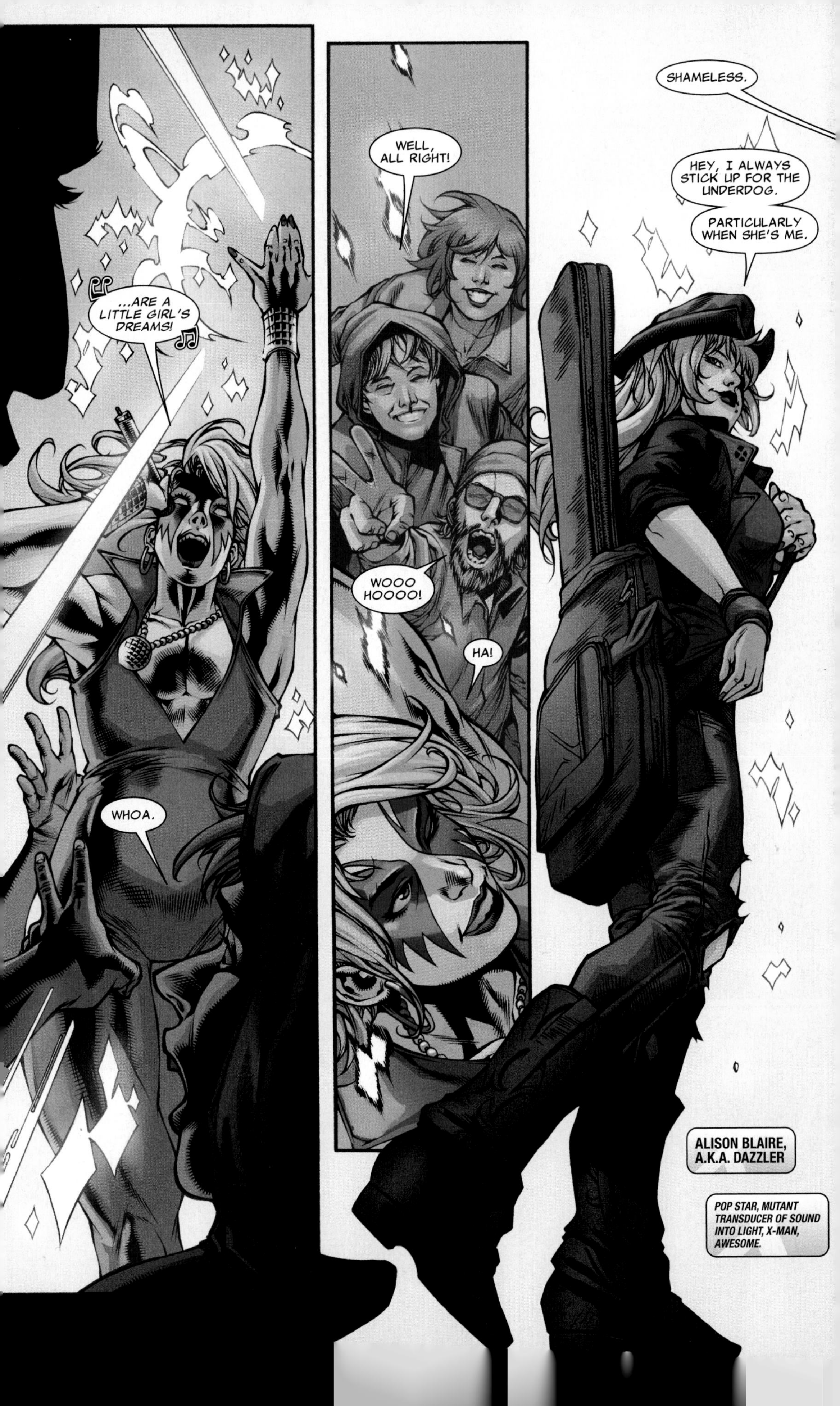
...ARE A LITTLE GIRL'S DREAMS!
WHOA.
WELL, ALL RIGHT!
WOOO HOOOO!
HA!
SHAMELESS.
HEY, I ALWAYS STICK UP FOR THE UNDERDOG.
PARTICULARLY WHEN SHE'S ME.
ALISON BLAIRE, A.K.A. DAZZLER
POP STAR, MUTANT TRANSDUCER OF SOUND INTO LIGHT, X-MAN, AWESOME.

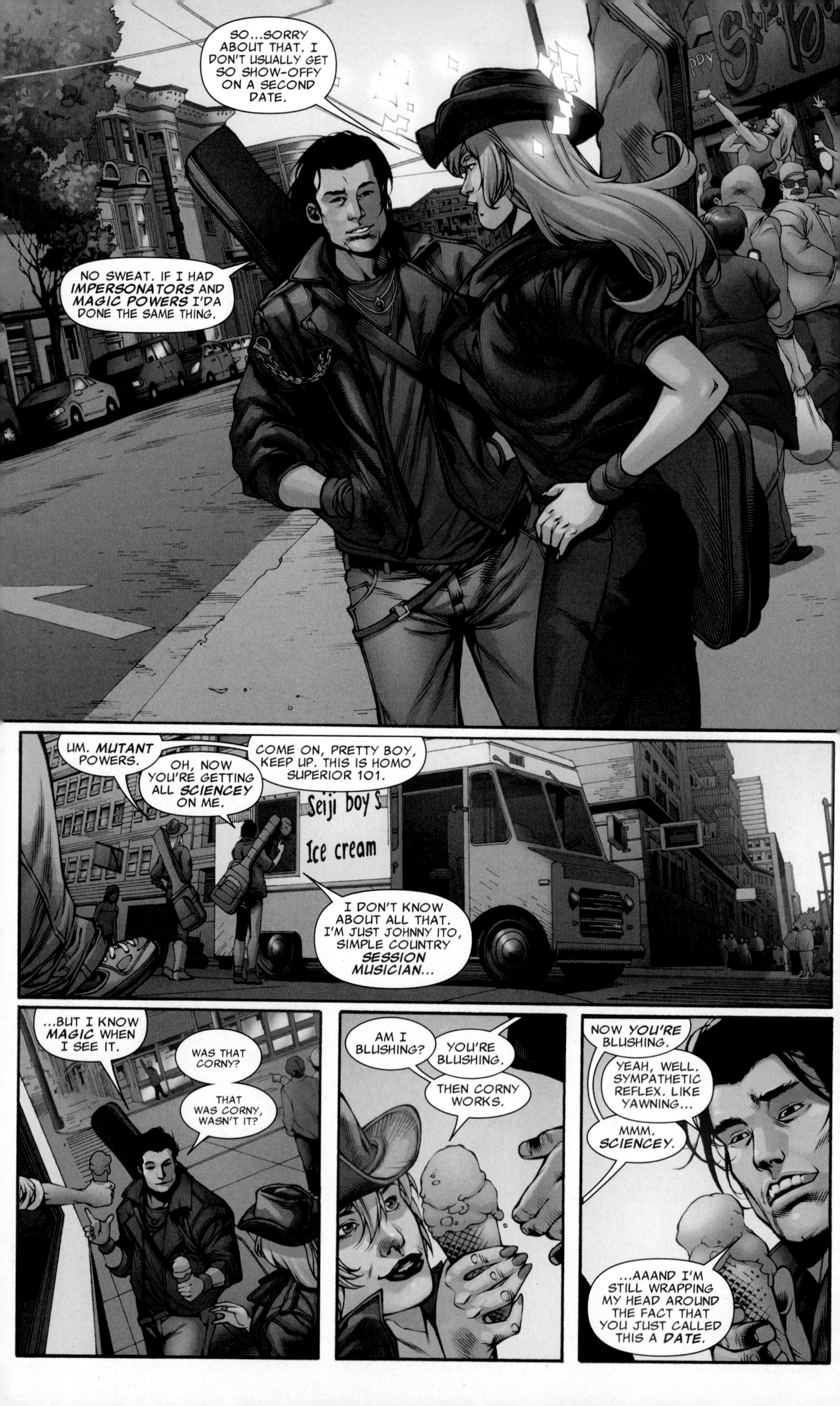
SO...SORRY ABOUT THAT. I DON'T USUALLY GET SO SHOW-OFFY ON A SECOND DATE.
NO SWEAT. IF I HAD IMPERSONATORS AND MAGIC POWERS I'DA DONE THE SAME THING.
UM. MUTANT POWERS.
OH, NOW YOU'RE GETTING ALL SCIENCEY ON ME.
COME ON, PRETTY BOY, KEEP UP. THIS IS HOMO SUPERIOR 101.
Seiji boy's
Ice cream
I DON'T KNOW ABOUT ALL THAT. I'M JUST JOHNNY ITO, SIMPLE COUNTRY SESSION MUSICIAN...
...BUT I KNOW MAGIC WHEN I SEE IT.
WAS THAT CORNY?
THAT WAS CORNY, WASN'T IT?
AM I BLUSHING?
YOU'RE BLUSHING.
THEN CORNY WORKS.
NOW YOU'RE BLUSHING.
YEAH, WELL. SYMPATHETIC REFLEX. LIKE YAWNING...
MMM. SCIENCEY.
...AAAND I'M STILL WRAPPING MY HEAD AROUND THE FACT THAT YOU JUST CALLED THIS A DATE.

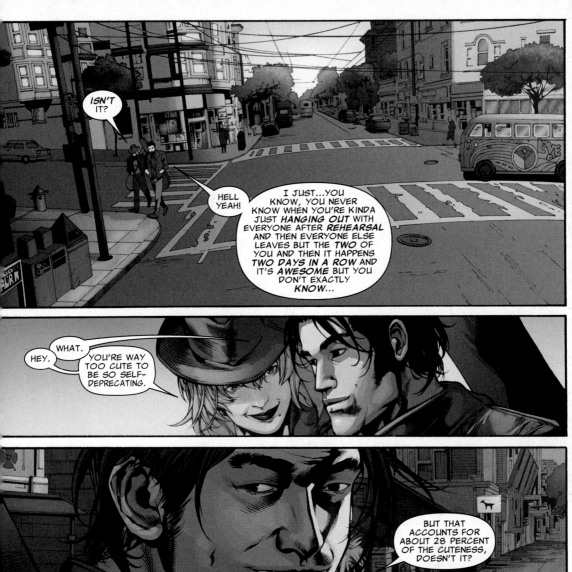

ISN'T IT?

HELL YEAH!

I JUST...YOU KNOW, YOU NEVER KNOW WHEN YOU'RE KINDA JUST *HANGING OUT* WITH EVERYONE AFTER *REHEARSAL* AND THEN EVERYONE ELSE LEAVES BUT THE *TWO OF YOU* AND THEN IT HAPPENS *TWO DAYS IN A ROW* AND IT'S *AWESOME* BUT YOU DON'T EXACTLY *KNOW*...

HEY.

WHAT.

YOU'RE WAY TOO CUTE TO BE SO SELF-DEPRECATING.

BUT THAT ACCOUNTS FOR ABOUT 28 PERCENT OF THE CUTENESS, DOESN'T IT?

ALL RIGHT.

I THINK I'M ABOUT TO MAKE SOME RASH DECISIONS.

SWEET.

RING RING

OH, HELL.

DAZZLER-- REPORT TO UTOPIA

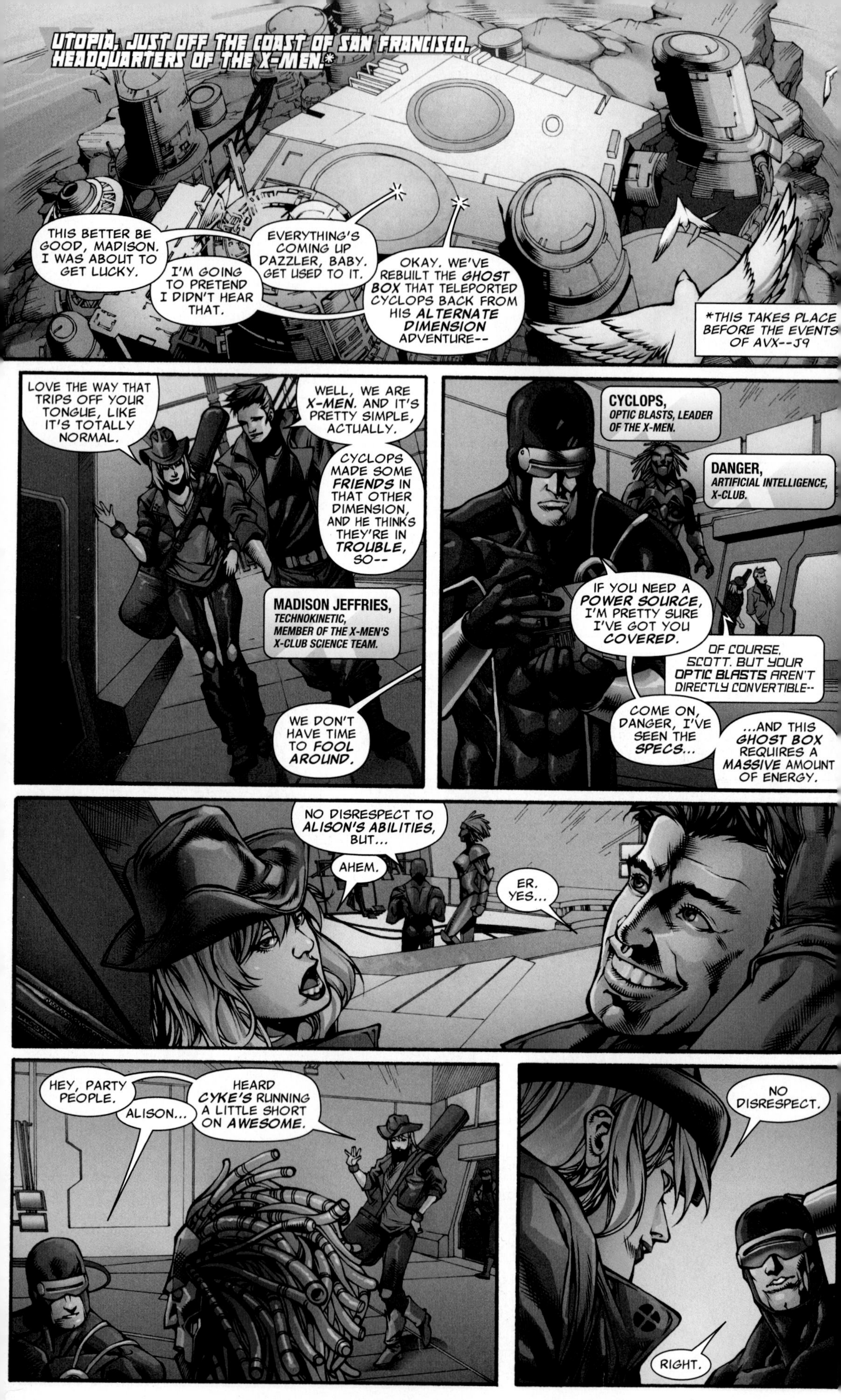
UTOPIA, JUST OFF THE COAST OF SAN FRANCISCO. HEADQUARTERS OF THE X-MEN.*
THIS BETTER BE GOOD, MADISON. I WAS ABOUT TO GET LUCKY.
EVERYTHING'S COMING UP DAZZLER, BABY. GET USED TO IT.
I'M GOING TO PRETEND I DIDN'T HEAR THAT.
OKAY. WE'VE REBUILT THE GHOST BOX THAT TELEPORTED CYCLOPS BACK FROM HIS ALTERNATE DIMENSION ADVENTURE--
*THIS TAKES PLACE BEFORE THE EVENTS OF AVX--J9
LOVE THE WAY THAT TRIPS OFF YOUR TONGUE, LIKE IT'S TOTALLY NORMAL.
WELL, WE ARE X-MEN. AND IT'S PRETTY SIMPLE, ACTUALLY.
CYCLOPS MADE SOME FRIENDS IN THAT OTHER DIMENSION, AND HE THINKS THEY'RE IN TROUBLE, SO--
MADISON JEFFRIES, TECHNOKINETIC, MEMBER OF THE X-MEN'S X-CLUB SCIENCE TEAM.
WE DON'T HAVE TIME TO FOOL AROUND.
CYCLOPS, OPTIC BLASTS, LEADER OF THE X-MEN.
DANGER, ARTIFICIAL INTELLIGENCE, X-CLUB.
IF YOU NEED A POWER SOURCE, I'M PRETTY SURE I'VE GOT YOU COVERED.
OF COURSE, SCOTT. BUT YOUR OPTIC BLASTS AREN'T DIRECTLY CONVERTIBLE--
COME ON, DANGER, I'VE SEEN THE SPECS...
...AND THIS GHOST BOX REQUIRES A MASSIVE AMOUNT OF ENERGY.
NO DISRESPECT TO ALISON'S ABILITIES, BUT...
AHEM.
ER. YES...
HEY, PARTY PEOPLE.
ALISON...
HEARD CYKE'S RUNNING A LITTLE SHORT ON AWESOME.
NO DISRESPECT.
RIGHT.

ALISON, WE CAN GENERATE ANY KIND OF SOUND YOU NEED...

S'ALL RIGHT. I GET BETTER CONTROL THIS WAY.

GOOD. THE SYSTEM'S BUILT AROUND A NETWORK OF CONCENTRATED PHOTOVOLTAICS--

JUST TELL ME WHERE TO HIT IT, BABY.

THE LITTLE RED DOT.

DON'T SWEAT IT, SCOTT. I UNDERSTAND.

WASN'T AWARE I WAS SWEATING ANYTHING.

HEH. IT'S EASY TO UNDERESTIMATE THE DAZZ.

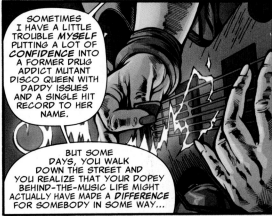

SOMETIMES I HAVE A LITTLE TROUBLE MYSELF PUTTING A LOT OF CONFIDENCE INTO A FORMER DRUG ADDICT MUTANT DISCO QUEEN WITH DADDY ISSUES AND A SINGLE HIT RECORD TO HER NAME.

BUT SOME DAYS, YOU WALK DOWN THE STREET AND YOU REALIZE THAT YOUR DOPEY BEHIND-THE-MUSIC LIFE MIGHT ACTUALLY HAVE MADE A DIFFERENCE FOR SOMEBODY IN SOME WAY...

...SO IT'S ALL GOOD.

NO, ALISON...

...IT'S PERFECT.

GHOST BOX IS 100 PERCENT POWERED. OBSERVATION PORTAL IS OPENING.

THANKS, DAZZLER.

NO SWEAT.

ALL RIGHT. NOW STEP BACK. WE DON'T KNOW WHAT--

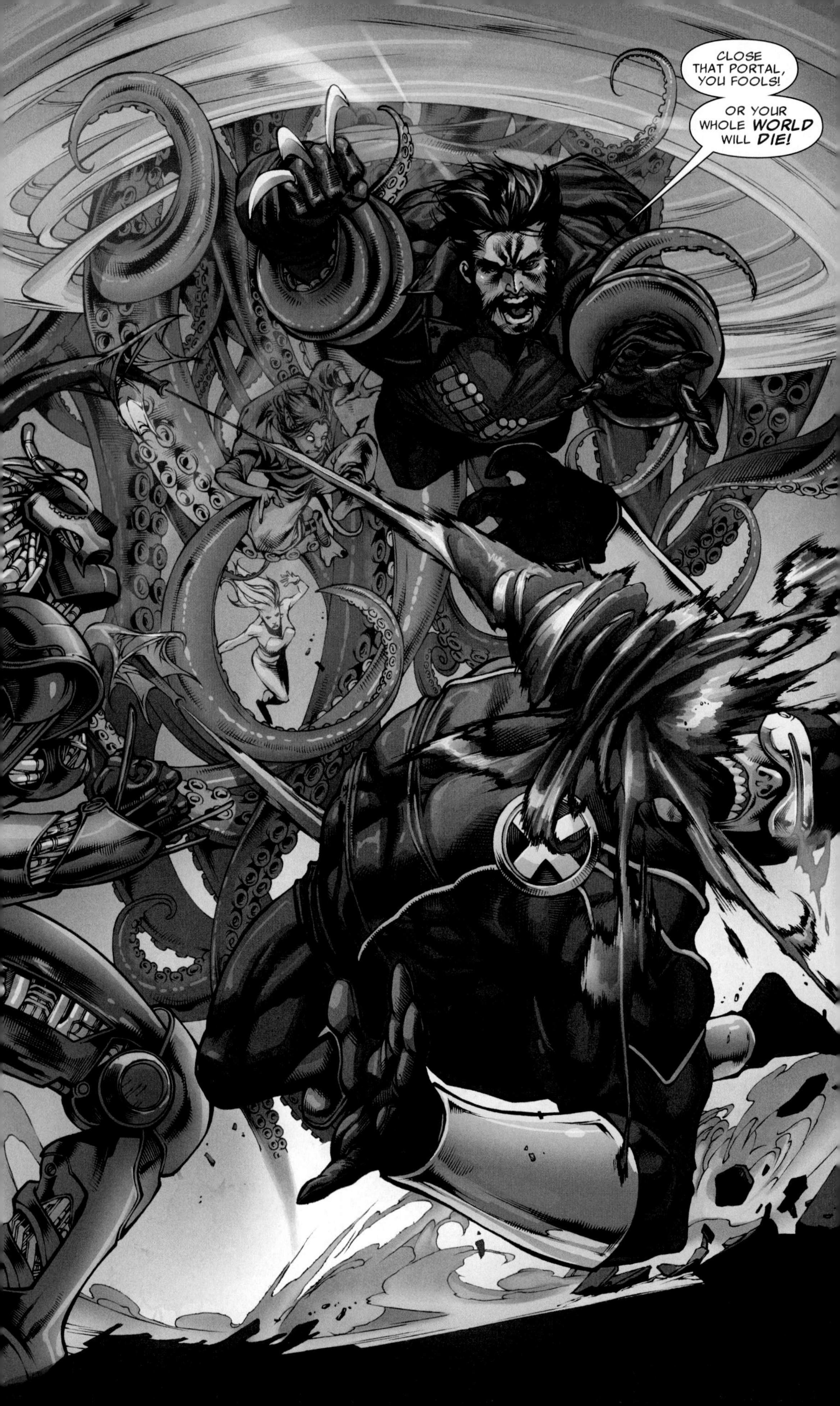
CLOSE THAT PORTAL, YOU FOOLS!
OR YOUR WHOLE WORLD WILL DIE!

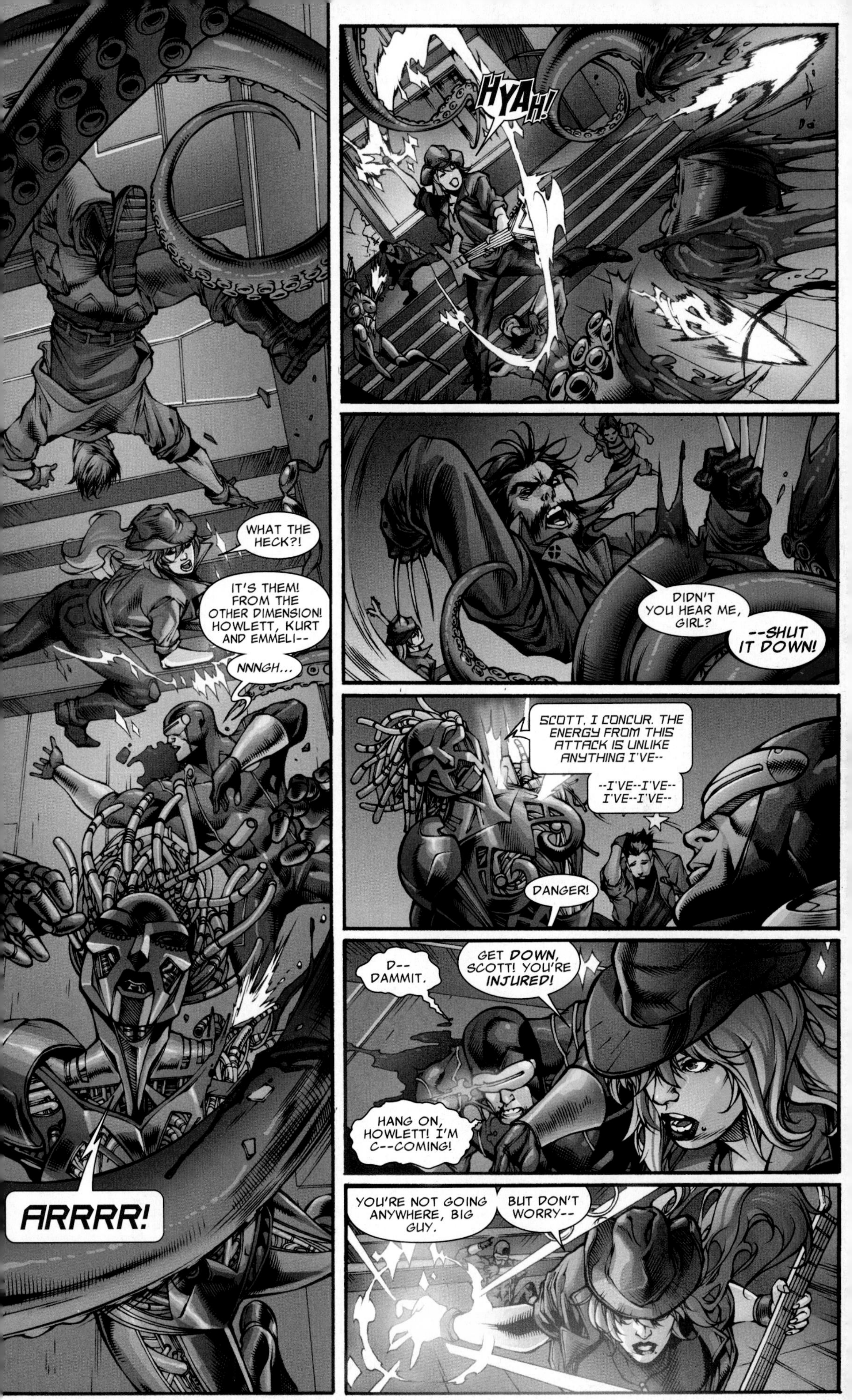
WHAT THE HECK?!
IT'S THEM! FROM THE OTHER DIMENSION! HOWLETT, KURT AND EMMELI--
NNNGH...
ARRRR!
HYAH!
DIDN'T YOU HEAR ME, GIRL?
--SHUT IT DOWN!
SCOTT, I CONCUR. THE ENERGY FROM THIS ATTACK IS UNLIKE ANYTHING I'VE--
--I'VE--I'VE--I'VE--I'VE--
DANGER!
D--DAMMIT.
GET DOWN, SCOTT! YOU'RE INJURED!
HANG ON, HOWLETT! I'M C--COMING!
YOU'RE NOT GOING ANYWHERE, BIG GUY.
BUT DON'T WORRY--

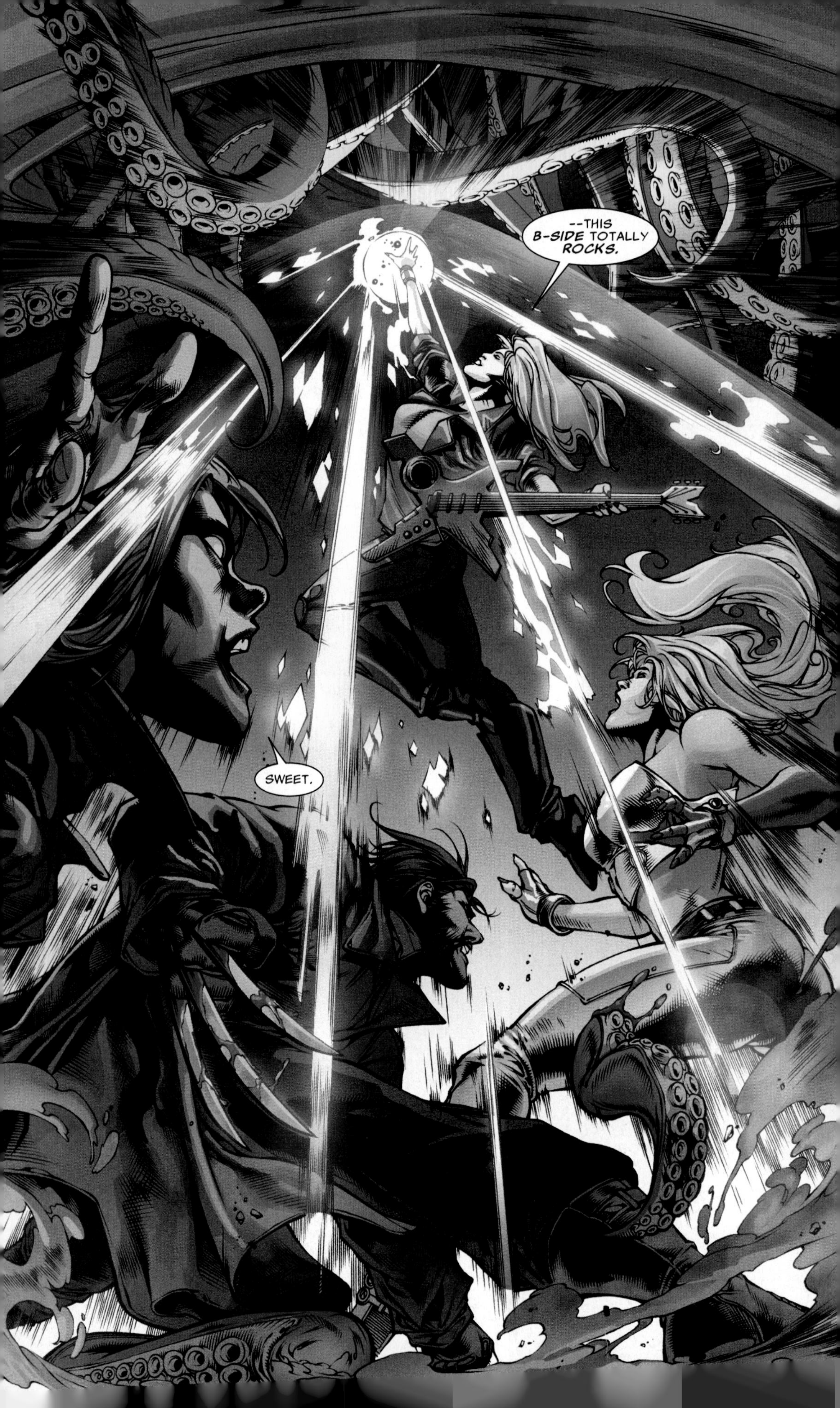
--THIS B-SIDE TOTALLY ROCKS.
SWEET.

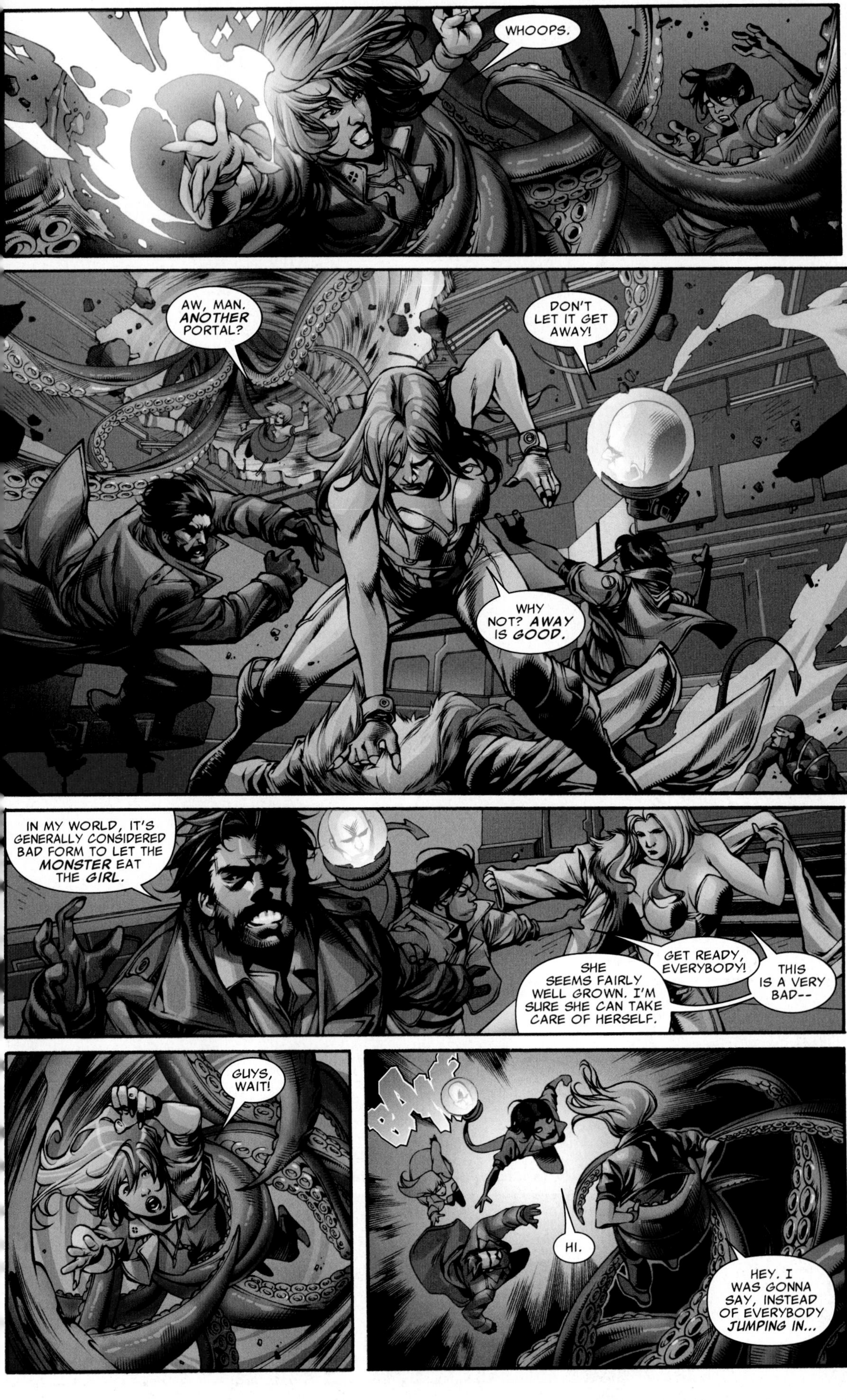
WHOOPS.
AW, MAN. ANOTHER PORTAL?
DON'T LET IT GET AWAY!
WHY NOT? AWAY IS GOOD.
IN MY WORLD, IT'S GENERALLY CONSIDERED BAD FORM TO LET THE MONSTER EAT THE GIRL.
SHE SEEMS FAIRLY WELL GROWN. I'M SURE SHE CAN TAKE CARE OF HERSELF.
GET READY, EVERYBODY!
THIS IS A VERY BAD--
GUYS, WAIT!
HI.
HEY. I WAS GONNA SAY, INSTEAD OF EVERYBODY JUMPING IN...

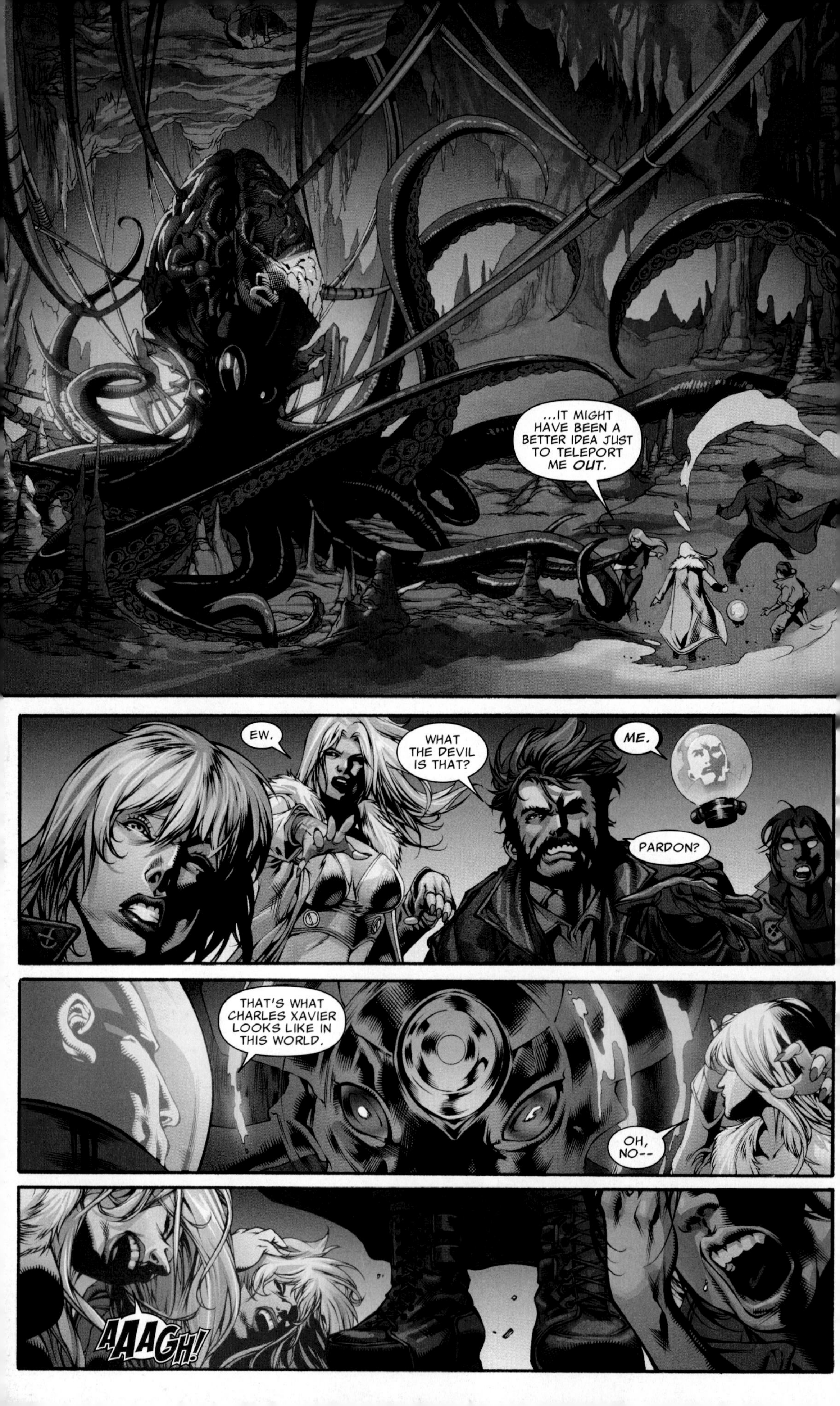
...IT MIGHT HAVE BEEN A BETTER IDEA JUST TO TELEPORT ME OUT.
EW.
WHAT THE DEVIL IS THAT?
ME.
PARDON?
THAT'S WHAT CHARLES XAVIER LOOKS LIKE IN THIS WORLD.
OH, NO--
AAAGH!

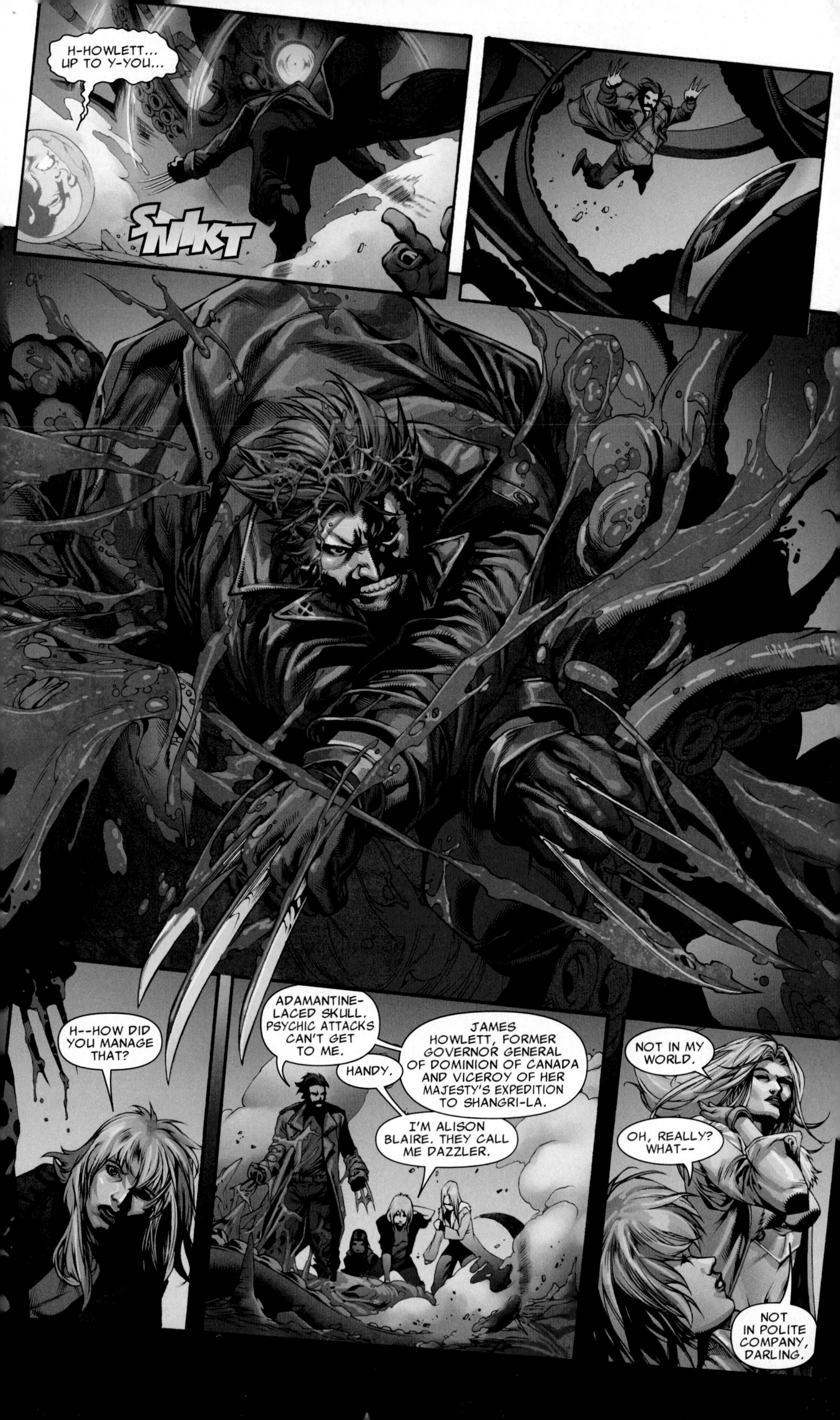
H-HOWLETT... UP TO Y-YOU...
SNIKT
H--HOW DID YOU MANAGE THAT?
ADAMANTINE-LACED SKULL. PSYCHIC ATTACKS CAN'T GET TO ME.
HANDY.
JAMES HOWLETT, FORMER GOVERNOR GENERAL OF DOMINION OF CANADA AND VICEROY OF HER MAJESTY'S EXPEDITION TO SHANGRI-LA.
I'M ALISON BLAIRE. THEY CALL ME DAZZLER.
NOT IN MY WORLD.
OH, REALLY? WHAT--
NOT IN POLITE COMPANY, DARLING.

THAT'S EMMELINE FROST-SUMMERS OF THE NEW ALBION X-SOCIETY.

SHE'S ACTUALLY NOT SO POLITE.

I GATHERED.

I'M KURT WAGGONER. P.S. 1214, BROOKLYN, UNITED STATES OF CALIFORNIA.

I GOT YOUR ALBUM. OR THE ALBUM OF THE *YOU* FROM *MY* WORLD.

YOU I LIKE.

YEAH, I'VE NEVER HEARD ANYONE PLAY THE ACCORDION THE WAY *YOU* DO.

UH...

AND I'M CHARLES XAVIER.

RIGHT. FROM THE NO-BODY ALTERNA-WORLD?

IT'S A LONG STORY. IF YOU DON'T MIND, I'LL CUT TO THE CHASE...

PLEASE.

A HUNDRED OTHER XAVIERS AND I JUST SAVED THE ENTIRE HUMAN POPULATION OF A DYING PLANET WITH THE LARGEST TRANS-DIMENSIONAL TELEPORTATION EVER ATTEMPTED.

IT WAS AWESOME. THEY MOVED THE CATS, TOO.

THAT'S...IMPRESSIVE. I DON'T THINK MY WORLD'S XAVIER HAS THAT KIND OF POWER.

NEITHER DID ANY OF US-- ALONE.

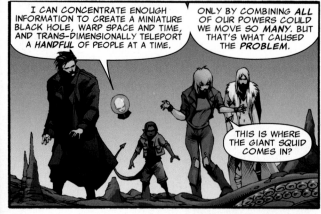

I CAN CONCENTRATE ENOUGH INFORMATION TO CREATE A MINIATURE BLACK HOLE, WARP SPACE AND TIME, AND TRANS-DIMENSIONALLY TELEPORT A *HANDFUL* OF PEOPLE AT A TIME.

ONLY BY COMBINING *ALL* OF OUR POWERS COULD WE MOVE SO *MANY.* BUT THAT'S WHAT CAUSED THE *PROBLEM.*

THIS IS WHERE THE GIANT SQUID COMES IN?

WE...*BROKE* SOMETHING IN THE MULTIVERSE.

OR MAYBE...*MADE* SOMETHING.

LOSING TRACK OF THE "CUT TO THE CHASE" PART, PROFESSOR.

RIGHT.

I HAVE A *MISSION* FOR YOU, MY X-MEN...

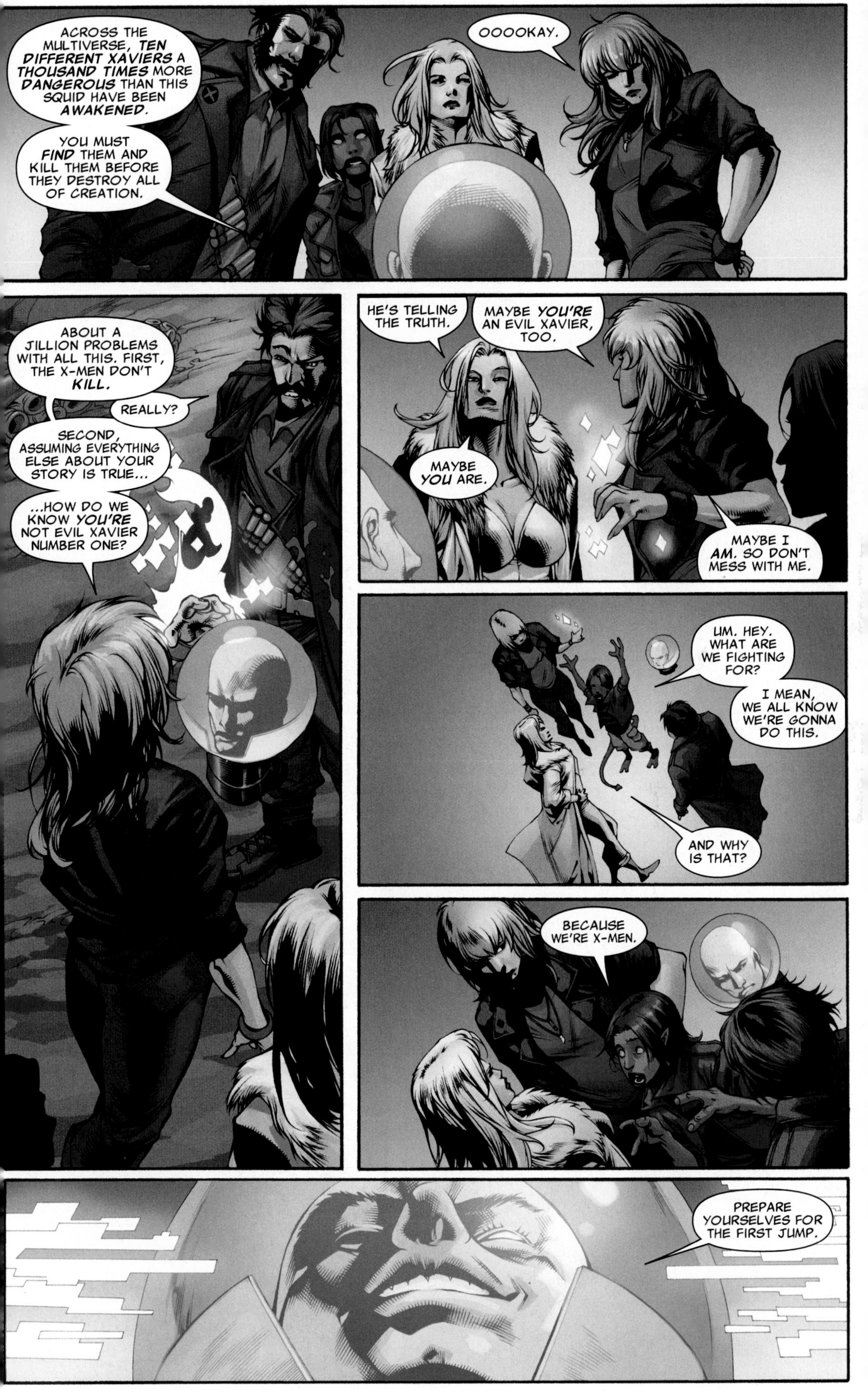

ACROSS THE MULTIVERSE, TEN DIFFERENT XAVIERS A THOUSAND TIMES MORE DANGEROUS THAN THIS SQUID HAVE BEEN AWAKENED.
YOU MUST FIND THEM AND KILL THEM BEFORE THEY DESTROY ALL OF CREATION.
OOOOKAY.
ABOUT A JILLION PROBLEMS WITH ALL THIS. FIRST, THE X-MEN DON'T KILL.
REALLY?
SECOND, ASSUMING EVERYTHING ELSE ABOUT YOUR STORY IS TRUE...
...HOW DO WE KNOW YOU'RE NOT EVIL XAVIER NUMBER ONE?
HE'S TELLING THE TRUTH.
MAYBE YOU'RE AN EVIL XAVIER, TOO.
MAYBE YOU ARE.
MAYBE I AM. SO DON'T MESS WITH ME.
UM. HEY. WHAT ARE WE FIGHTING FOR?
I MEAN, WE ALL KNOW WE'RE GONNA DO THIS.
AND WHY IS THAT?
BECAUSE WE'RE X-MEN.
PREPARE YOURSELVES FOR THE FIRST JUMP.

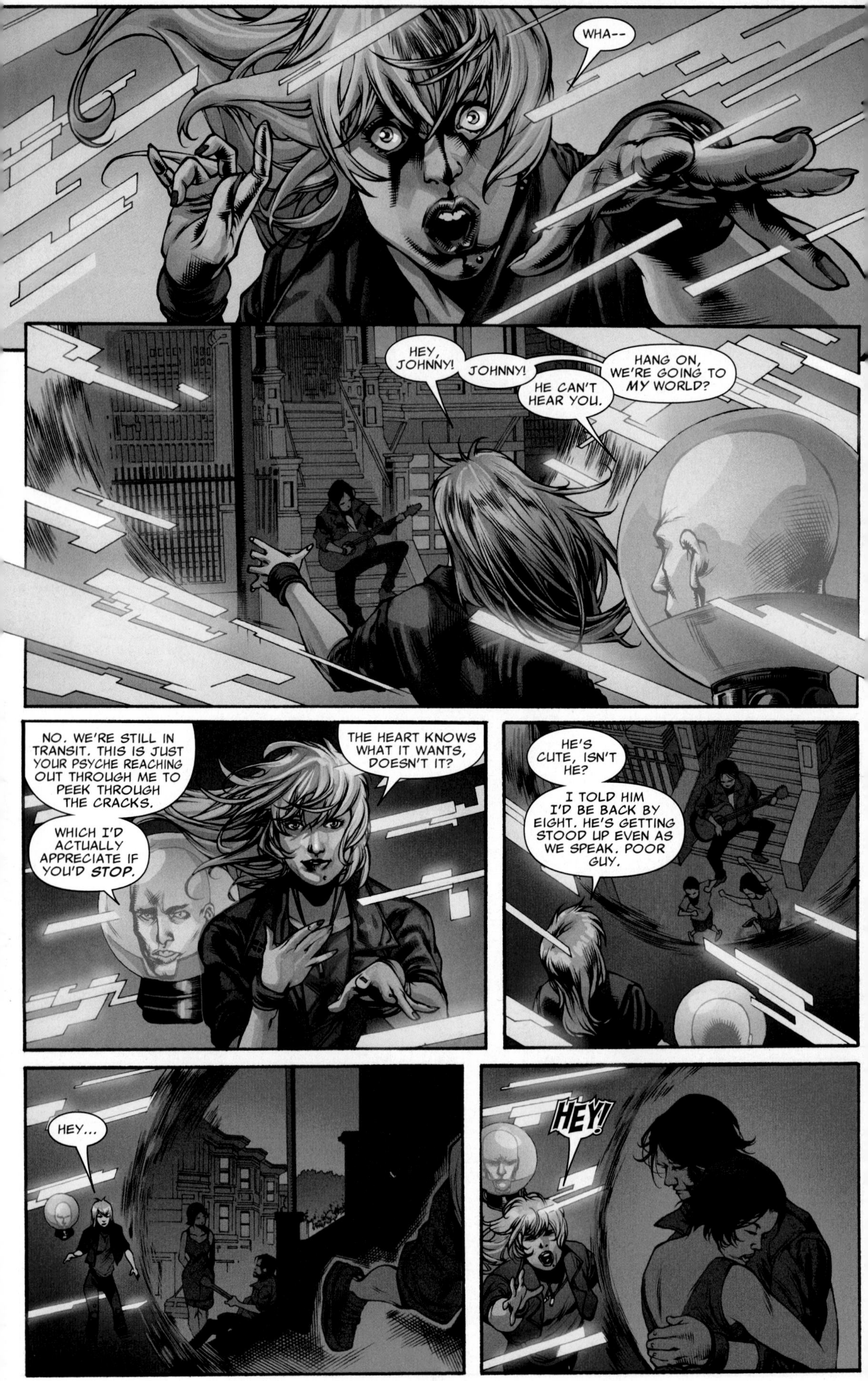
WHA--
HEY, JOHNNY!
JOHNNY!
HE CAN'T HEAR YOU.
HANG ON, WE'RE GOING TO *MY* WORLD?
NO. WE'RE STILL IN TRANSIT. THIS IS JUST YOUR PSYCHE REACHING OUT THROUGH ME TO PEEK THROUGH THE CRACKS.
WHICH I'D ACTUALLY APPRECIATE IF YOU'D **STOP**.
THE HEART KNOWS WHAT IT WANTS, DOESN'T IT?
HE'S CUTE, ISN'T HE?
I TOLD HIM I'D BE BACK BY EIGHT. HE'S GETTING STOOD UP EVEN AS WE SPEAK. POOR GUY.
HEY...
HEY!

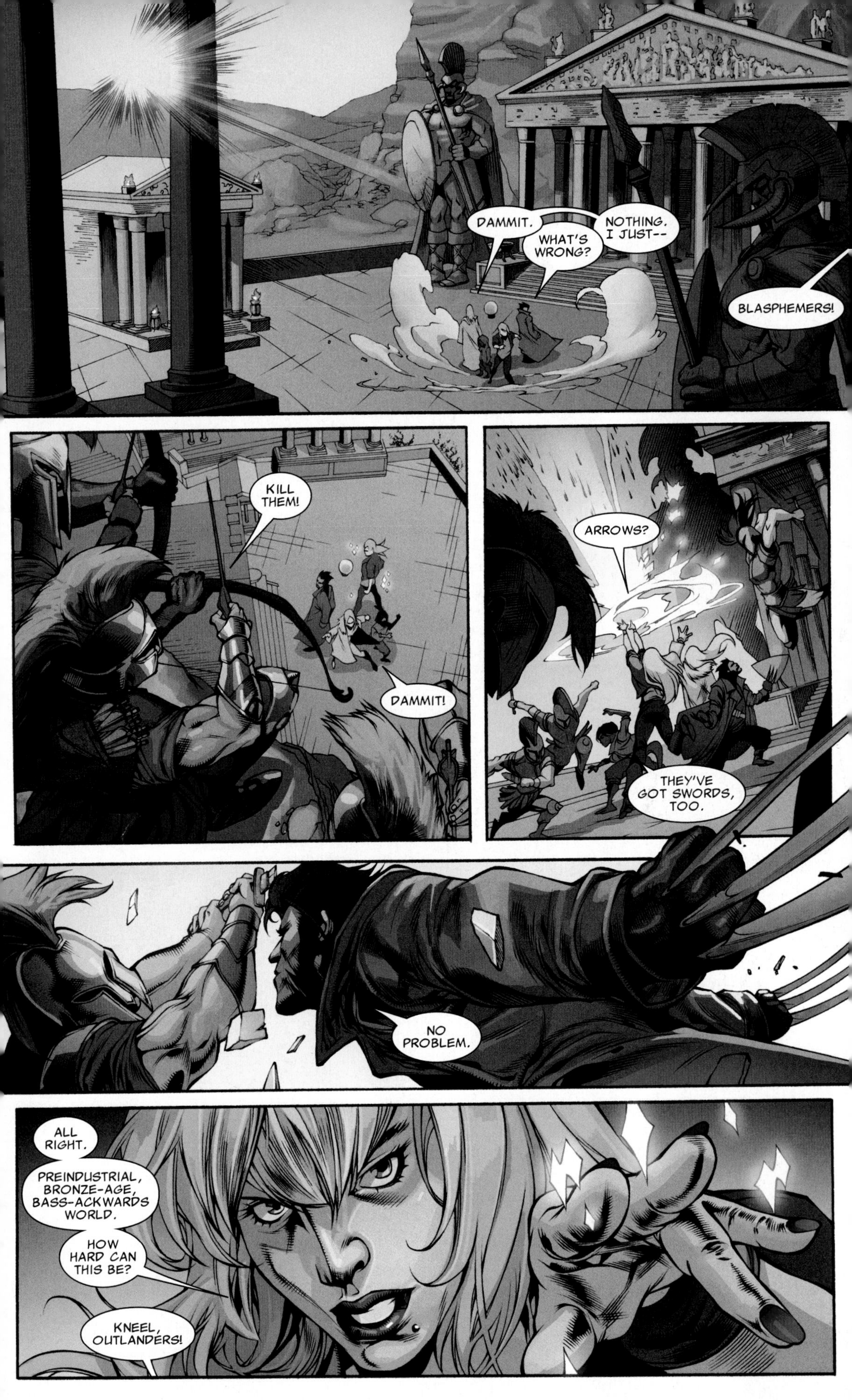
DAMMIT.
WHAT'S WRONG?
NOTHING. I JUST--
BLASPHEMERS!
KILL THEM!
DAMMIT!
ARROWS?
THEY'VE GOT SWORDS, TOO.
NO PROBLEM.
ALL RIGHT.
PREINDUSTRIAL, BRONZE-AGE, BASS-ACKWARDS WORLD.
HOW HARD CAN THIS BE?
KNEEL, OUTLANDERS!

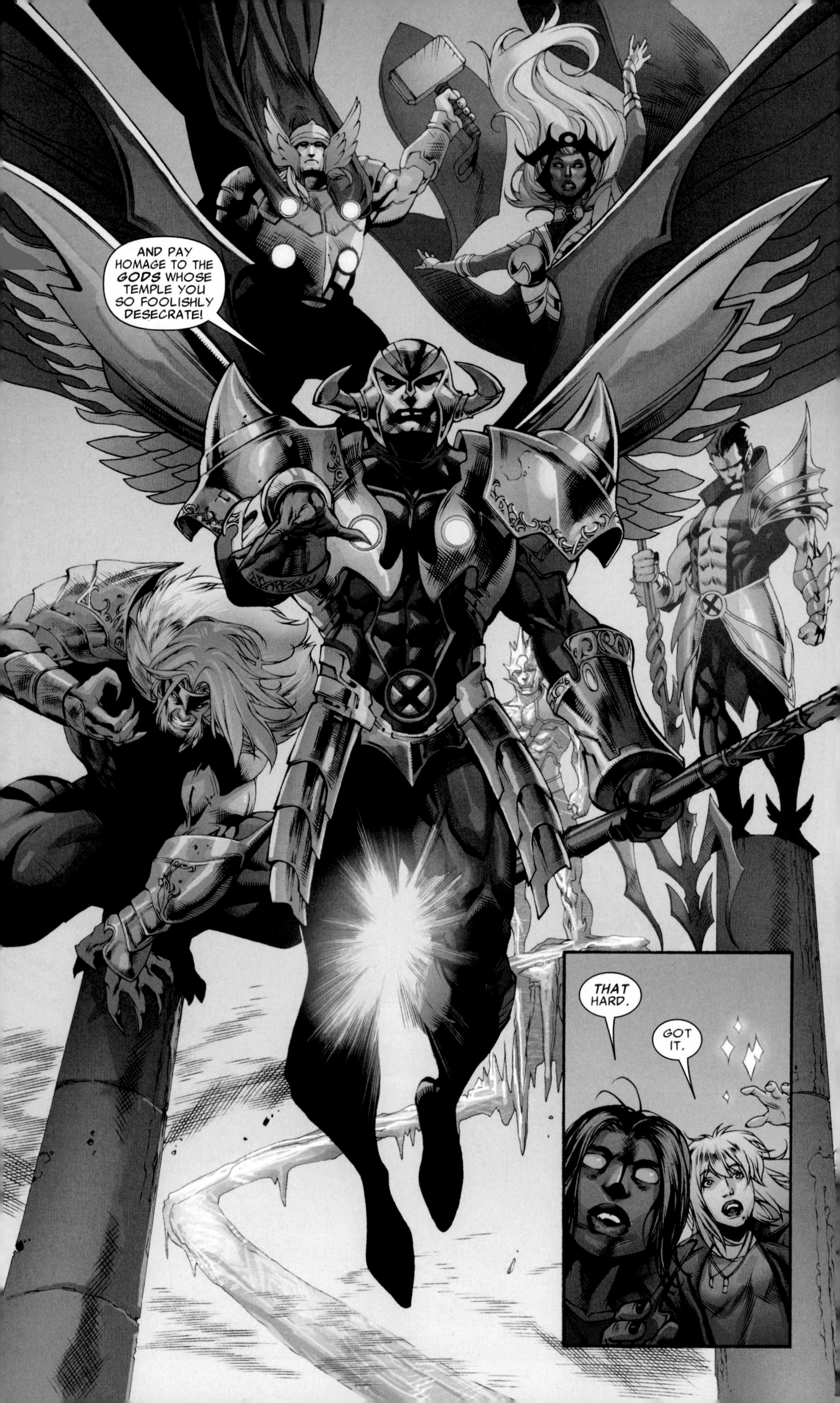
AND PAY HOMAGE TO THE GODS WHOSE TEMPLE YOU SO FOOLISHLY DESECRATE!
THAT HARD.
GOT IT.

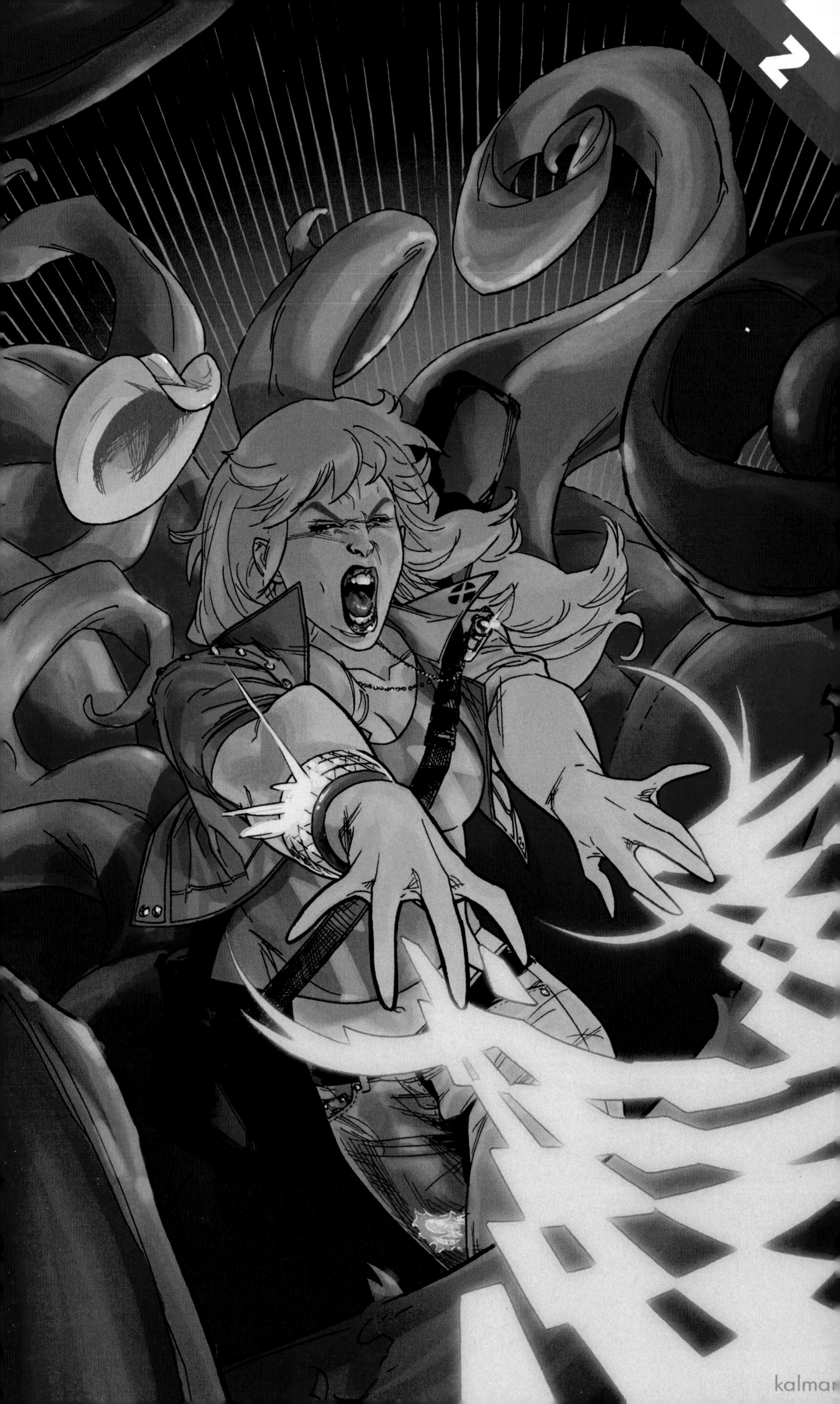
2

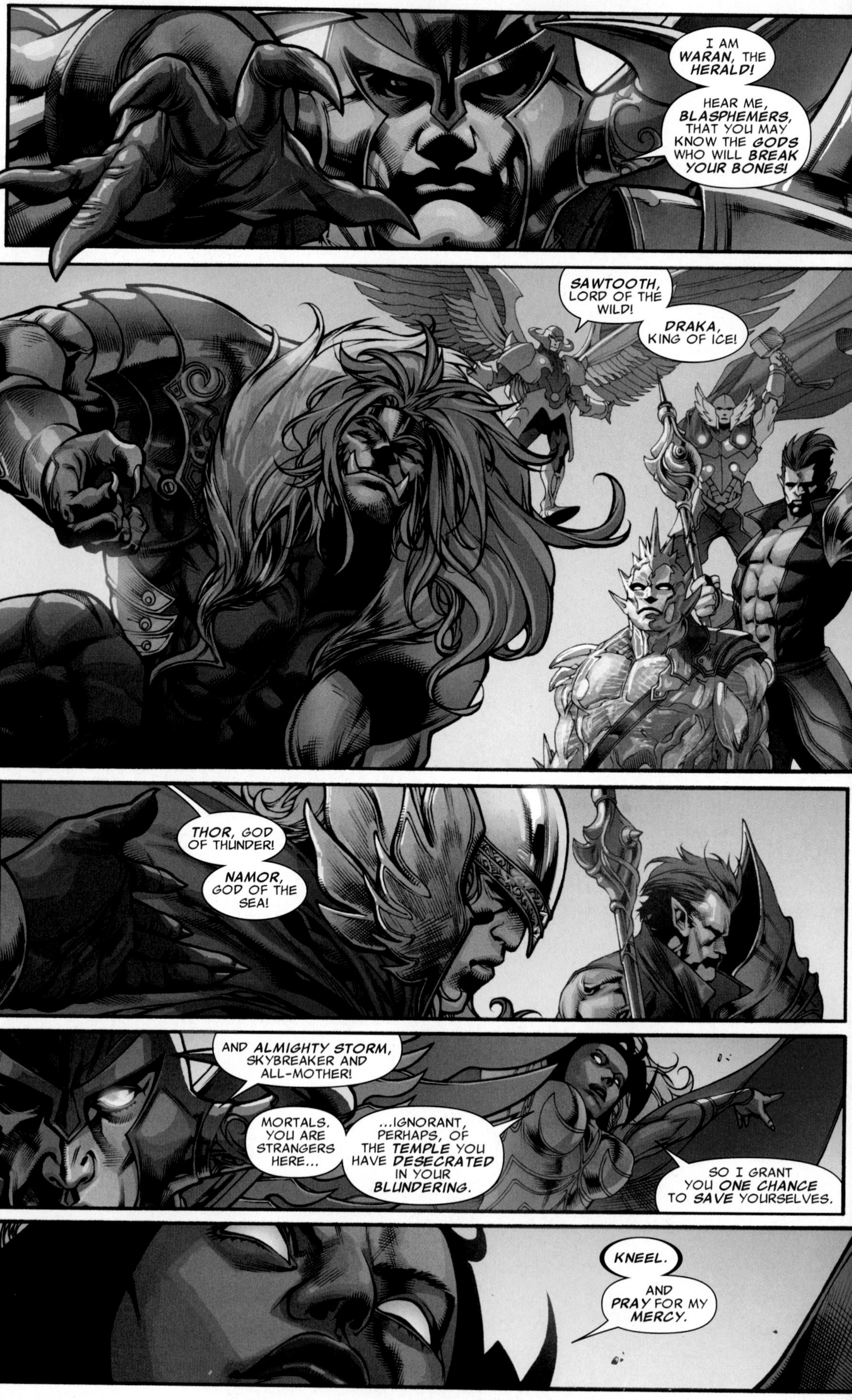
I AM WARAN, THE HERALD!
HEAR ME, BLASPHEMERS, THAT YOU MAY KNOW THE GODS WHO WILL BREAK YOUR BONES!
SAWTOOTH, LORD OF THE WILD!
DRAKA, KING OF ICE!
THOR, GOD OF THUNDER!
NAMOR, GOD OF THE SEA!
AND ALMIGHTY STORM, SKYBREAKER AND ALL-MOTHER!
MORTALS. YOU ARE STRANGERS HERE...
...IGNORANT, PERHAPS, OF THE TEMPLE YOU HAVE DESECRATED IN YOUR BLUNDERING.
SO I GRANT YOU ONE CHANCE TO SAVE YOURSELVES.
KNEEL.
AND PRAY FOR MY MERCY.

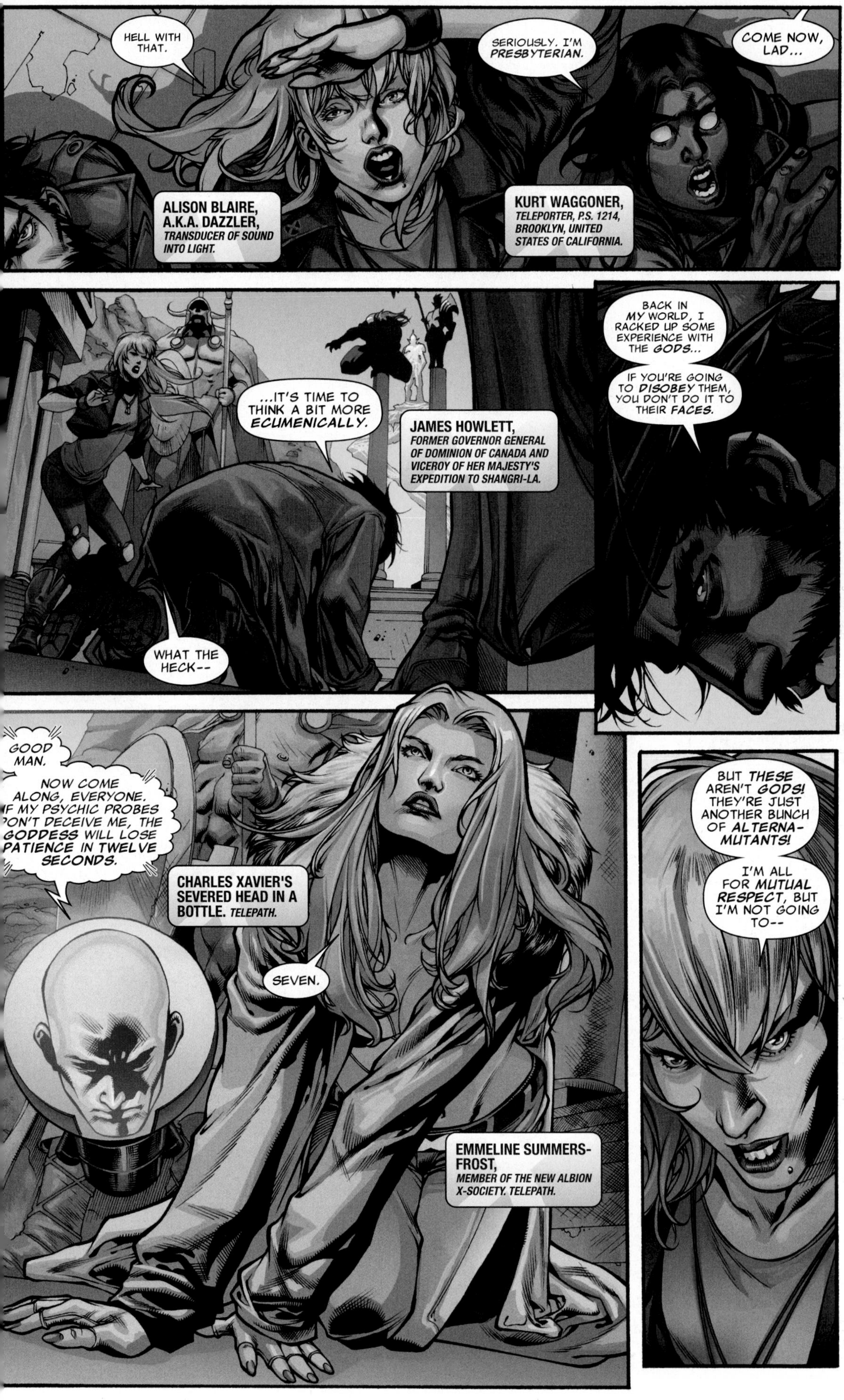
HELL WITH THAT.
SERIOUSLY. I'M PRESBYTERIAN.
COME NOW, LAD...
ALISON BLAIRE, A.K.A. DAZZLER, TRANSDUCER OF SOUND INTO LIGHT.
KURT WAGGONER, TELEPORTER, P.S. 1214, BROOKLYN, UNITED STATES OF CALIFORNIA.
...IT'S TIME TO THINK A BIT MORE ECUMENICALLY.
JAMES HOWLETT, FORMER GOVERNOR GENERAL OF DOMINION OF CANADA AND VICEROY OF HER MAJESTY'S EXPEDITION TO SHANGRI-LA.
WHAT THE HECK--
BACK IN MY WORLD, I RACKED UP SOME EXPERIENCE WITH THE GODS...
IF YOU'RE GOING TO DISOBEY THEM, YOU DON'T DO IT TO THEIR FACES.
GOOD MAN.
NOW COME ALONG, EVERYONE. IF MY PSYCHIC PROBES DON'T DECEIVE ME, THE GODDESS WILL LOSE PATIENCE IN TWELVE SECONDS.
CHARLES XAVIER'S SEVERED HEAD IN A BOTTLE. TELEPATH.
SEVEN.
EMMELINE SUMMERS-FROST, MEMBER OF THE NEW ALBION X-SOCIETY. TELEPATH.
BUT THESE AREN'T GODS! THEY'RE JUST ANOTHER BUNCH OF ALTERNA-MUTANTS!
I'M ALL FOR MUTUAL RESPECT, BUT I'M NOT GOING TO--

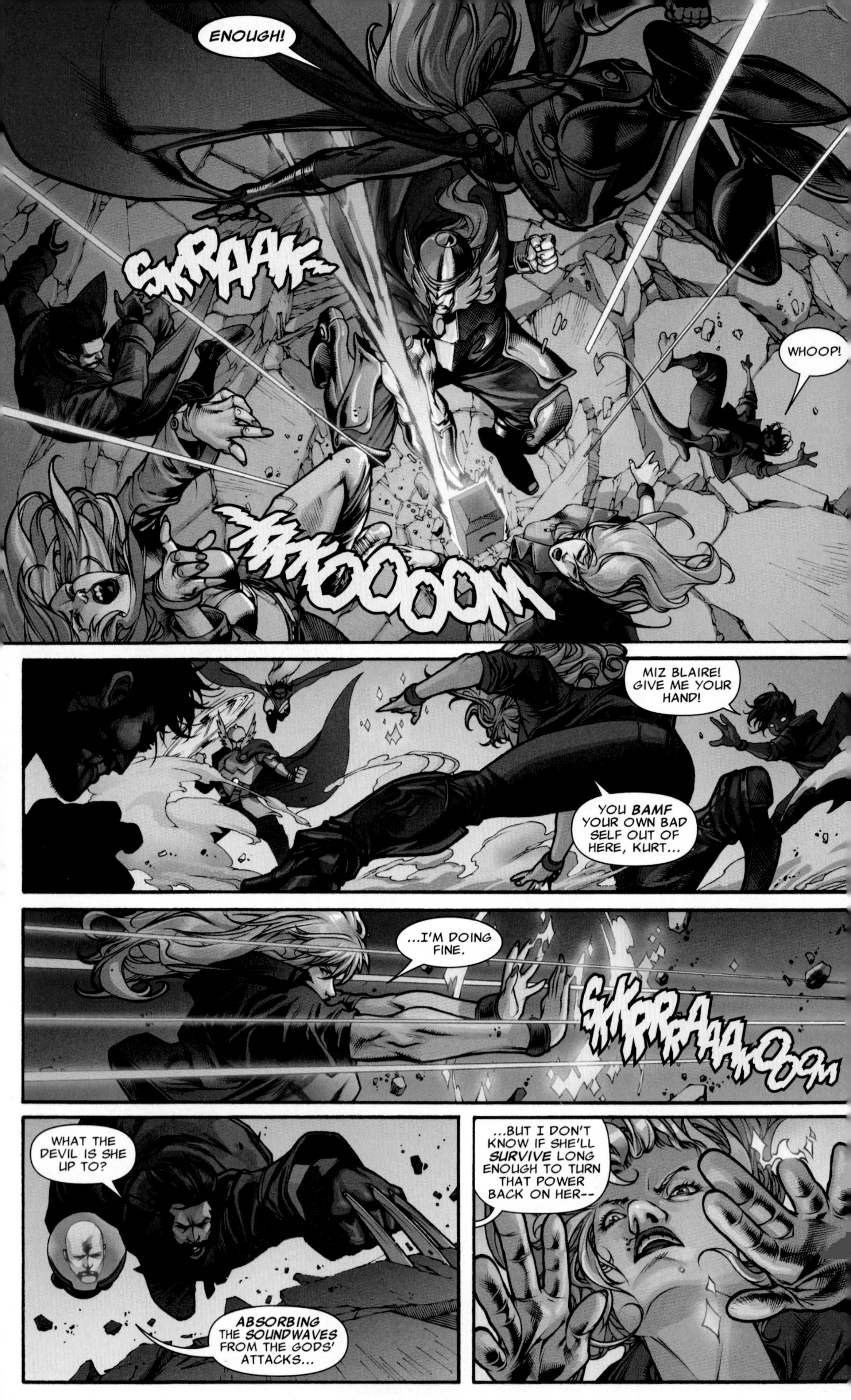
ENOUGH!
SKRAAK
WHOOP!
KRKOOOOM
MIZ BLAIRE! GIVE ME YOUR HAND!
YOU BAMF YOUR OWN BAD SELF OUT OF HERE, KURT...
...I'M DOING FINE.
SKRRAAAKOOOM
WHAT THE DEVIL IS SHE UP TO?
ABSORBING THE SOUNDWAVES FROM THE GODS' ATTACKS...
...BUT I DON'T KNOW IF SHE'LL SURVIVE LONG ENOUGH TO TURN THAT POWER BACK ON HER--

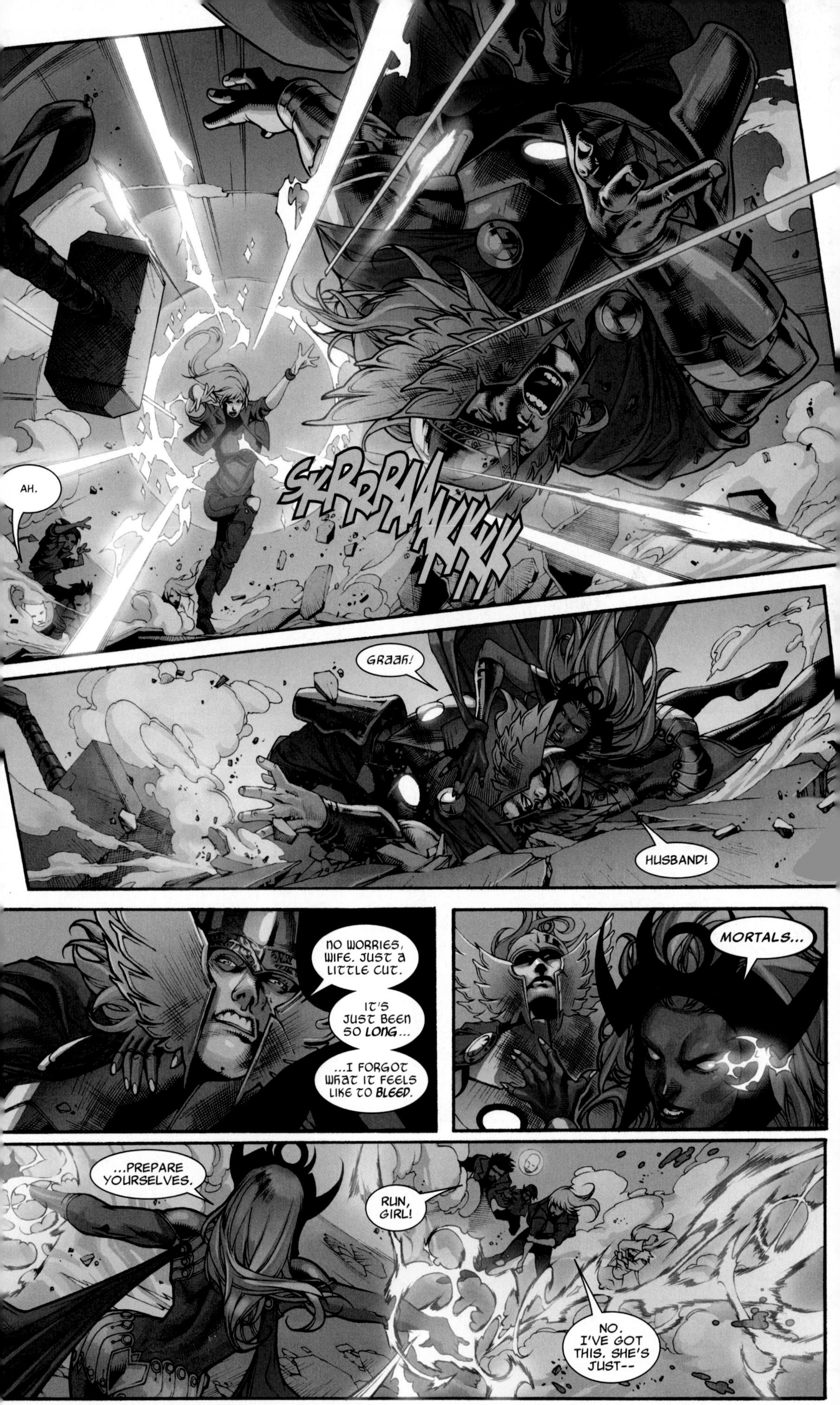
SKRRRAAAKKKK
AH.
GRAAH!
HUSBAND!
NO WORRIES, WIFE. JUST A LITTLE CUT.
IT'S JUST BEEN SO LONG...
...I FORGOT WHAT IT FEELS LIKE TO BLEED.
MORTALS...
...PREPARE YOURSELVES.
RUN, GIRL!
NO. I'VE GOT THIS. SHE'S JUST--

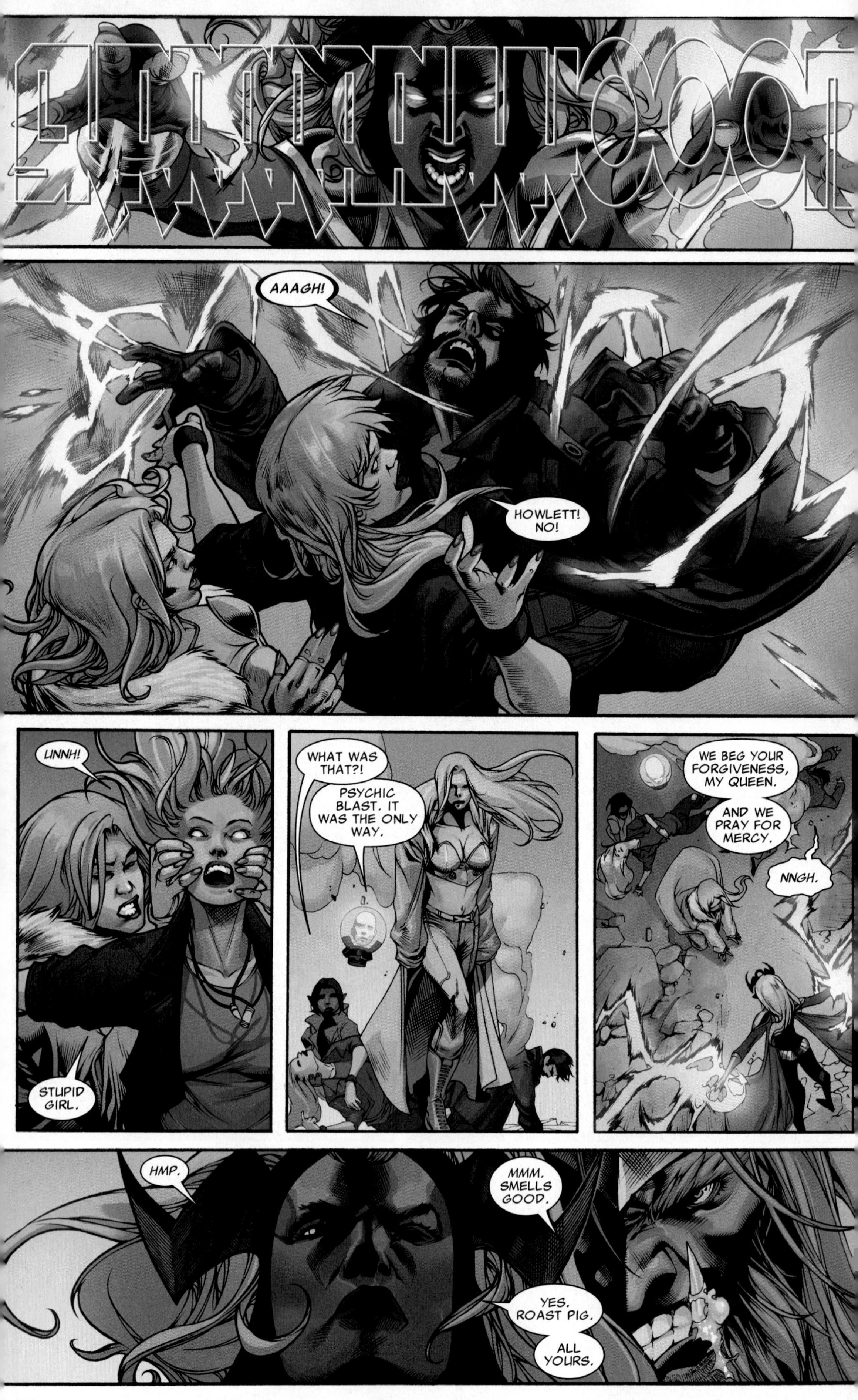
LINNNNNNNOOOOL
AAAGH!
HOWLETT! NO!
LINNH!
STUPID GIRL.
WHAT WAS THAT?!
PSYCHIC BLAST. IT WAS THE ONLY WAY.
WE BEG YOUR FORGIVENESS, MY QUEEN.
AND WE PRAY FOR MERCY.
NNGH.
HMP.
MMM. SMELLS GOOD.
YES. ROAST PIG.
ALL YOURS.

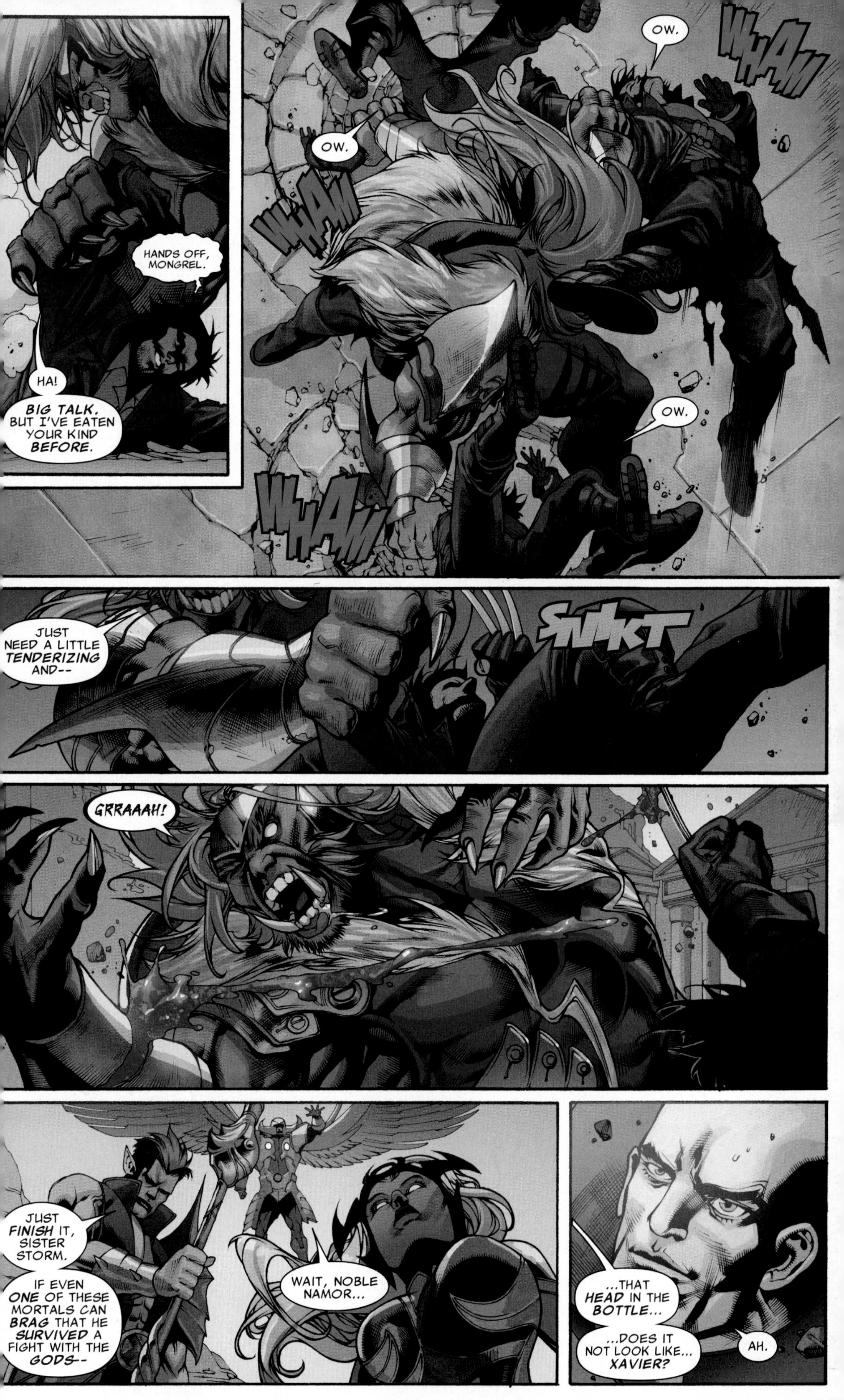

HANDS OFF, MONGREL.
HA!
BIG TALK. BUT I'VE EATEN YOUR KIND BEFORE.
OW.
WHAM
OW.
WHAM
OW.
WHAM
JUST NEED A LITTLE TENDERIZING AND--
SNIKT
GRRAAAH!
JUST FINISH IT, SISTER STORM.
IF EVEN ONE OF THESE MORTALS CAN BRAG THAT HE SURVIVED A FIGHT WITH THE GODS--
WAIT, NOBLE NAMOR...
...THAT HEAD IN THE BOTTLE...
...DOES IT NOT LOOK LIKE... XAVIER?
AH.

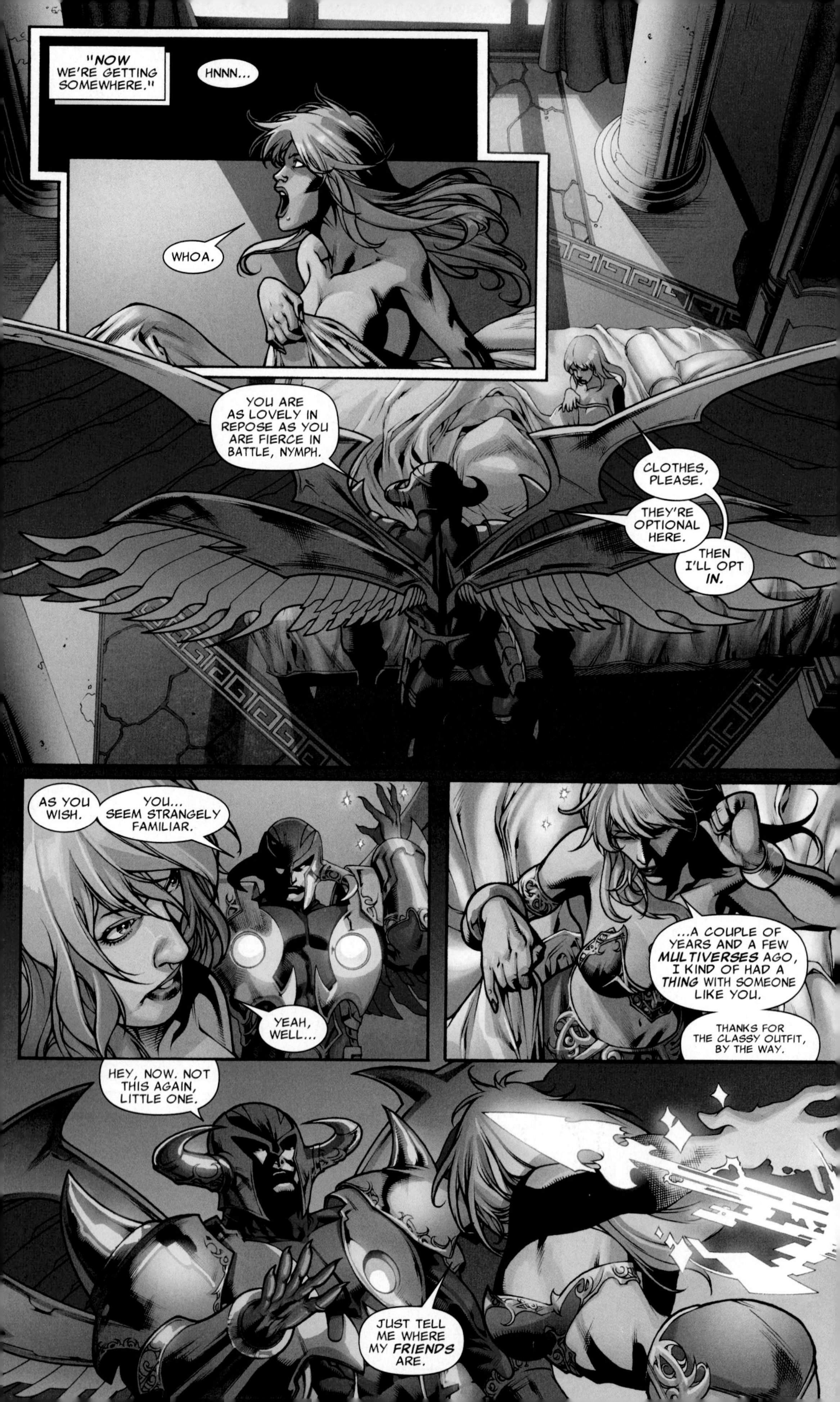
"NOW WE'RE GETTING SOMEWHERE."
HNNN...
WHOA.
YOU ARE AS LOVELY IN REPOSE AS YOU ARE FIERCE IN BATTLE, NYMPH.
CLOTHES, PLEASE.
THEY'RE OPTIONAL HERE.
THEN I'LL OPT IN.
AS YOU WISH.
YOU... SEEM STRANGELY FAMILIAR.
YEAH, WELL...
...A COUPLE OF YEARS AND A FEW MULTIVERSES AGO, I KIND OF HAD A THING WITH SOMEONE LIKE YOU.
THANKS FOR THE CLASSY OUTFIT, BY THE WAY.
HEY, NOW. NOT THIS AGAIN, LITTLE ONE.
JUST TELL ME WHERE MY FRIENDS ARE.

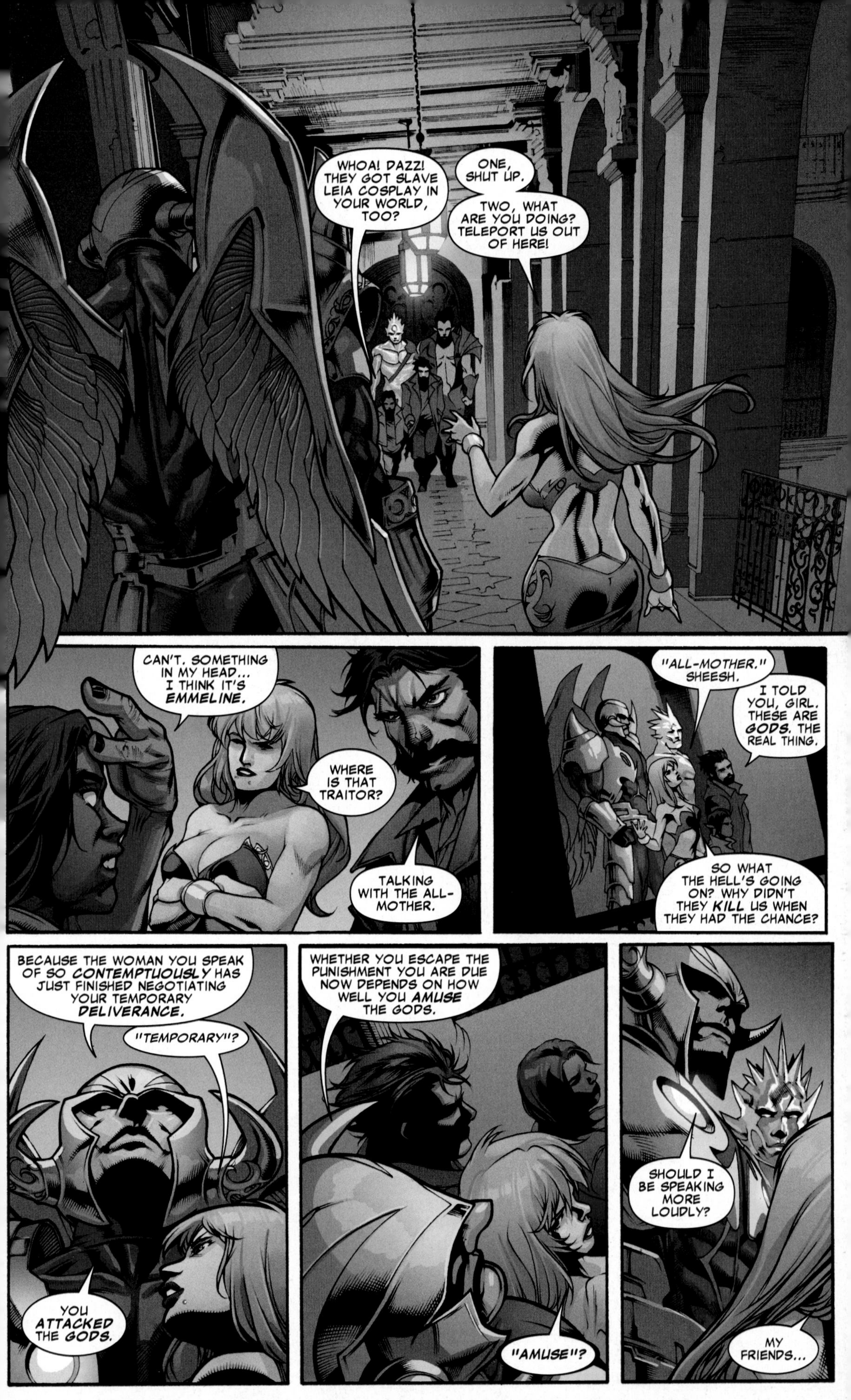

WHOA! DAZZ! THEY GOT SLAVE LEIA COSPLAY IN YOUR WORLD, TOO?
ONE, SHUT UP.
TWO, WHAT ARE YOU DOING? TELEPORT US OUT OF HERE!
CAN'T. SOMETHING IN MY HEAD... I THINK IT'S EMMELINE.
WHERE IS THAT TRAITOR?
TALKING WITH THE ALL-MOTHER.
"ALL-MOTHER." SHEESH.
I TOLD YOU, GIRL. THESE ARE GODS. THE REAL THING.
SO WHAT THE HELL'S GOING ON? WHY DIDN'T THEY KILL US WHEN THEY HAD THE CHANCE?
BECAUSE THE WOMAN YOU SPEAK OF SO CONTEMPTUOUSLY HAS JUST FINISHED NEGOTIATING YOUR TEMPORARY DELIVERANCE.
"TEMPORARY"?
YOU ATTACKED THE GODS.
WHETHER YOU ESCAPE THE PUNISHMENT YOU ARE DUE NOW DEPENDS ON HOW WELL YOU AMUSE THE GODS.
"AMUSE"?
SHOULD I BE SPEAKING MORE LOUDLY?
MY FRIENDS...

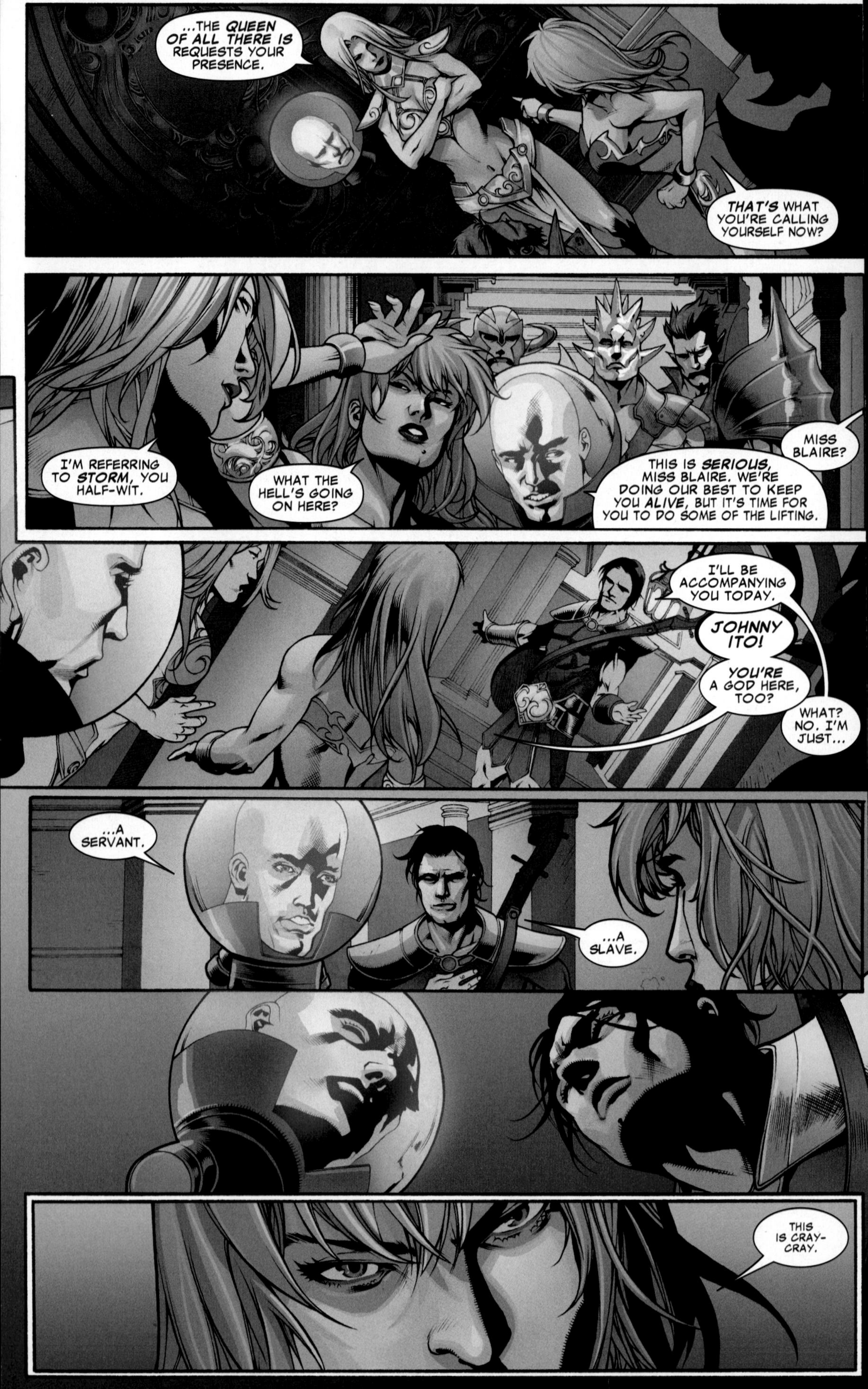
...THE QUEEN OF ALL THERE IS REQUESTS YOUR PRESENCE.
THAT'S WHAT YOU'RE CALLING YOURSELF NOW?
I'M REFERRING TO STORM, YOU HALF-WIT.
WHAT THE HELL'S GOING ON HERE?
THIS IS SERIOUS, MISS BLAIRE. WE'RE DOING OUR BEST TO KEEP YOU ALIVE, BUT IT'S TIME FOR YOU TO DO SOME OF THE LIFTING.
MISS BLAIRE?
I'LL BE ACCOMPANYING YOU TODAY.
JOHNNY ITO!
YOU'RE A GOD HERE, TOO?
WHAT? NO. I'M JUST...
...A SERVANT.
...A SLAVE.
THIS IS CRAY-CRAY.

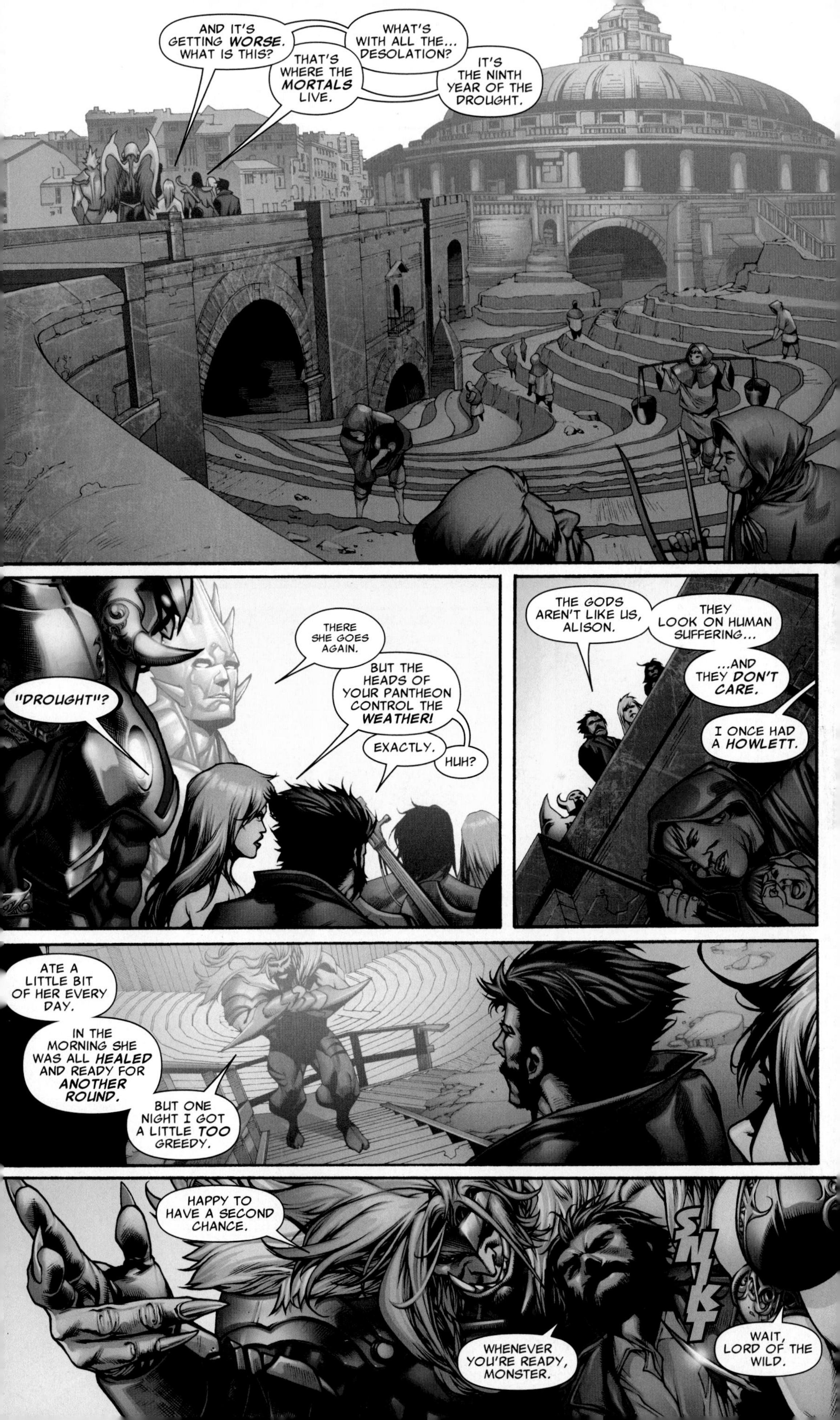

AND IT'S GETTING WORSE. WHAT IS THIS?
WHAT'S WITH ALL THE... DESOLATION?
THAT'S WHERE THE MORTALS LIVE.
IT'S THE NINTH YEAR OF THE DROUGHT.
"DROUGHT"?
THERE SHE GOES AGAIN.
BUT THE HEADS OF YOUR PANTHEON CONTROL THE WEATHER!
EXACTLY.
HUH?
THE GODS AREN'T LIKE US, ALISON.
THEY LOOK ON HUMAN SUFFERING...
...AND THEY DON'T CARE.
I ONCE HAD A HOWLETT.
ATE A LITTLE BIT OF HER EVERY DAY.
IN THE MORNING SHE WAS ALL HEALED AND READY FOR ANOTHER ROUND.
BUT ONE NIGHT I GOT A LITTLE TOO GREEDY.
HAPPY TO HAVE A SECOND CHANCE.
SNIKT
WHENEVER YOU'RE READY, MONSTER.
WAIT, LORD OF THE WILD.

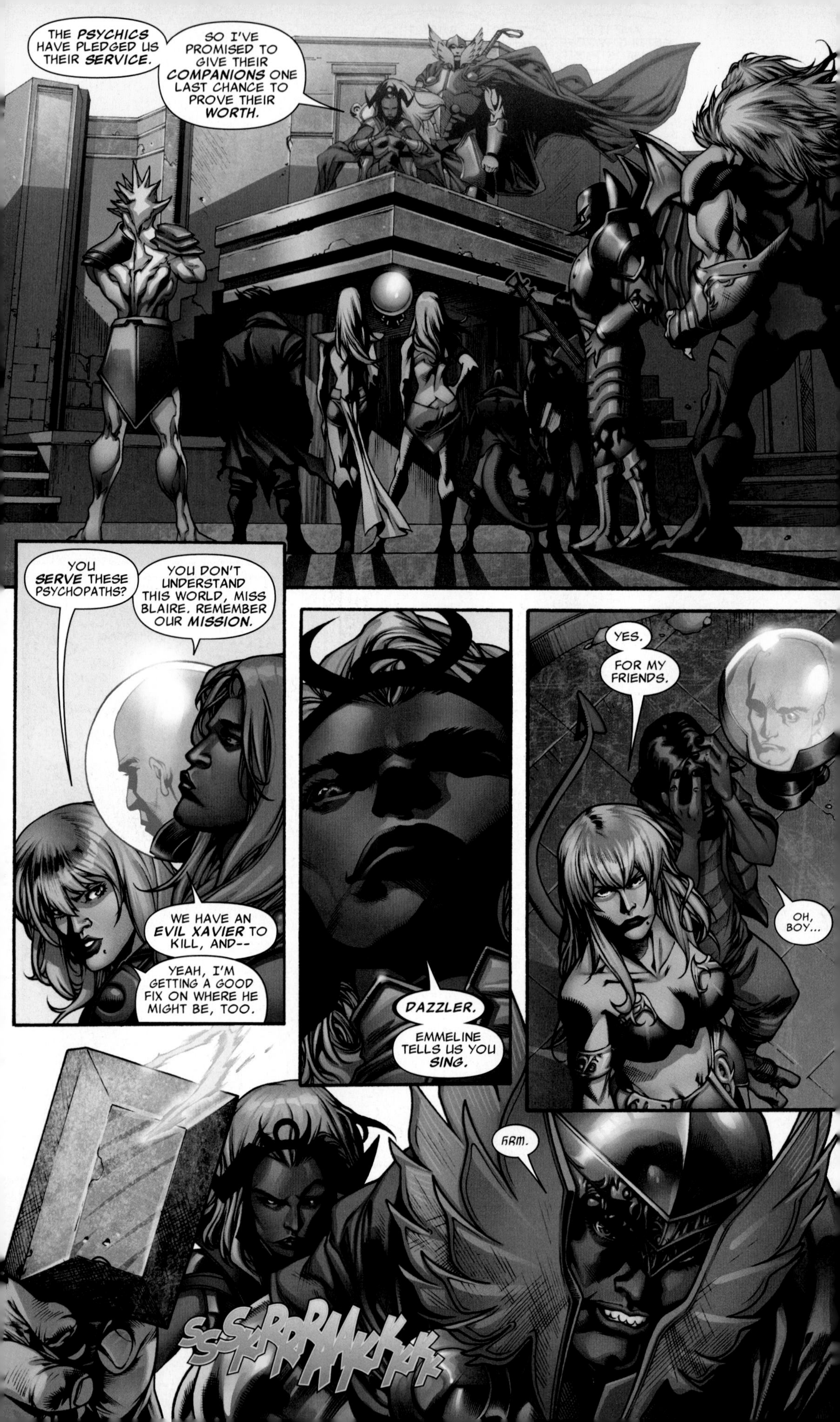
THE PSYCHICS HAVE PLEDGED US THEIR SERVICE.
SO I'VE PROMISED TO GIVE THEIR COMPANIONS ONE LAST CHANCE TO PROVE THEIR WORTH.
YOU SERVE THESE PSYCHOPATHS?
YOU DON'T UNDERSTAND THIS WORLD, MISS BLAIRE. REMEMBER OUR MISSION.
WE HAVE AN EVIL XAVIER TO KILL, AND--
YEAH, I'M GETTING A GOOD FIX ON WHERE HE MIGHT BE, TOO.
DAZZLER.
EMMELINE TELLS US YOU SING.
YES.
FOR MY FRIENDS.
OH, BOY...
HRM.
SSSKRRAAKKK

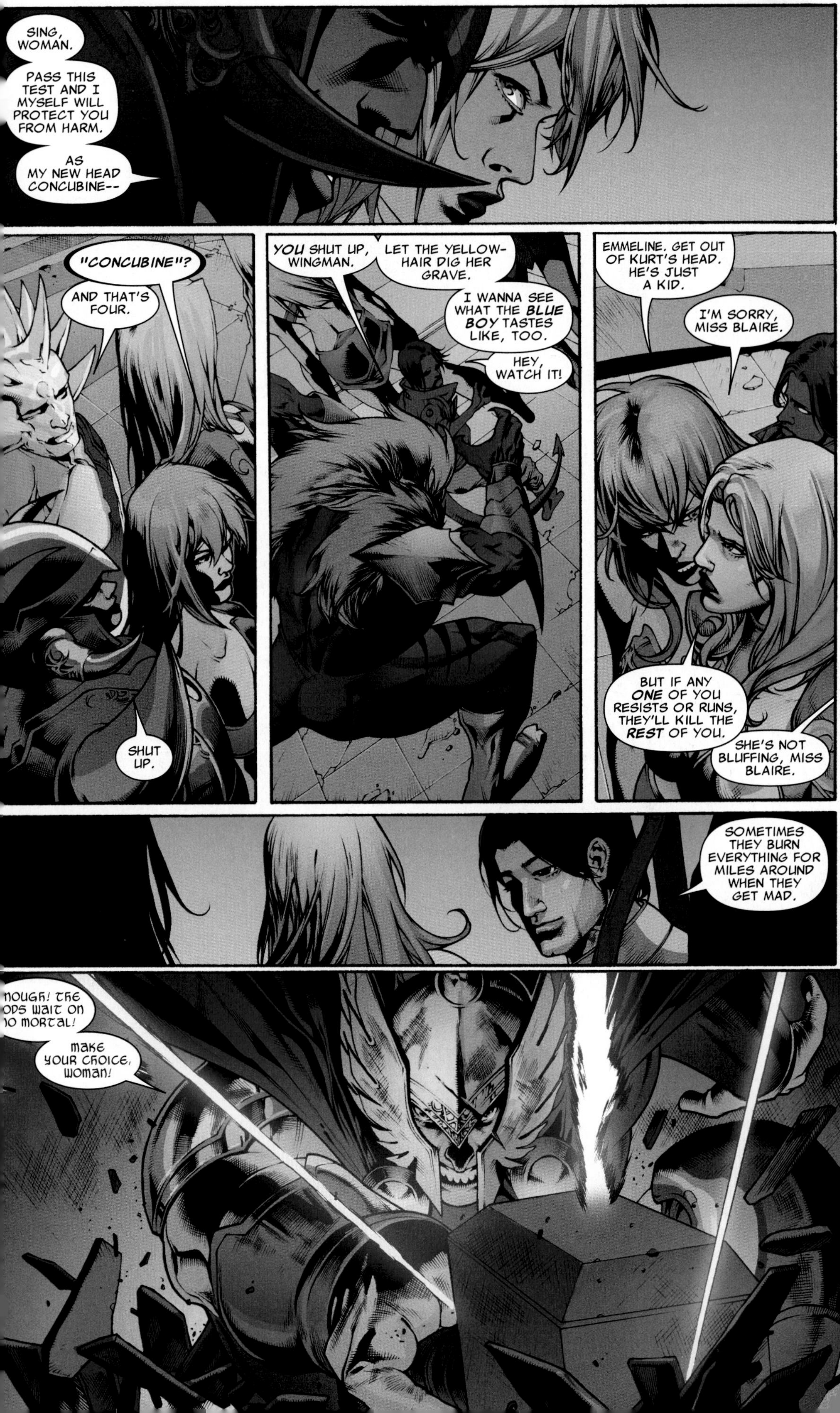
SING, WOMAN.
PASS THIS TEST AND I MYSELF WILL PROTECT YOU FROM HARM.
AS MY NEW HEAD CONCUBINE--
"CONCUBINE"?
AND THAT'S FOUR.
SHUT UP.
YOU SHUT UP, WINGMAN.
LET THE YELLOW-HAIR DIG HER GRAVE.
I WANNA SEE WHAT THE BLUE BOY TASTES LIKE, TOO.
HEY, WATCH IT!
EMMELINE. GET OUT OF KURT'S HEAD. HE'S JUST A KID.
I'M SORRY, MISS BLAIRE.
BUT IF ANY ONE OF YOU RESISTS OR RUNS, THEY'LL KILL THE REST OF YOU.
SHE'S NOT BLUFFING, MISS BLAIRE.
SOMETIMES THEY BURN EVERYTHING FOR MILES AROUND WHEN THEY GET MAD.
NOUGH! THE ODS WAIT ON O MORTAL!
MAKE YOUR CHOICE, WOMAN!

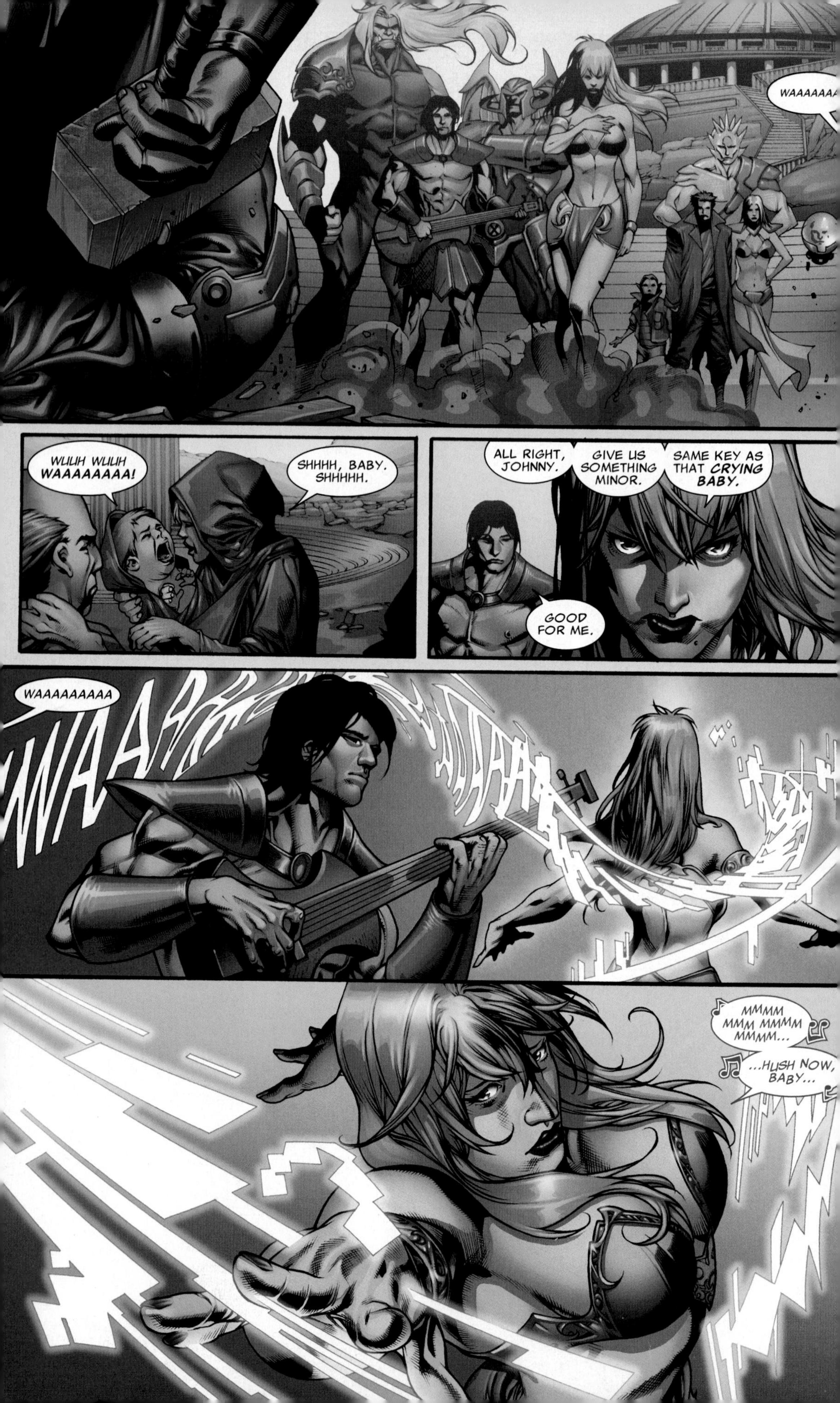
WAAAAAAA
WUUH WUUH WAAAAAAAA!
SHHHH, BABY. SHHHHH.
ALL RIGHT, JOHNNY.
GIVE US SOMETHING MINOR.
SAME KEY AS THAT CRYING BABY.
GOOD FOR ME.
WAAAAAAAAA
MMMM MMM MMMM MMMM...
...HUSH NOW, BABY...

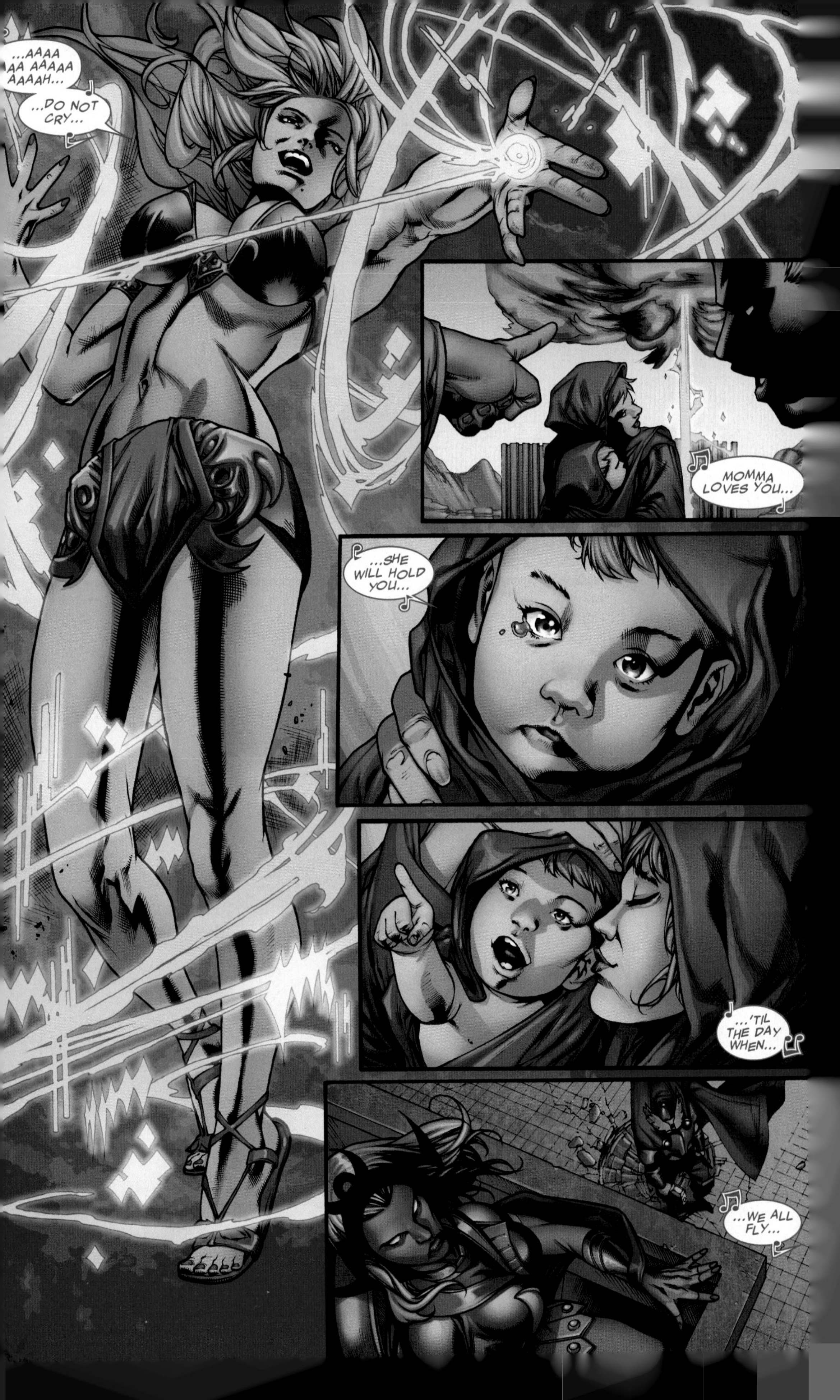
...AAAA AA AAAAA AAAAH...
...DO NOT CRY...
MOMMA LOVES YOU...
...SHE WILL HOLD YOU...
...'TIL THE DAY WHEN...
...WE ALL FLY...

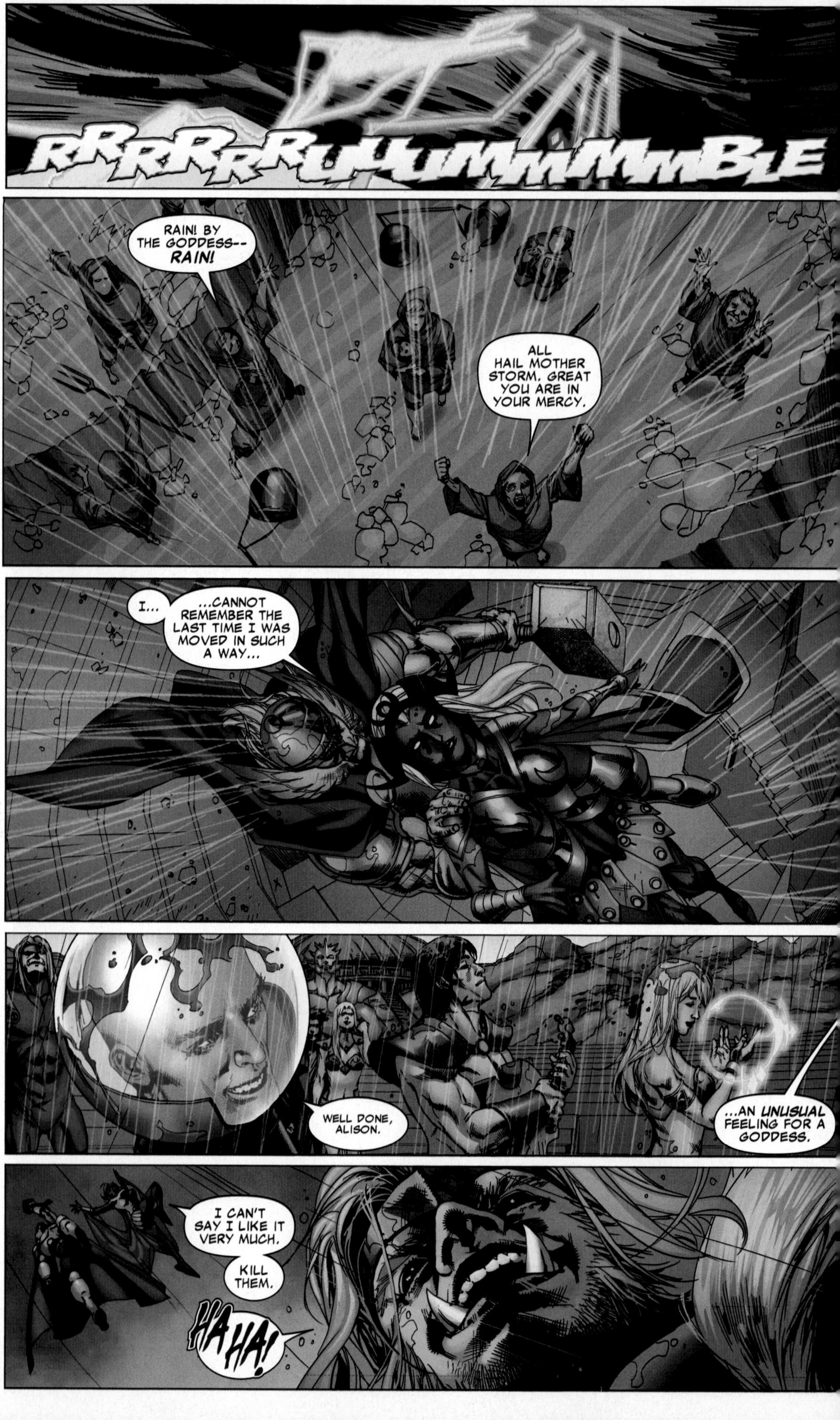
RRRRRRUHHUMMMMMBLE
RAIN! BY THE GODDESS-- RAIN!
ALL HAIL MOTHER STORM. GREAT YOU ARE IN YOUR MERCY.
I...
...CANNOT REMEMBER THE LAST TIME I WAS MOVED IN SUCH A WAY...
...AN UNUSUAL FEELING FOR A GODDESS.
WELL DONE, ALISON.
I CAN'T SAY I LIKE IT VERY MUCH.
KILL THEM.
HA HA!

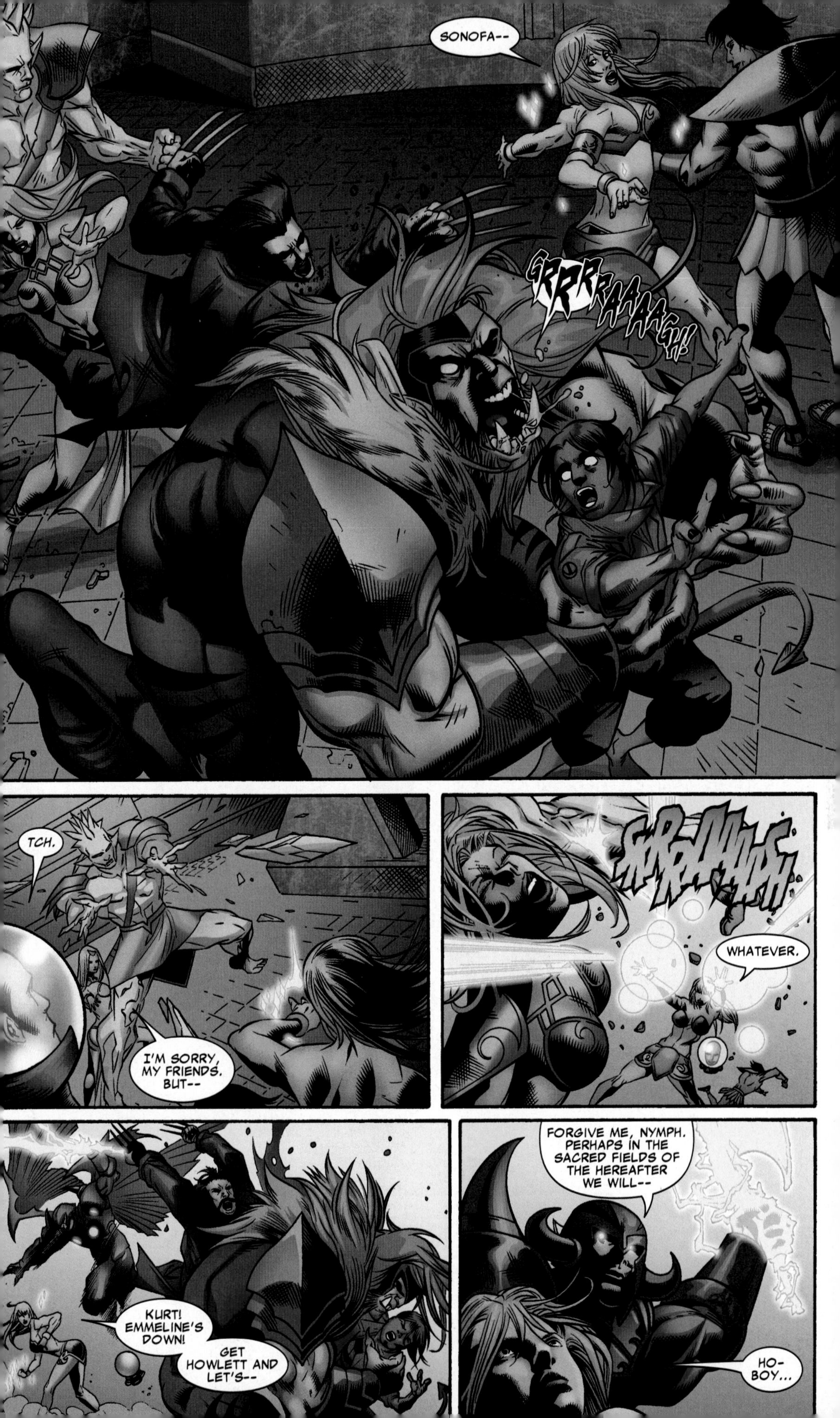
SONOFA--
GRRRRAAAAGH!
TCH.
I'M SORRY, MY FRIENDS. BUT--
WHATEVER.
KURT! EMMELINE'S DOWN!
GET HOWLETT AND LET'S--
FORGIVE ME, NYMPH. PERHAPS IN THE SACRED FIELDS OF THE HEREAFTER WE WILL--
HO-BOY...

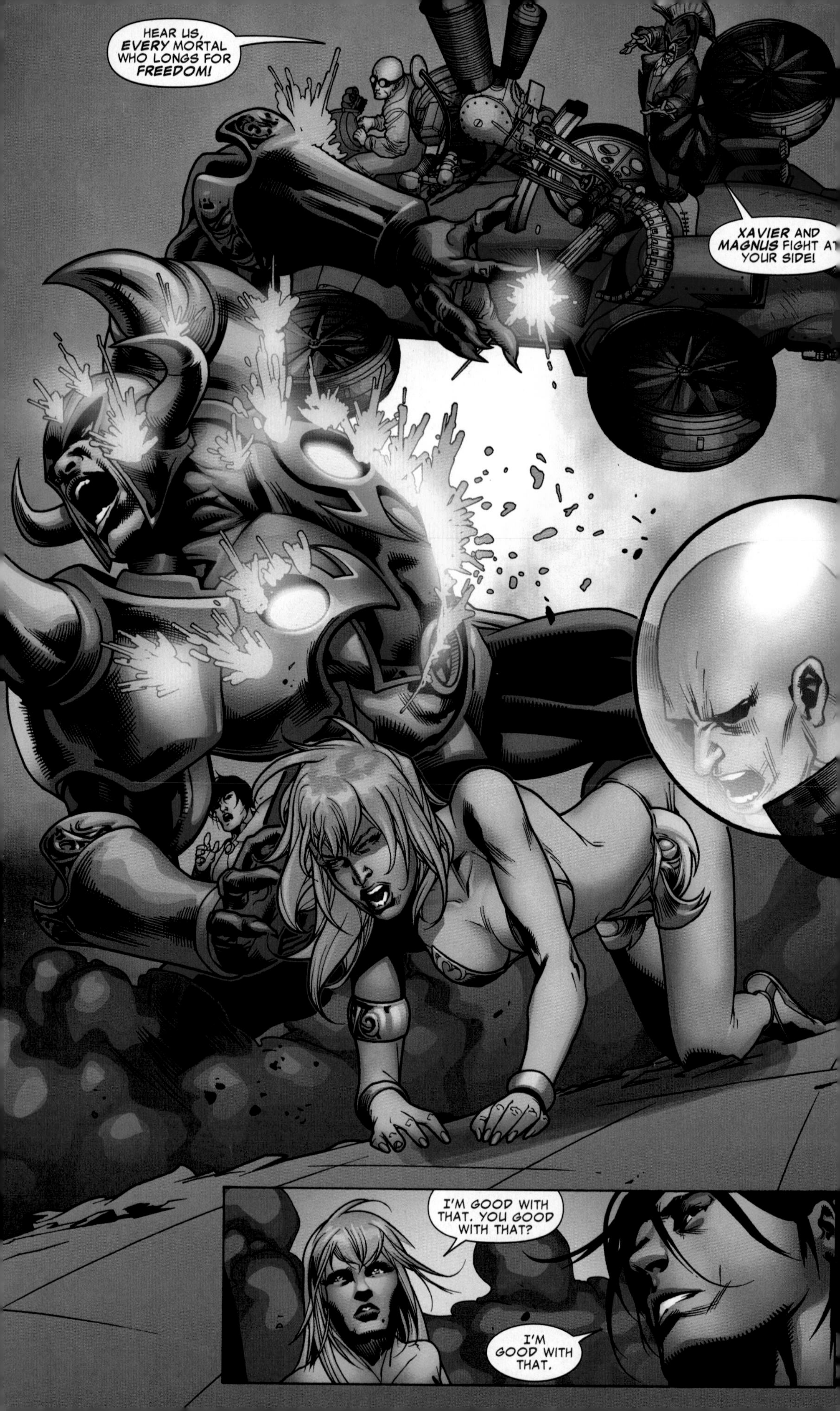
HEAR US, EVERY MORTAL WHO LONGS FOR FREEDOM!
XAVIER AND MAGNUS FIGHT AT YOUR SIDE!
I'M GOOD WITH THAT. YOU GOOD WITH THAT?
I'M GOOD WITH THAT.

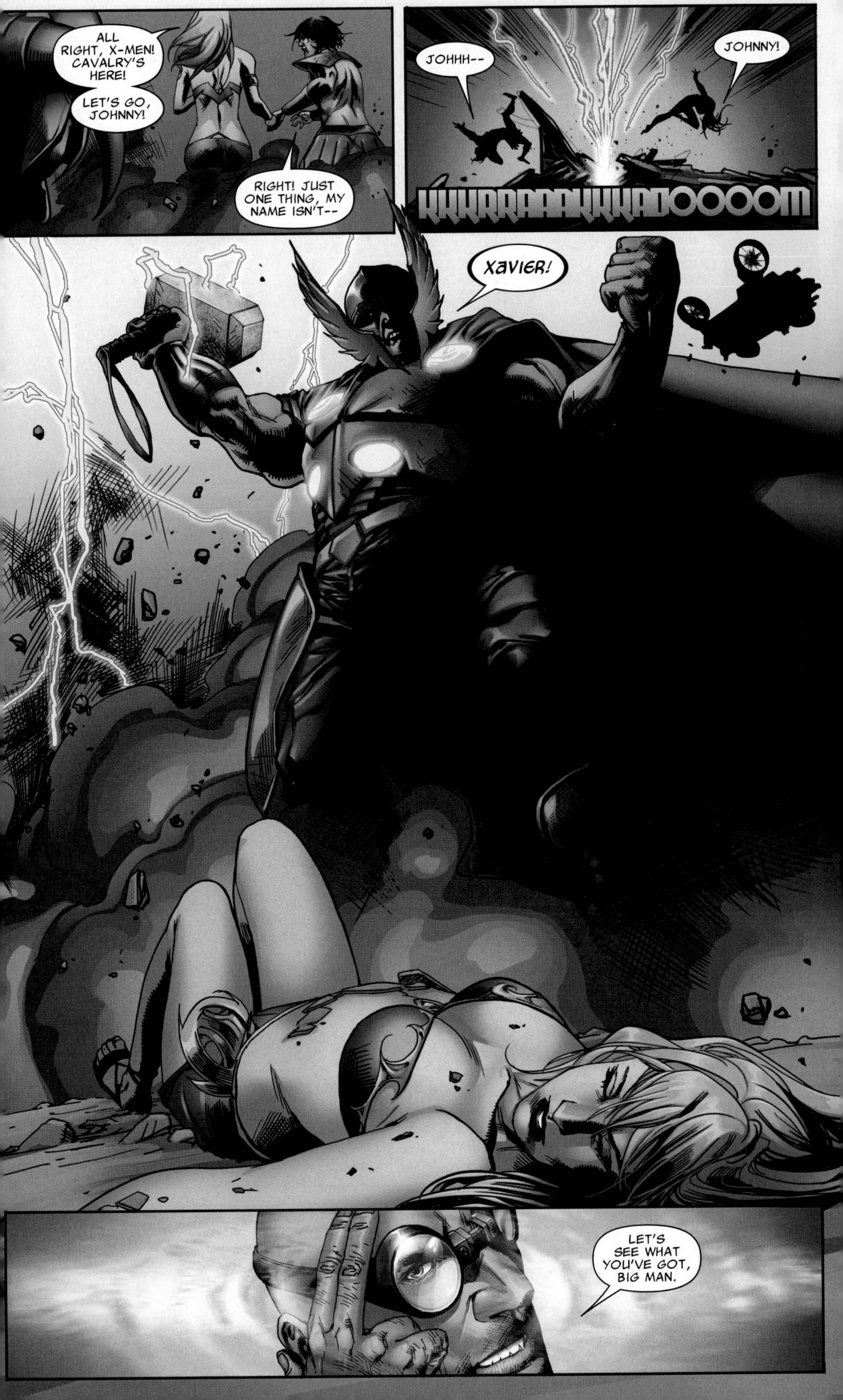
ALL RIGHT, X-MEN! CAVALRY'S HERE!
LET'S GO, JOHNNY!
RIGHT! JUST ONE THING, MY NAME ISN'T--
JOHHH--
JOHNNY!
KKKRRAAAKKKADOOOOM
XAVIER!
LET'S SEE WHAT YOU'VE GOT, BIG MAN.

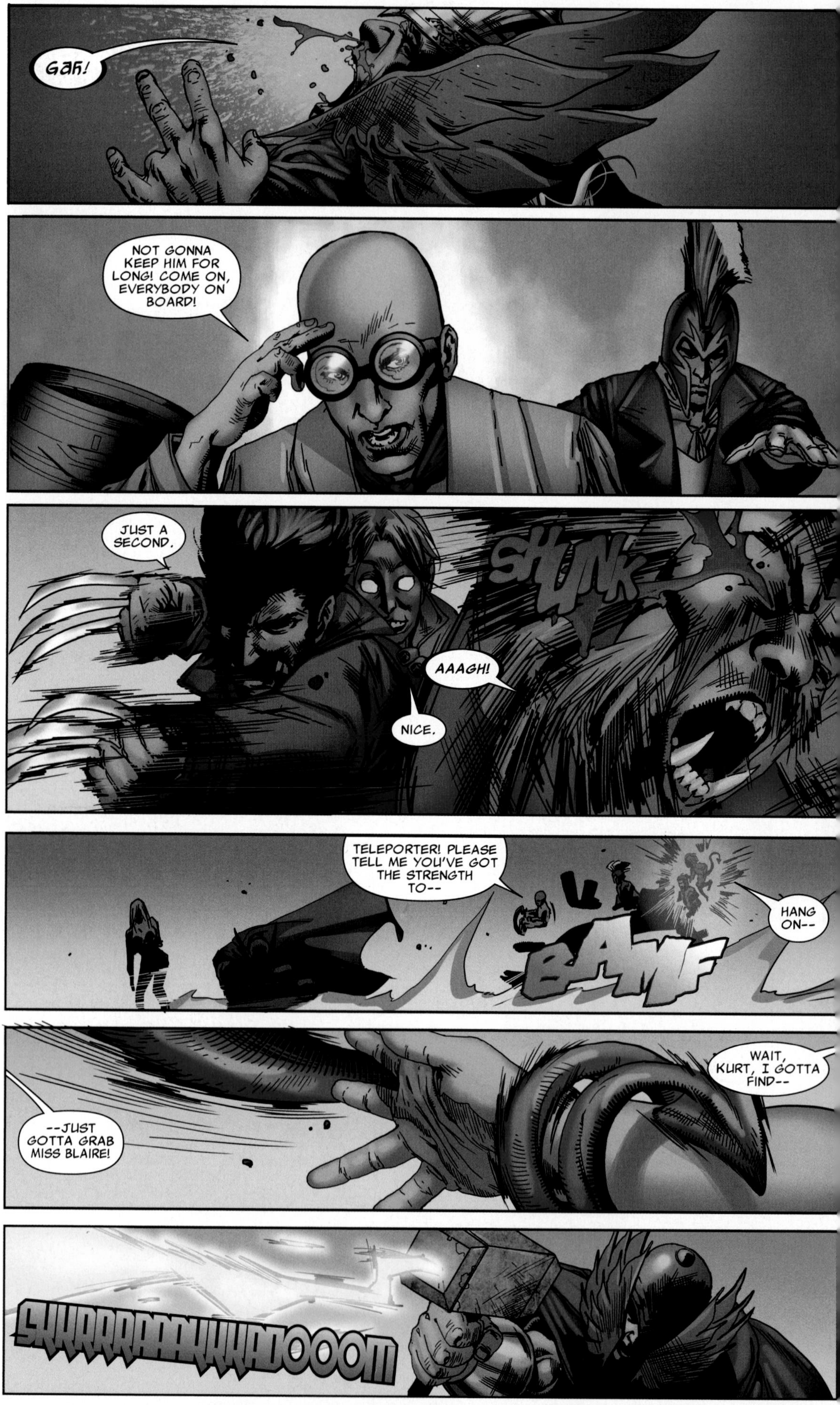
GAH!
NOT GONNA KEEP HIM FOR LONG! COME ON, EVERYBODY ON BOARD!
JUST A SECOND.
SHUNK
AAAGH!
NICE.
TELEPORTER! PLEASE TELL ME YOU'VE GOT THE STRENGTH TO--
HANG ON--
BAMF
WAIT, KURT, I GOTTA FIND--
--JUST GOTTA GRAB MISS BLAIRE!
SKRRRAAAKKKADOOOM

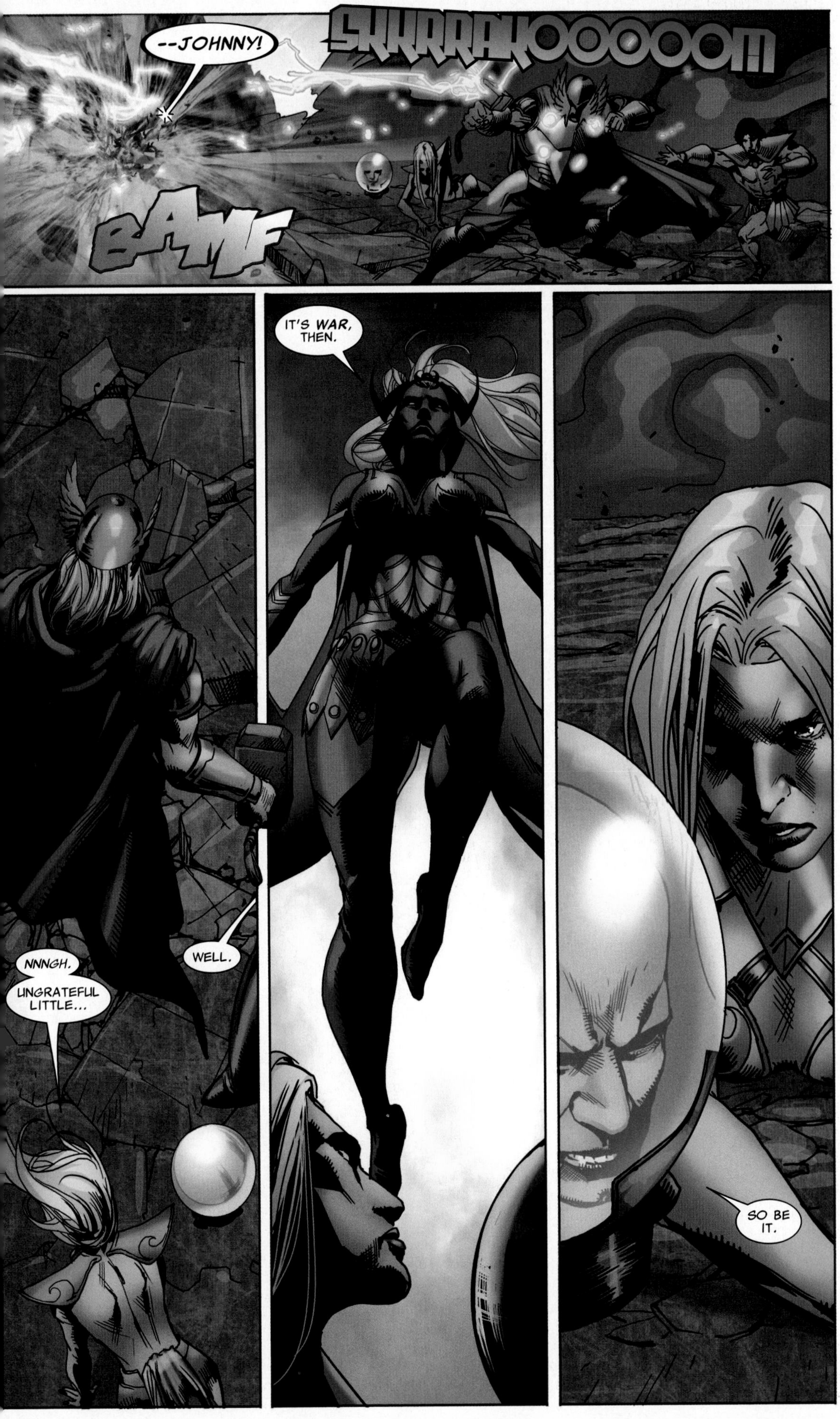
--JOHNNY!
SKRRRAKOOOOOOM!!
BAMF
IT'S WAR, THEN.
WELL.
NNNGH. UNGRATEFUL LITTLE...
SO BE IT.

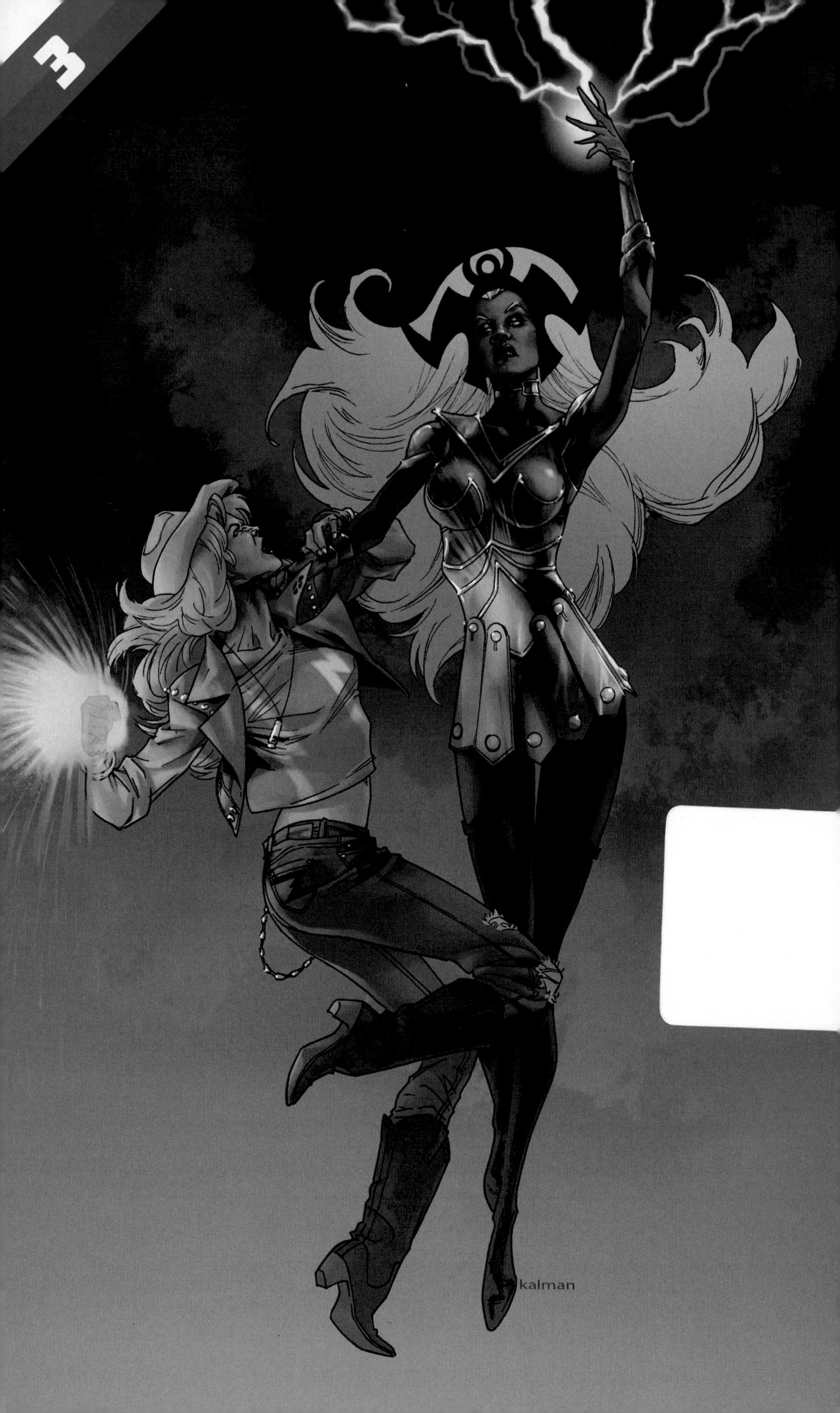
3
kalman

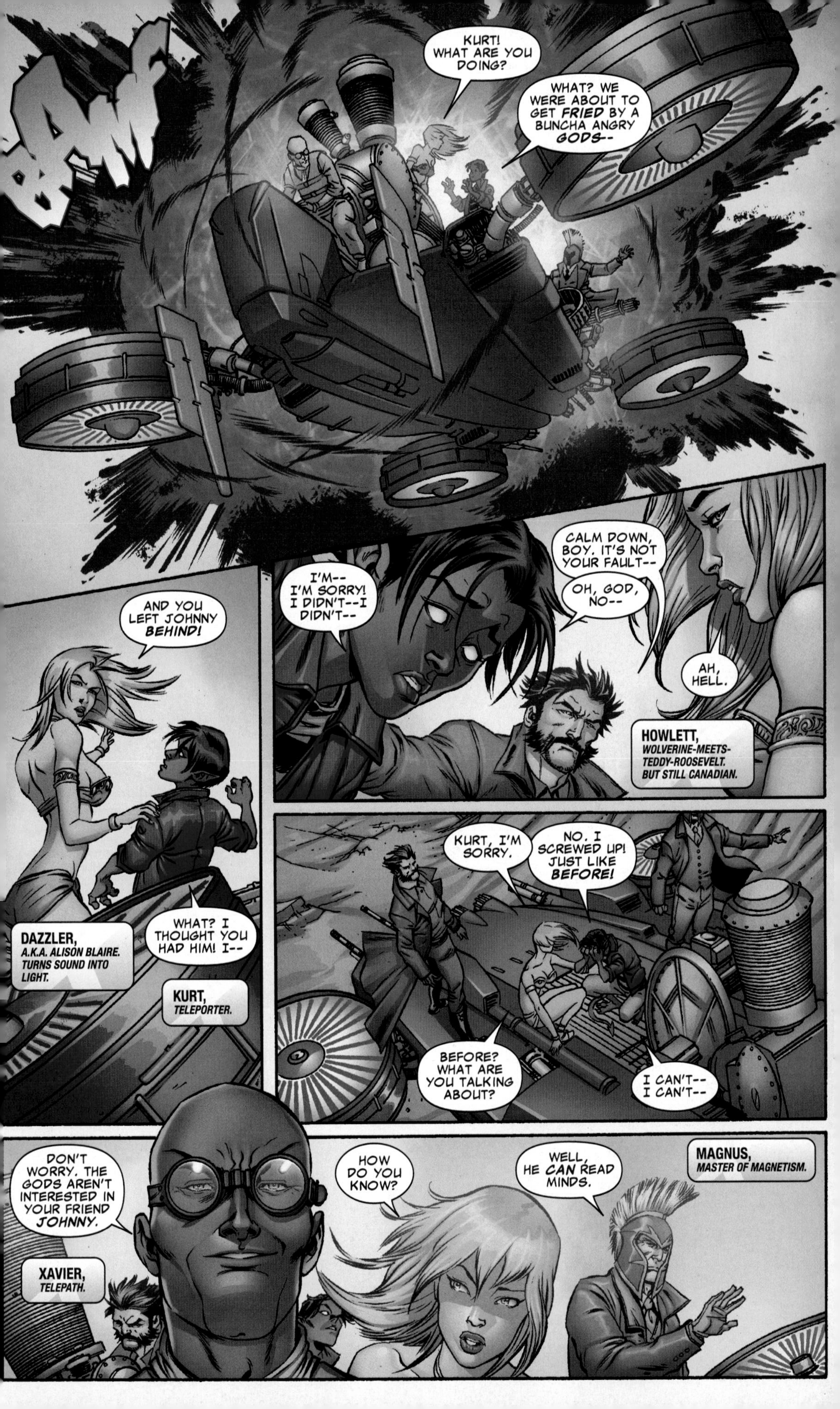

KURT! WHAT ARE YOU DOING?
WHAT? WE WERE ABOUT TO GET **FRIED** BY A BUNCHA ANGRY ***GODS--***
AND YOU LEFT JOHNNY ***BEHIND!***
DAZZLER, *A.K.A. ALISON BLAIRE. TURNS SOUND INTO LIGHT.*
WHAT? I THOUGHT YOU HAD HIM! I--
KURT, *TELEPORTER.*
I'M-- I'M SORRY! I DIDN'T--I DIDN'T--
CALM DOWN, BOY. IT'S NOT YOUR FAULT--
OH, GOD, NO--
AH, HELL.
HOWLETT, *WOLVERINE-MEETS-TEDDY-ROOSEVELT. BUT STILL CANADIAN.*
KURT, I'M SORRY.
NO. I SCREWED UP! JUST LIKE ***BEFORE!***
BEFORE? WHAT ARE YOU TALKING ABOUT?
I CAN'T-- I CAN'T--
DON'T WORRY. THE GODS AREN'T INTERESTED IN YOUR FRIEND *JOHNNY*.
XAVIER, *TELEPATH.*
HOW DO YOU KNOW?
WELL, HE ***CAN*** READ MINDS.
MAGNUS, *MASTER OF MAGNETISM.*

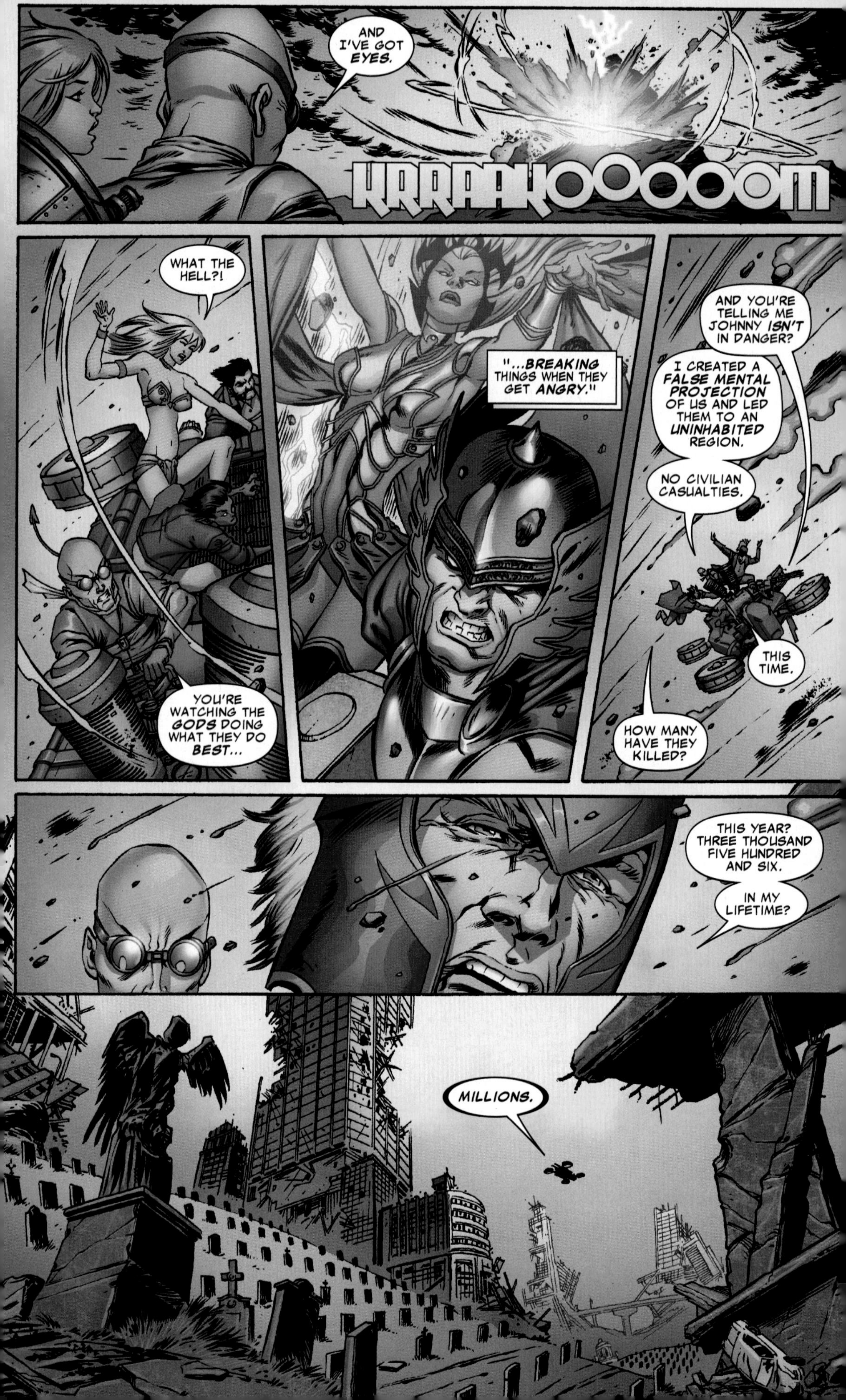
AND I'VE GOT EYES.
KRRAAKOOOOOOM
WHAT THE HELL?!
YOU'RE WATCHING THE GODS DOING WHAT THEY DO BEST...
"...BREAKING THINGS WHEN THEY GET ANGRY."
AND YOU'RE TELLING ME JOHNNY ISN'T IN DANGER?
I CREATED A FALSE MENTAL PROJECTION OF US AND LED THEM TO AN UNINHABITED REGION.
NO CIVILIAN CASUALTIES.
THIS TIME.
HOW MANY HAVE THEY KILLED?
THIS YEAR? THREE THOUSAND FIVE HUNDRED AND SIX.
IN MY LIFETIME?
MILLIONS.

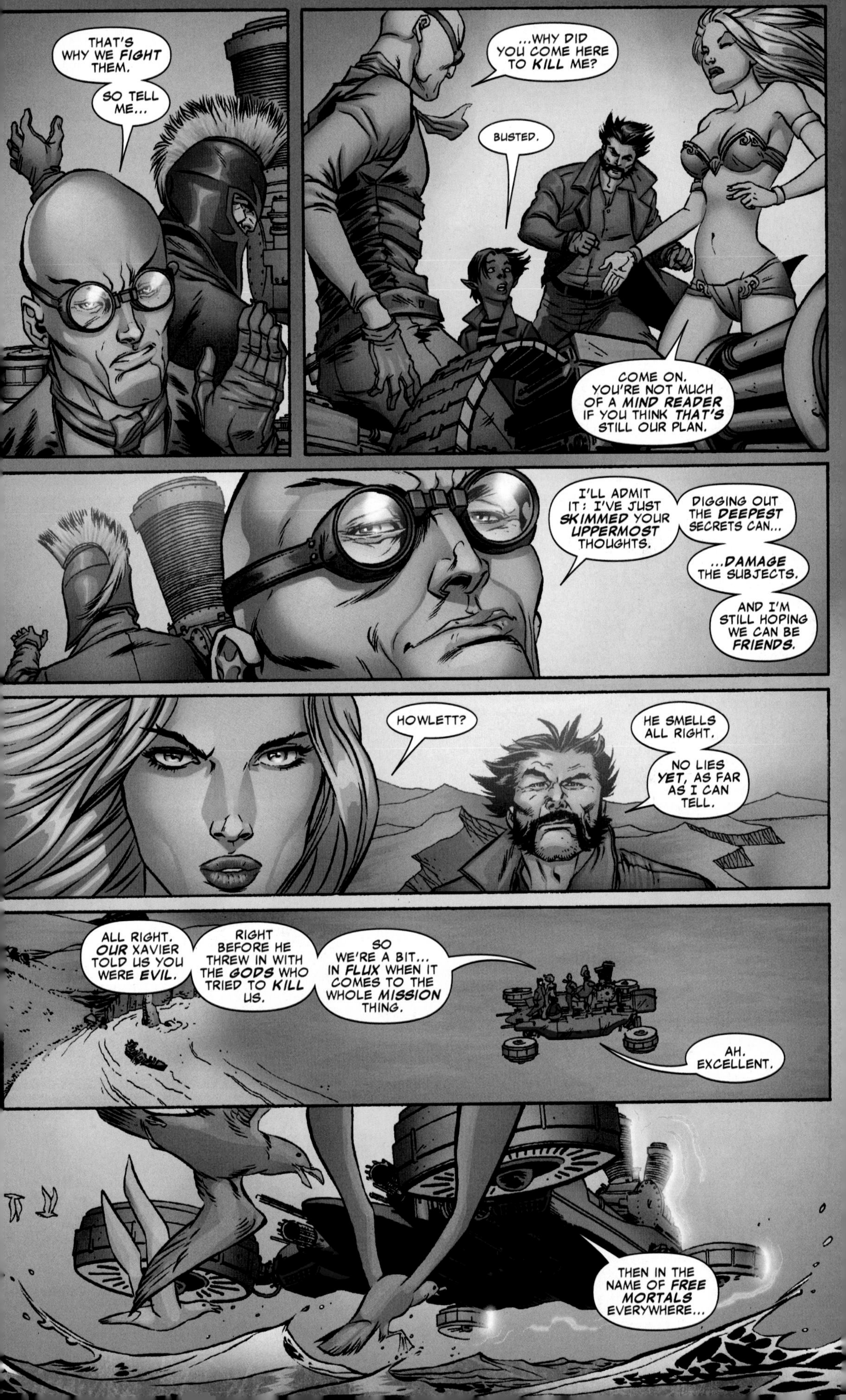
THAT'S WHY WE FIGHT THEM.
SO TELL ME...
...WHY DID YOU COME HERE TO KILL ME?
BUSTED.
COME ON. YOU'RE NOT MUCH OF A MIND READER IF YOU THINK THAT'S STILL OUR PLAN.
I'LL ADMIT IT: I'VE JUST SKIMMED YOUR UPPERMOST THOUGHTS.
DIGGING OUT THE DEEPEST SECRETS CAN...
...DAMAGE THE SUBJECTS.
AND I'M STILL HOPING WE CAN BE FRIENDS.
HOWLETT?
HE SMELLS ALL RIGHT.
NO LIES YET, AS FAR AS I CAN TELL.
ALL RIGHT. OUR XAVIER TOLD US YOU WERE EVIL.
RIGHT BEFORE HE THREW IN WITH THE GODS WHO TRIED TO KILL US.
SO WE'RE A BIT... IN FLUX WHEN IT COMES TO THE WHOLE MISSION THING.
AH. EXCELLENT.
THEN IN THE NAME OF FREE MORTALS EVERYWHERE...

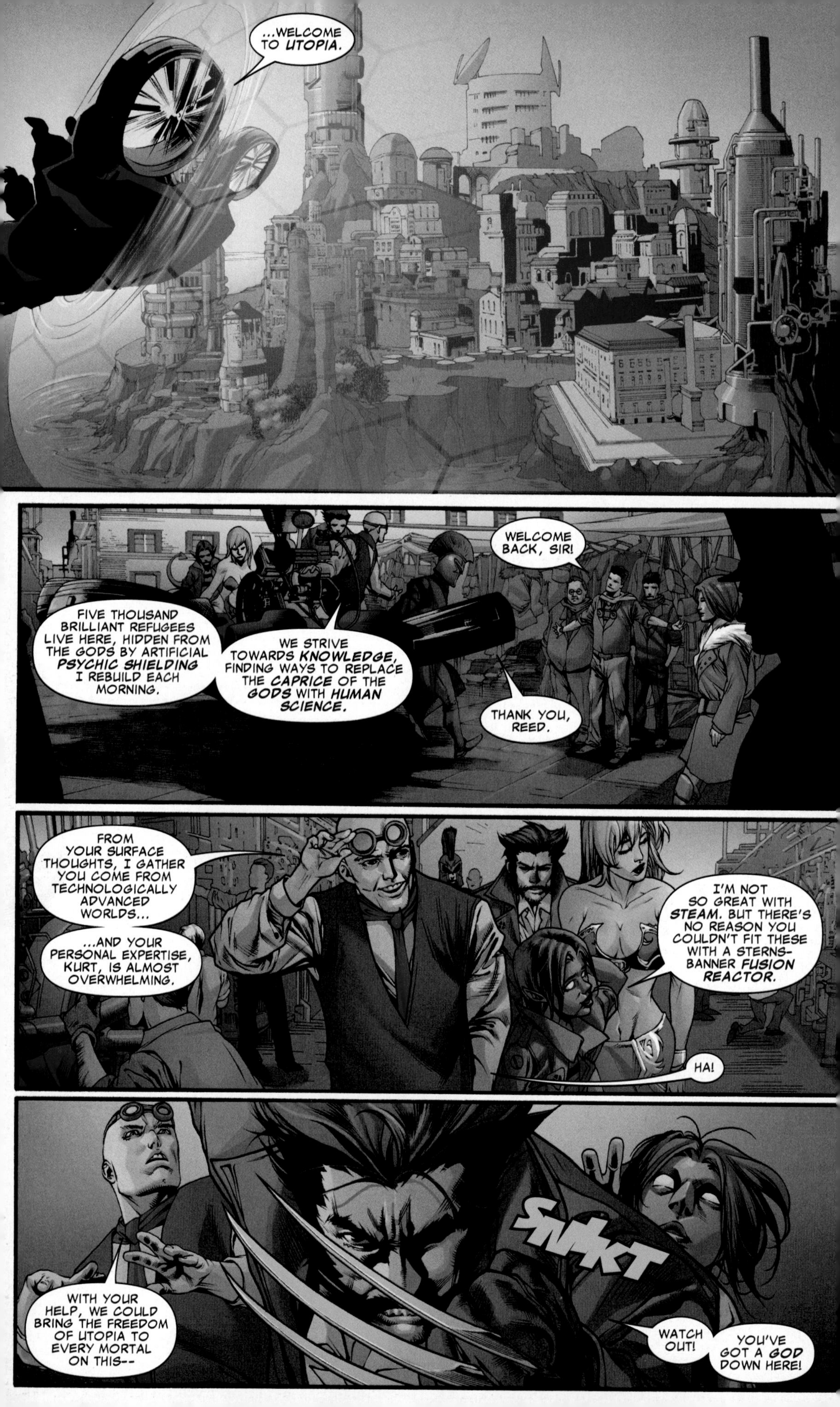
...WELCOME TO UTOPIA.
WELCOME BACK, SIR!
FIVE THOUSAND BRILLIANT REFUGEES LIVE HERE, HIDDEN FROM THE GODS BY ARTIFICIAL PSYCHIC SHIELDING I REBUILD EACH MORNING.
WE STRIVE TOWARDS KNOWLEDGE, FINDING WAYS TO REPLACE THE CAPRICE OF THE GODS WITH HUMAN SCIENCE.
THANK YOU, REED.
FROM YOUR SURFACE THOUGHTS, I GATHER YOU COME FROM TECHNOLOGICALLY ADVANCED WORLDS...
...AND YOUR PERSONAL EXPERTISE, KURT, IS ALMOST OVERWHELMING.
I'M NOT SO GREAT WITH STEAM. BUT THERE'S NO REASON YOU COULDN'T FIT THESE WITH A STERNS-BANNER FUSION REACTOR.
HA!
SNIKT
WITH YOUR HELP, WE COULD BRING THE FREEDOM OF UTOPIA TO EVERY MORTAL ON THIS--
WATCH OUT!
YOU'VE GOT A GOD DOWN HERE!

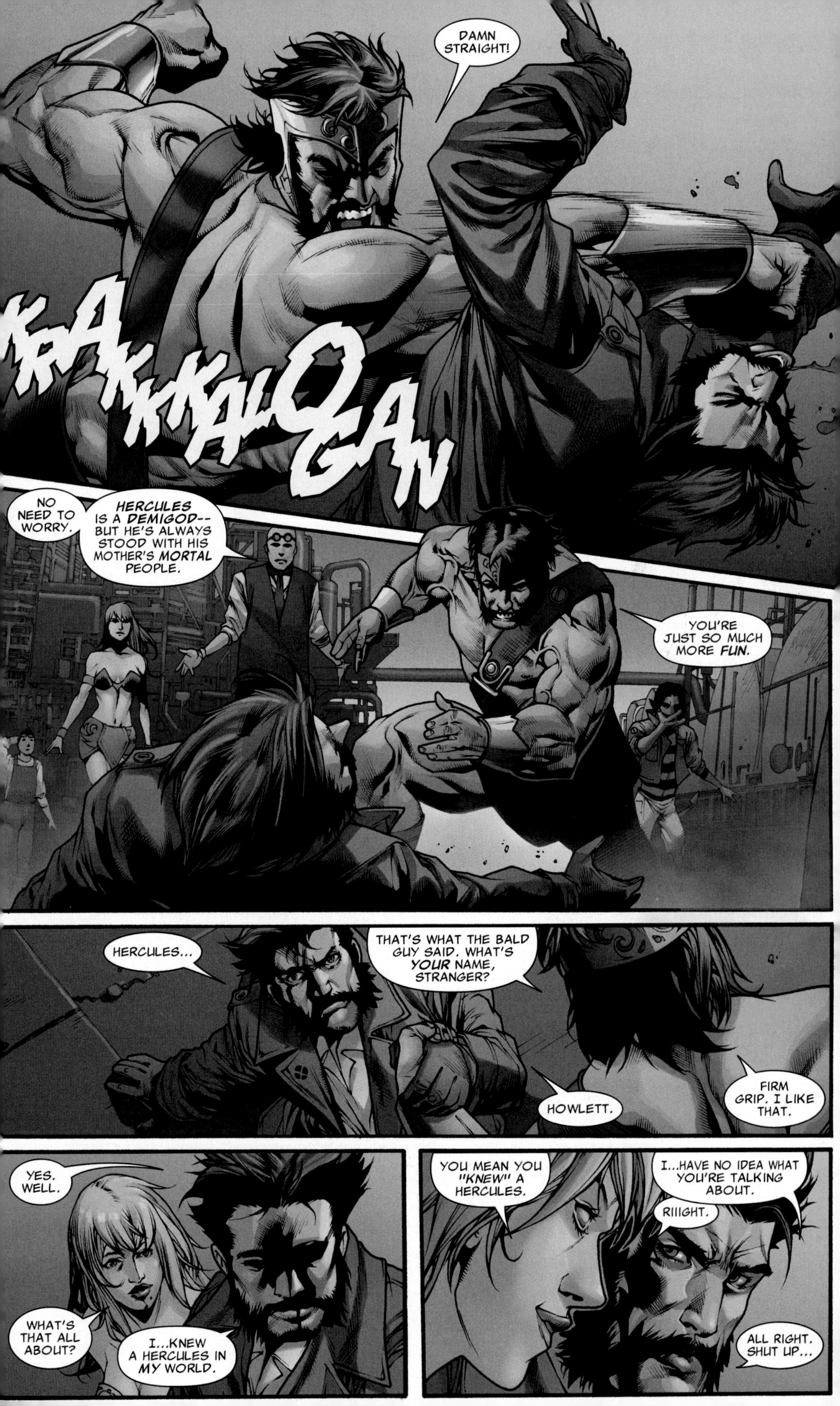
DAMN STRAIGHT!
KRAKKKALOOGAN
NO NEED TO WORRY.
HERCULES IS A DEMIGOD-- BUT HE'S ALWAYS STOOD WITH HIS MOTHER'S MORTAL PEOPLE.
YOU'RE JUST SO MUCH MORE FUN.
HERCULES...
THAT'S WHAT THE BALD GUY SAID. WHAT'S YOUR NAME, STRANGER?
HOWLETT.
FIRM GRIP. I LIKE THAT.
YES. WELL.
WHAT'S THAT ALL ABOUT?
I...KNEW A HERCULES IN MY WORLD.
YOU MEAN YOU "KNEW" A HERCULES.
I...HAVE NO IDEA WHAT YOU'RE TALKING ABOUT.
RIIIGHT.
ALL RIGHT. SHUT UP...

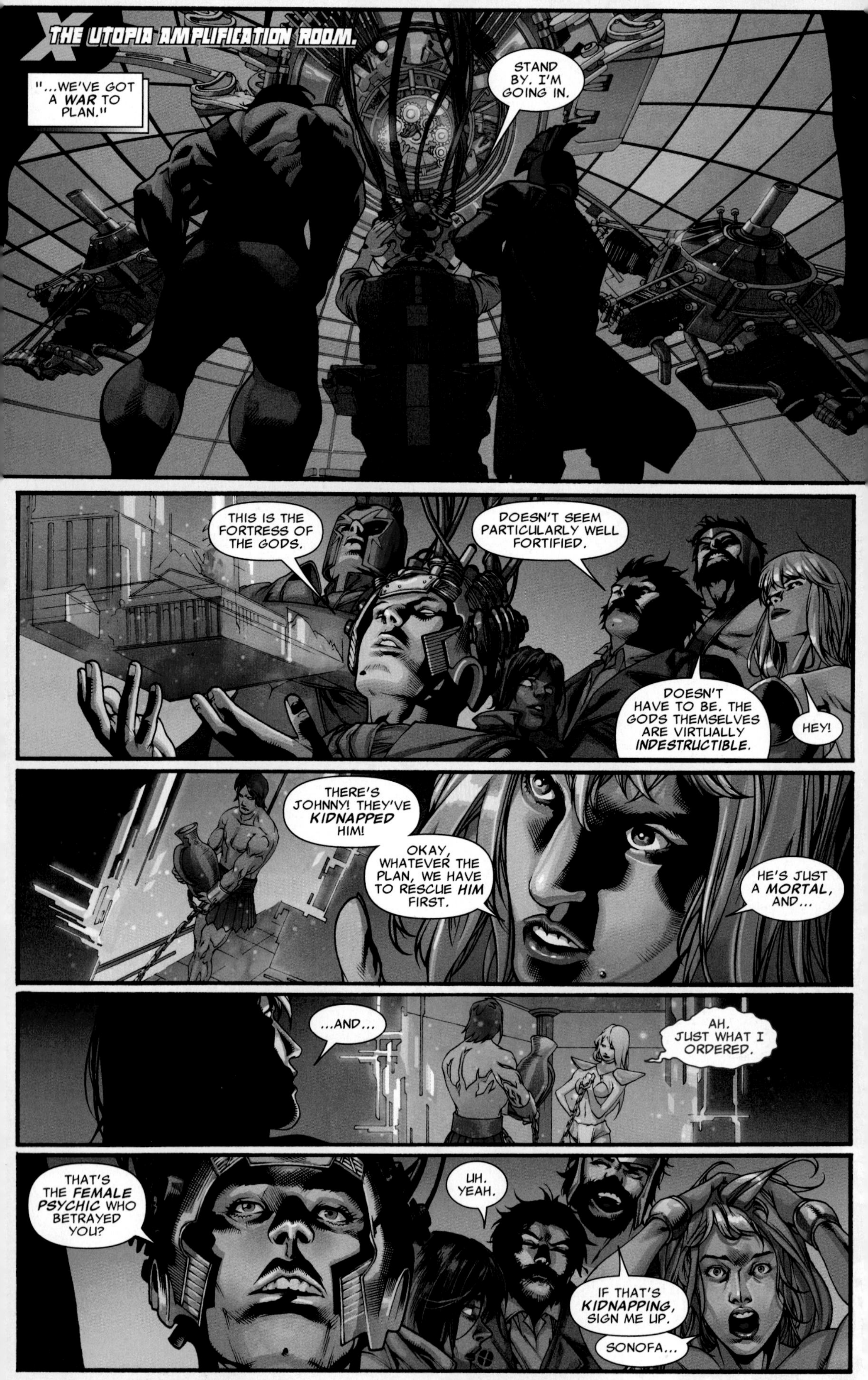
THE UTOPIA AMPLIFICATION ROOM.
"...WE'VE GOT A WAR TO PLAN."
STAND BY. I'M GOING IN.
THIS IS THE FORTRESS OF THE GODS.
DOESN'T SEEM PARTICULARLY WELL FORTIFIED.
DOESN'T HAVE TO BE. THE GODS THEMSELVES ARE VIRTUALLY INDESTRUCTIBLE.
HEY!
THERE'S JOHNNY! THEY'VE KIDNAPPED HIM!
OKAY, WHATEVER THE PLAN, WE HAVE TO RESCUE HIM FIRST.
HE'S JUST A MORTAL, AND...
...AND...
AH. JUST WHAT I ORDERED.
THAT'S THE FEMALE PSYCHIC WHO BETRAYED YOU?
UH. YEAH.
IF THAT'S KIDNAPPING, SIGN ME UP.
SONOFA...

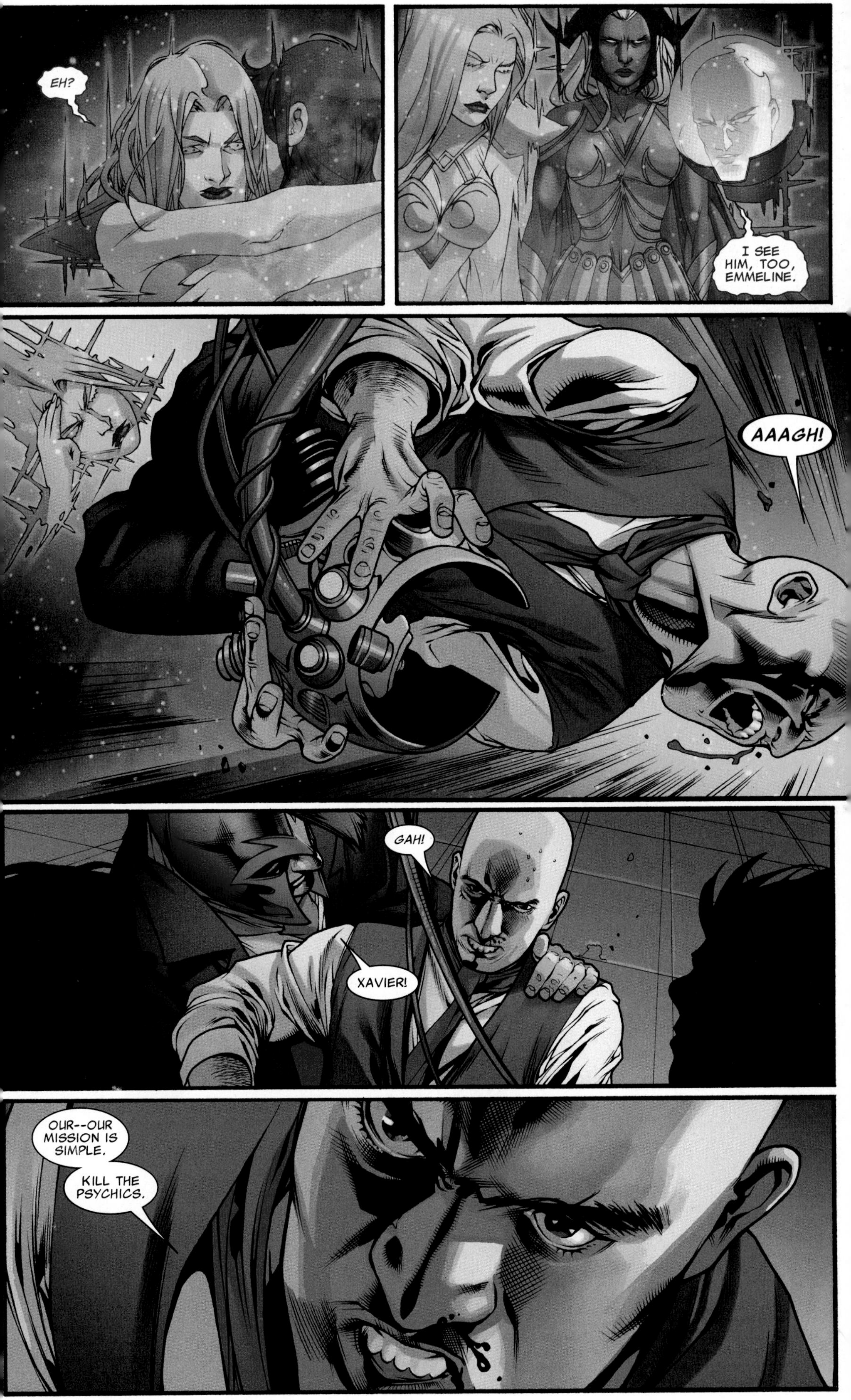
EH?
I SEE HIM, TOO, EMMELINE.
AAAGH!
GAH!
XAVIER!
OUR--OUR MISSION IS SIMPLE.
KILL THE PSYCHICS.

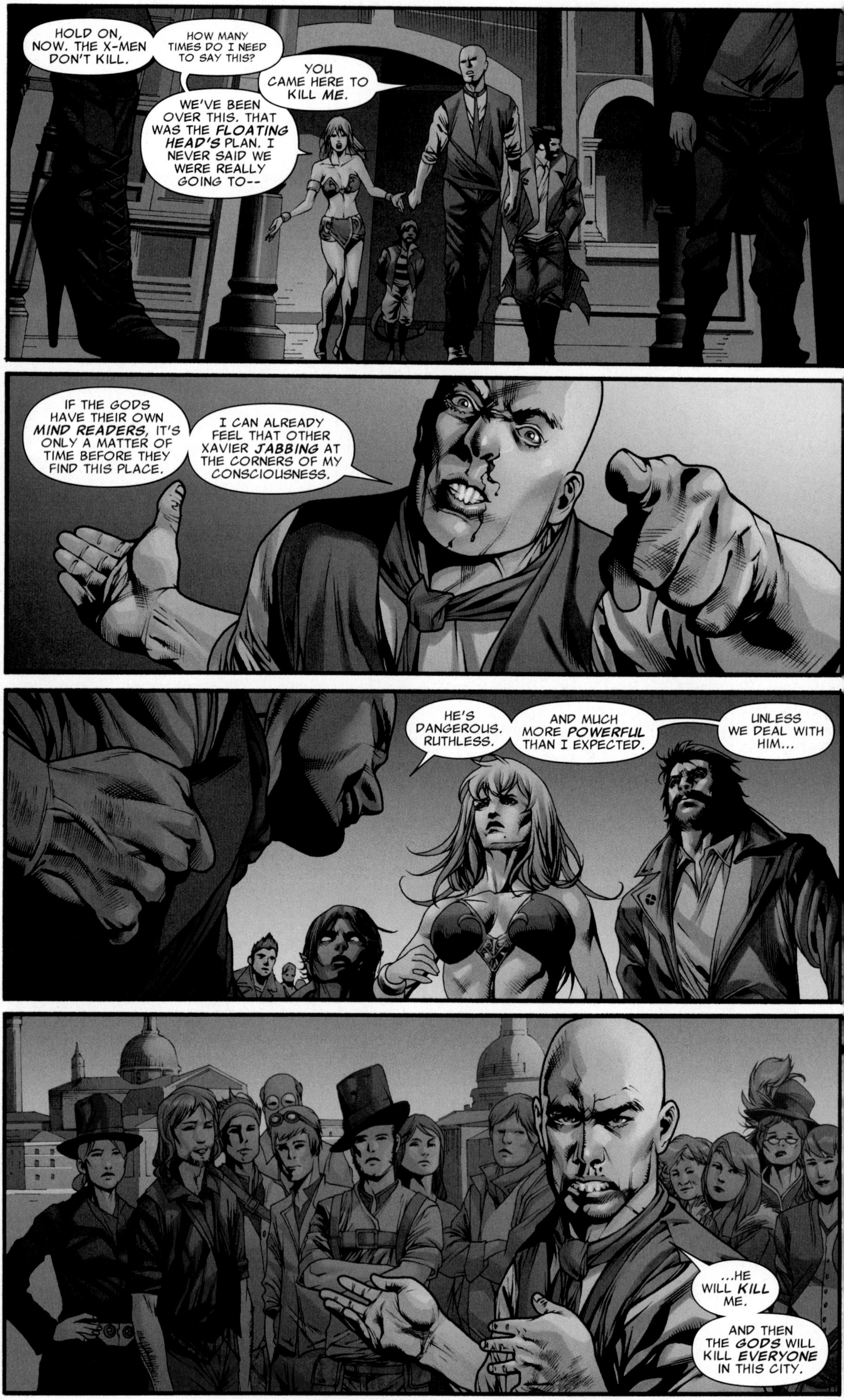
HOLD ON, NOW. THE X-MEN DON'T KILL.
HOW MANY TIMES DO I NEED TO SAY THIS?
WE'VE BEEN OVER THIS. THAT WAS THE FLOATING HEAD'S PLAN. I NEVER SAID WE WERE REALLY GOING TO--
YOU CAME HERE TO KILL ME.
IF THE GODS HAVE THEIR OWN MIND READERS, IT'S ONLY A MATTER OF TIME BEFORE THEY FIND THIS PLACE.
I CAN ALREADY FEEL THAT OTHER XAVIER JABBING AT THE CORNERS OF MY CONSCIOUSNESS.
HE'S DANGEROUS. RUTHLESS.
AND MUCH MORE POWERFUL THAN I EXPECTED.
UNLESS WE DEAL WITH HIM...
...HE WILL KILL ME.
AND THEN THE GODS WILL KILL EVERYONE IN THIS CITY.

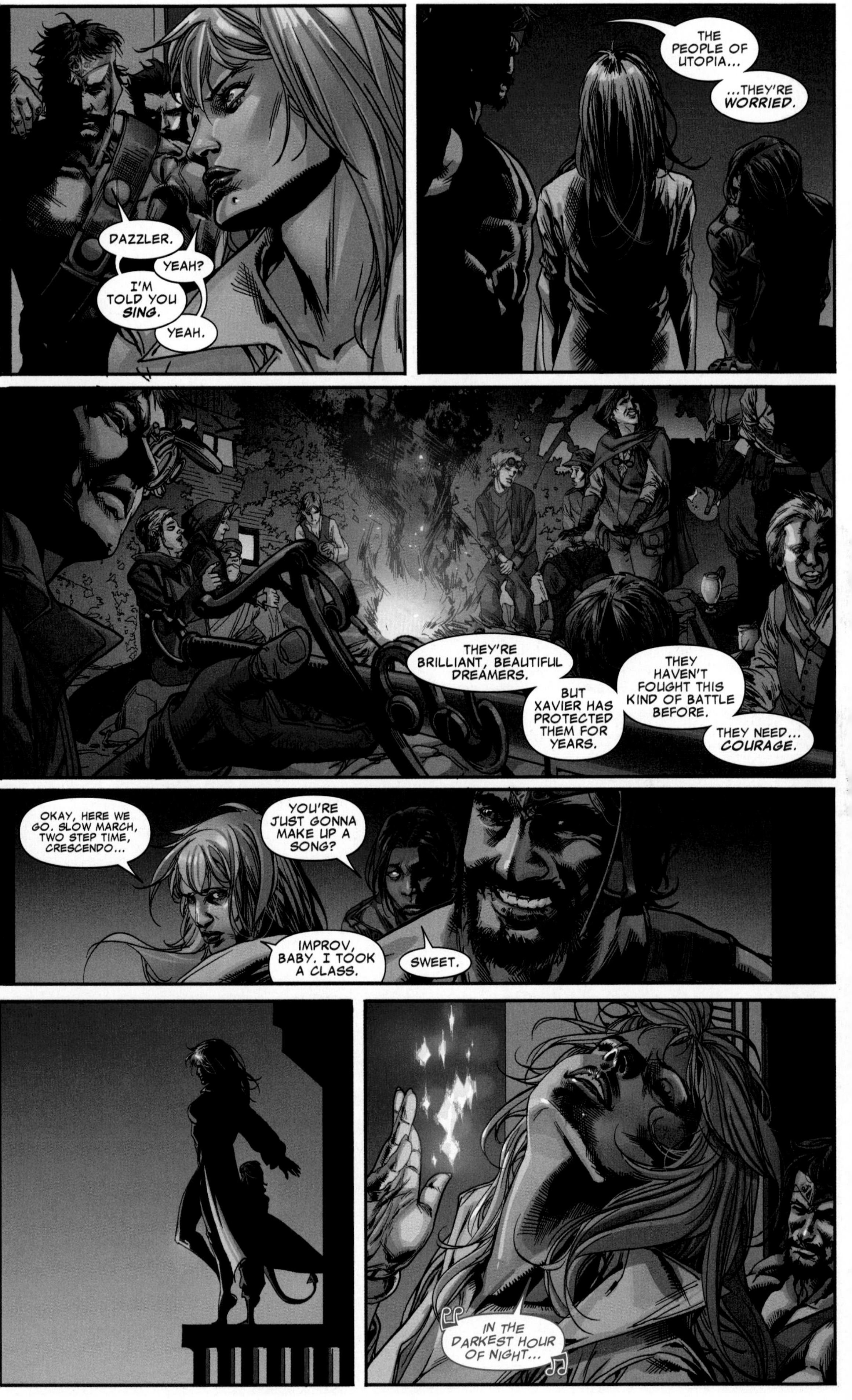
DAZZLER.
YEAH?
I'M TOLD YOU SING.
YEAH.
THE PEOPLE OF UTOPIA...
...THEY'RE WORRIED.
THEY'RE BRILLIANT, BEAUTIFUL DREAMERS.
BUT XAVIER HAS PROTECTED THEM FOR YEARS.
THEY HAVEN'T FOUGHT THIS KIND OF BATTLE BEFORE.
THEY NEED... COURAGE.
OKAY, HERE WE GO. SLOW MARCH, TWO STEP TIME, CRESCENDO...
YOU'RE JUST GONNA MAKE UP A SONG?
IMPROV, BABY. I TOOK A CLASS.
SWEET.
IN THE DARKEST HOUR OF NIGHT...

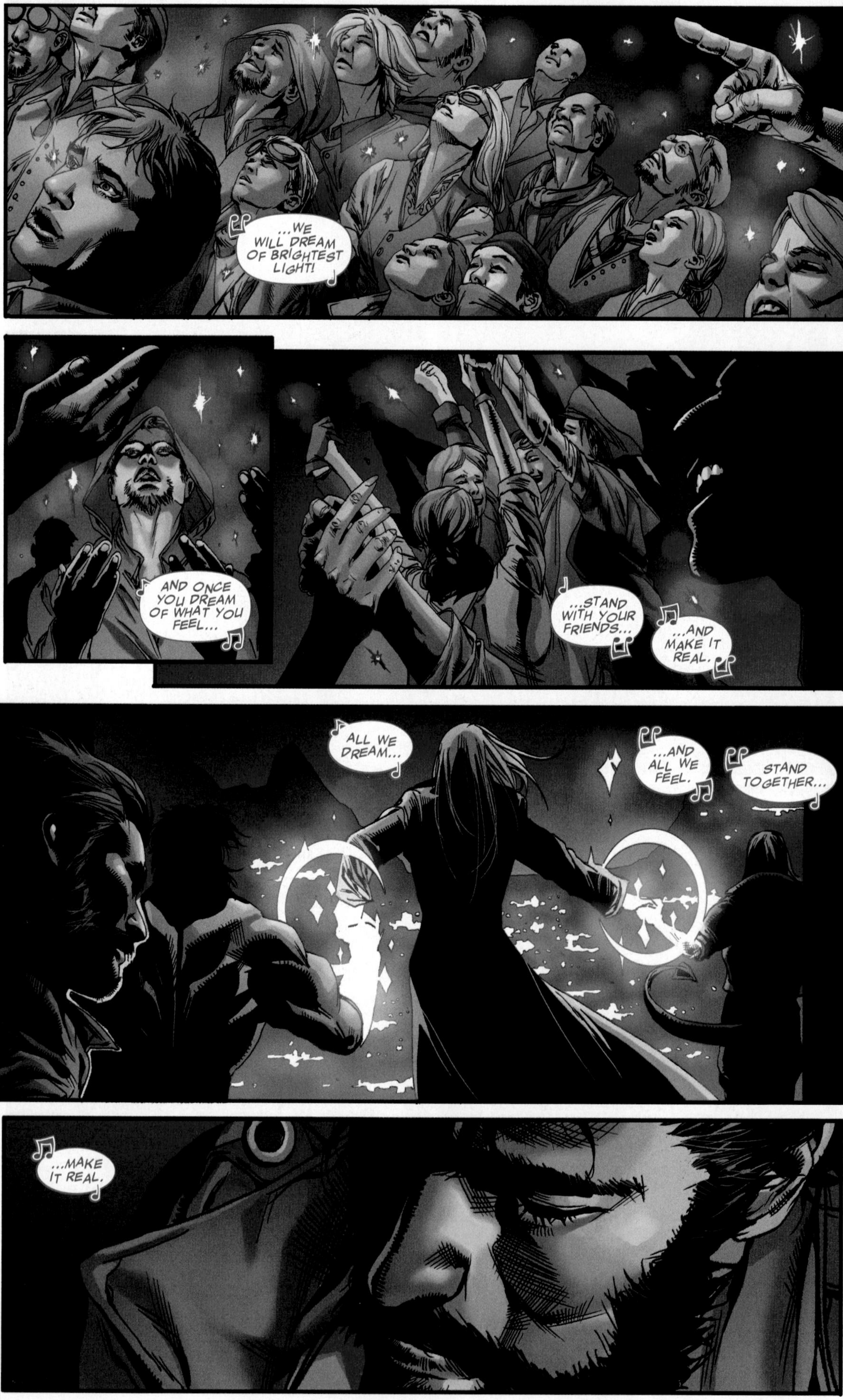
...WE WILL DREAM OF BRIGHTEST LIGHT!
AND ONCE YOU DREAM OF WHAT YOU FEEL...
...STAND WITH YOUR FRIENDS...
...AND MAKE IT REAL.
ALL WE DREAM...
...AND ALL WE FEEL.
STAND TOGETHER...
...MAKE IT REAL.

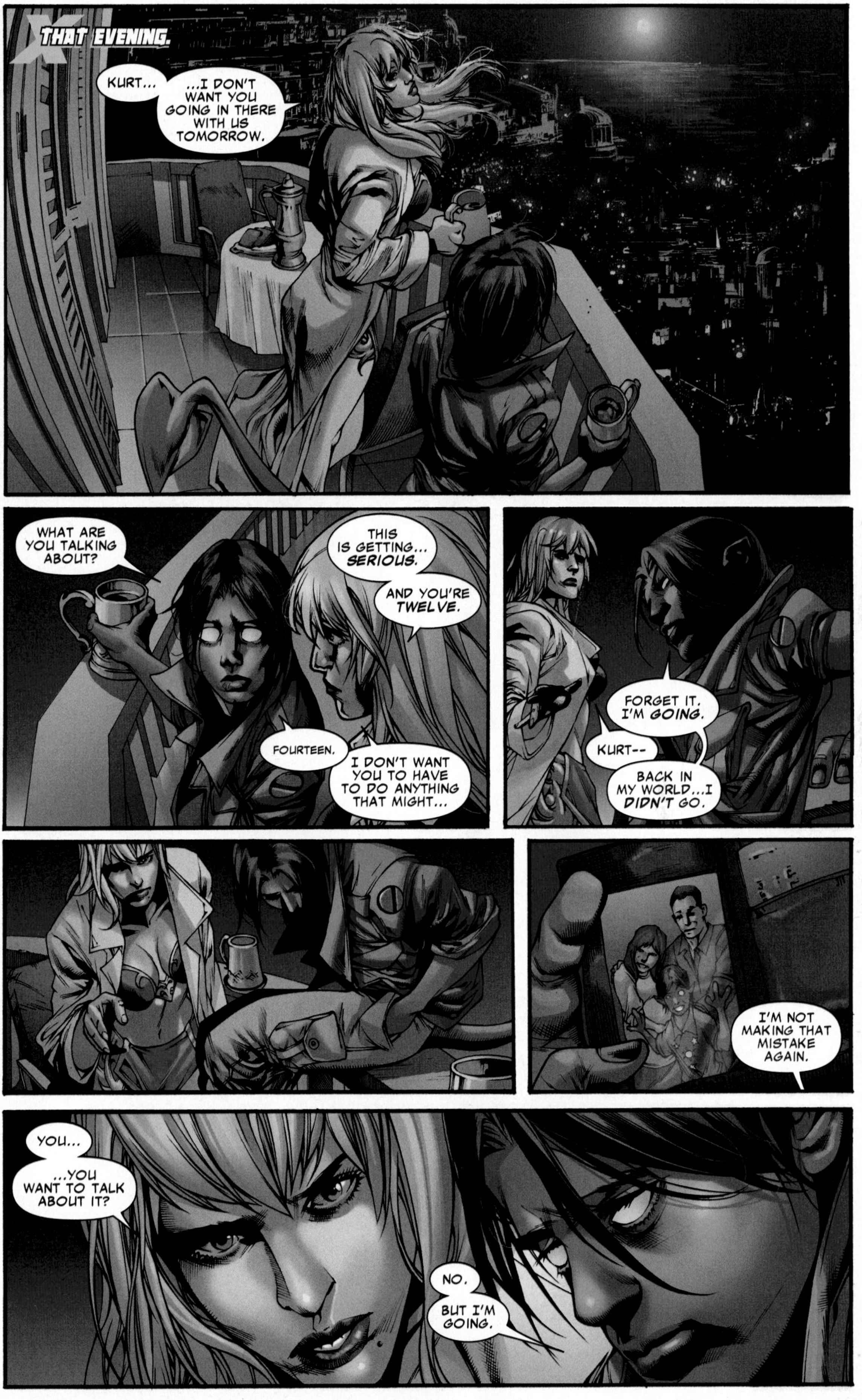
THAT EVENING.
KURT...
...I DON'T WANT YOU GOING IN THERE WITH US TOMORROW.
WHAT ARE YOU TALKING ABOUT?
THIS IS GETTING... SERIOUS.
AND YOU'RE TWELVE.
FOURTEEN.
I DON'T WANT YOU TO HAVE TO DO ANYTHING THAT MIGHT...
FORGET IT. I'M GOING.
KURT--
BACK IN MY WORLD...I DIDN'T GO.
I'M NOT MAKING THAT MISTAKE AGAIN.
YOU...
...YOU WANT TO TALK ABOUT IT?
NO.
BUT I'M GOING.

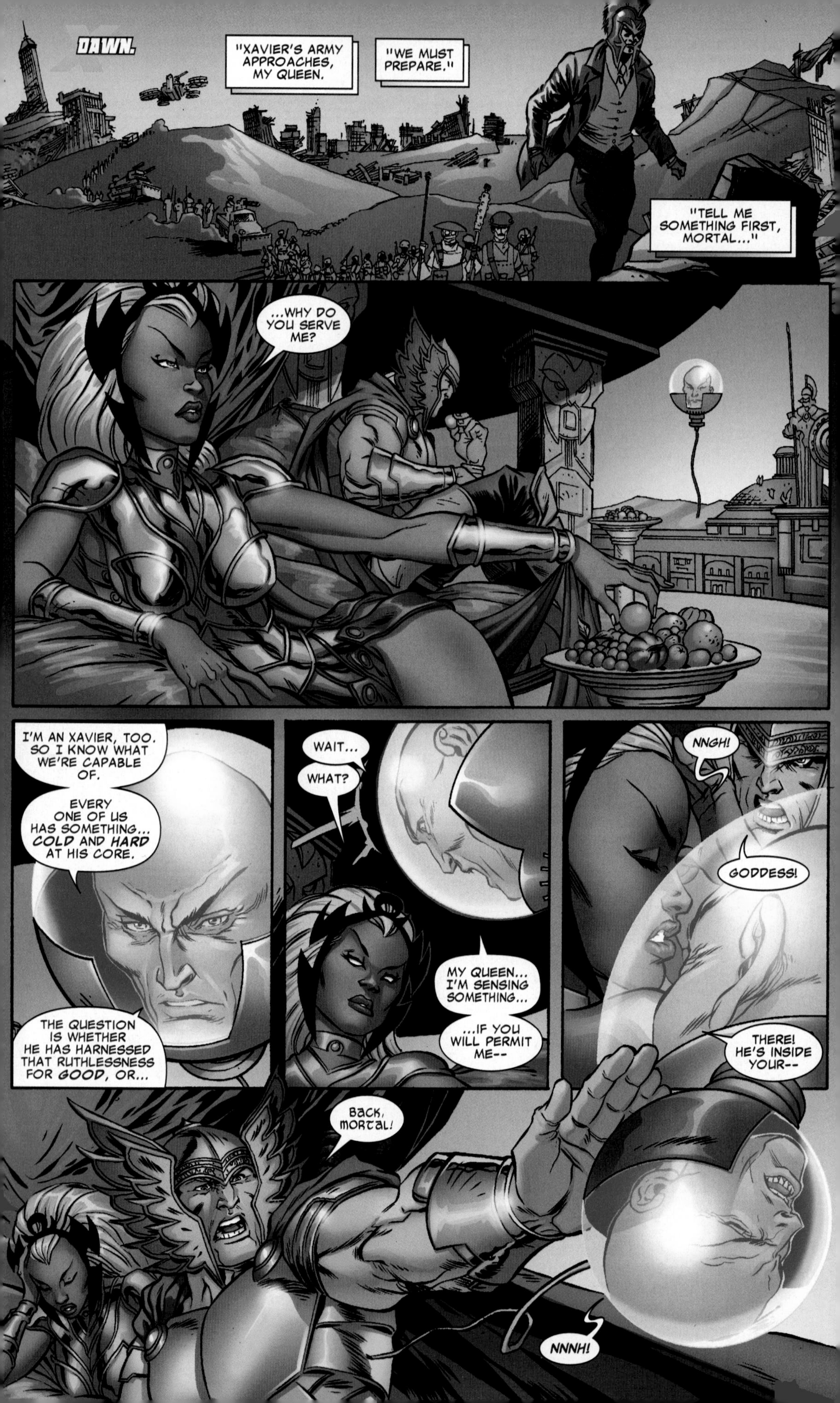
DAWN.
"XAVIER'S ARMY APPROACHES, MY QUEEN.
"WE MUST PREPARE."
"TELL ME SOMETHING FIRST, MORTAL..."
...WHY DO YOU SERVE ME?
I'M AN XAVIER, TOO. SO I KNOW WHAT WE'RE CAPABLE OF.
EVERY ONE OF US HAS SOMETHING... COLD AND HARD AT HIS CORE.
THE QUESTION IS WHETHER HE HAS HARNESSED THAT RUTHLESSNESS FOR GOOD, OR...
WAIT...
WHAT?
MY QUEEN... I'M SENSING SOMETHING...
...IF YOU WILL PERMIT ME--
NNGH!
GODDESS!
THERE! HE'S INSIDE YOUR--
BACK, MORTAL!
NNNH!

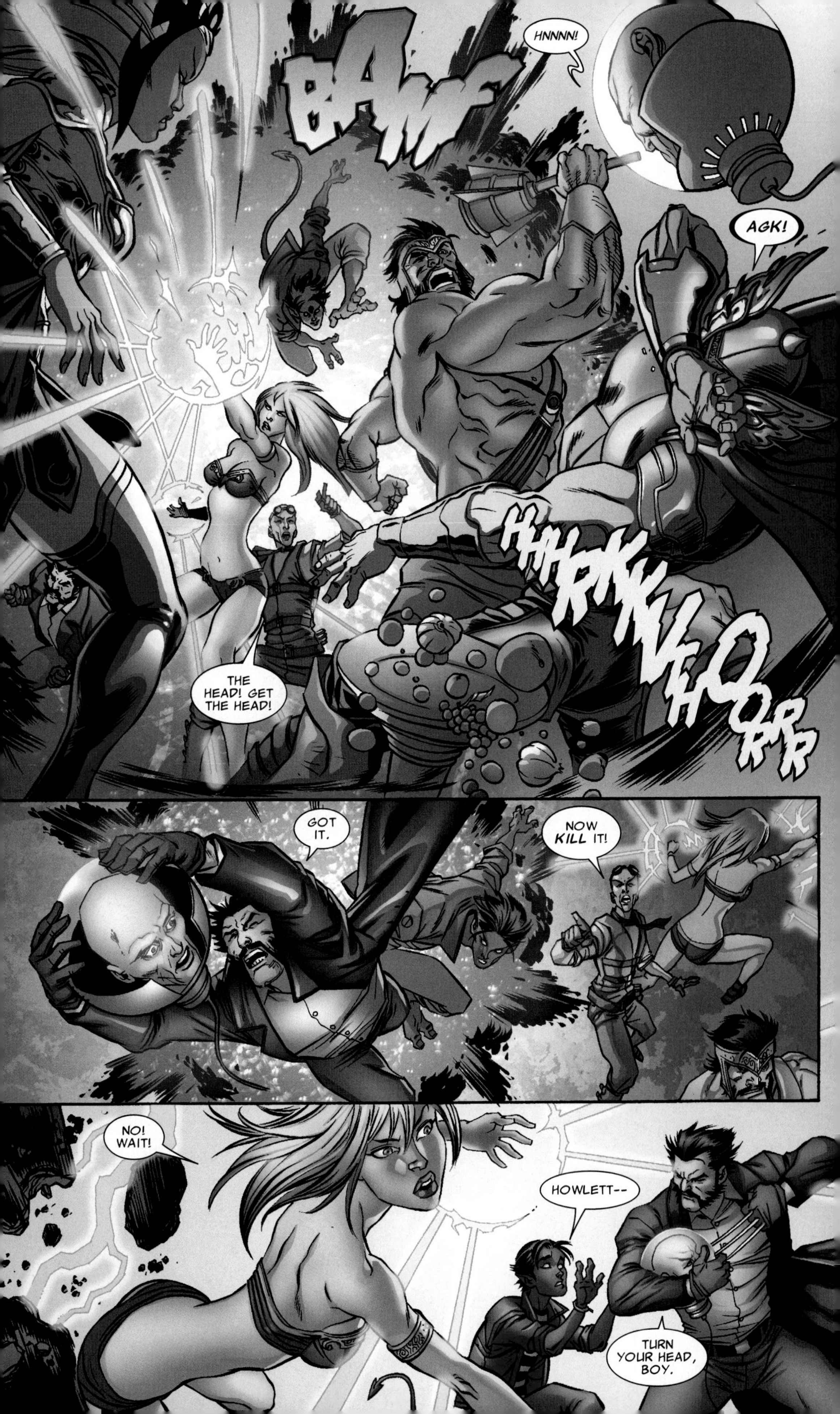
BAM
HNNNN!
AGK!
HHHRKKKHORRR
THE HEAD! GET THE HEAD!
GOT IT.
NOW KILL IT!
NO! WAIT!
HOWLETT--
TURN YOUR HEAD, BOY.

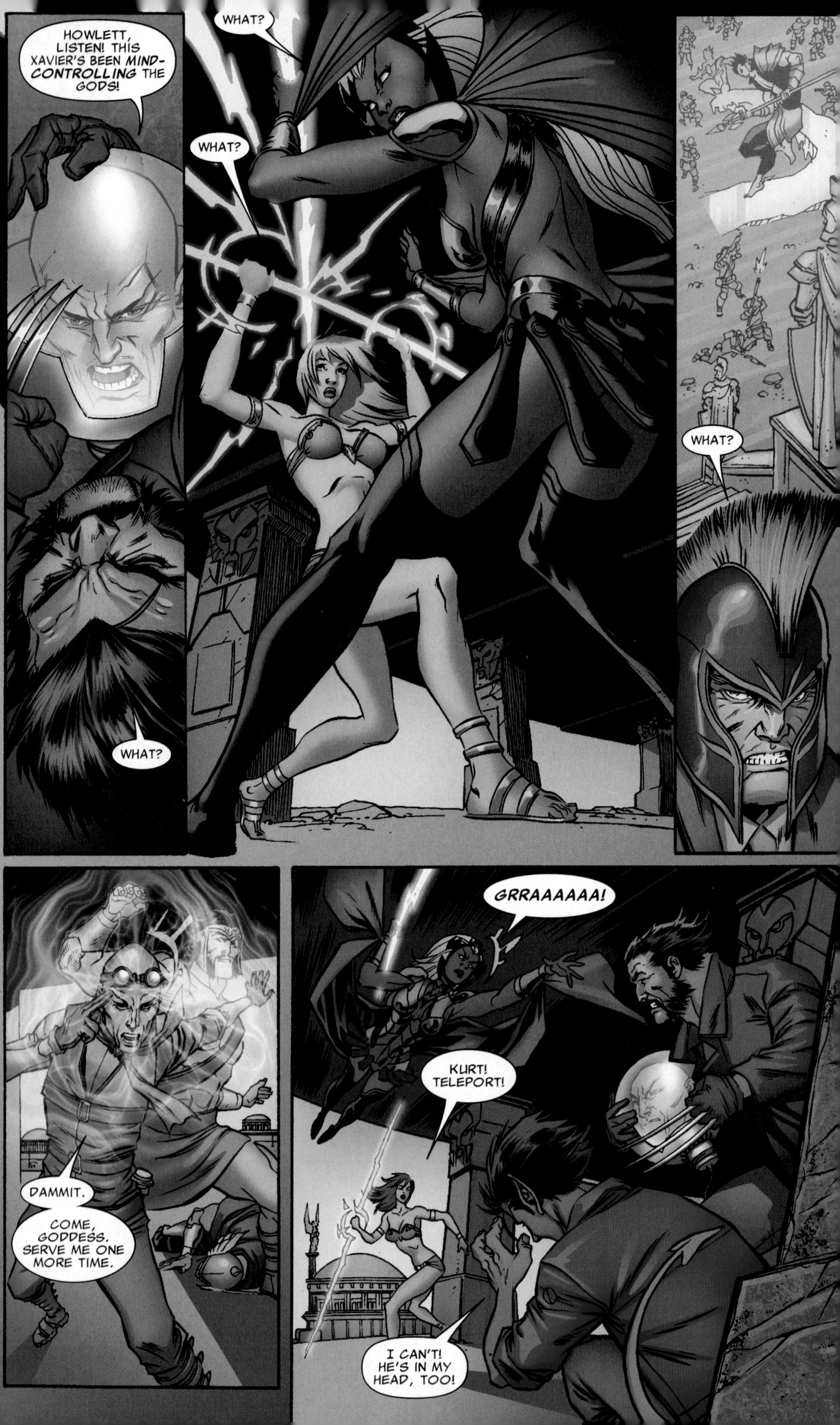
HOWLETT, LISTEN! THIS XAVIER'S BEEN *MIND-CONTROLLING* THE GODS!
WHAT?
WHAT?
WHAT?
WHAT?
DAMMIT.
COME, GODDESS. SERVE ME ONE MORE TIME.
GRRAAAAAA!
KURT! TELEPORT!
I CAN'T! HE'S IN MY HEAD, TOO!

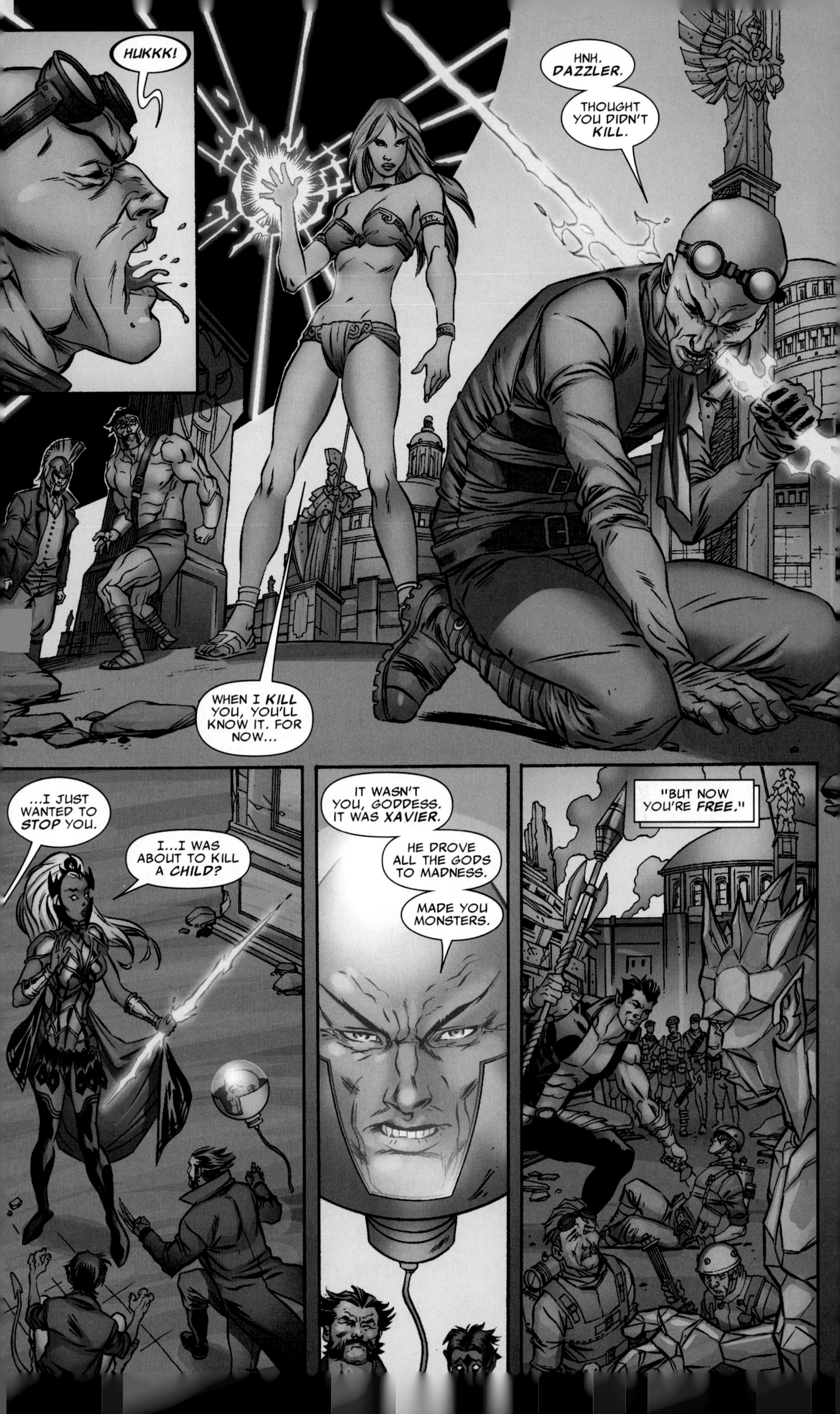
HUKKK!
HNH. DAZZLER.
THOUGHT YOU DIDN'T KILL.
WHEN I KILL YOU, YOU'LL KNOW IT. FOR NOW...
...I JUST WANTED TO STOP YOU.
I...I WAS ABOUT TO KILL A CHILD?
IT WASN'T YOU, GODDESS. IT WAS XAVIER.
HE DROVE ALL THE GODS TO MADNESS.
MADE YOU MONSTERS.
"BUT NOW YOU'RE FREE."

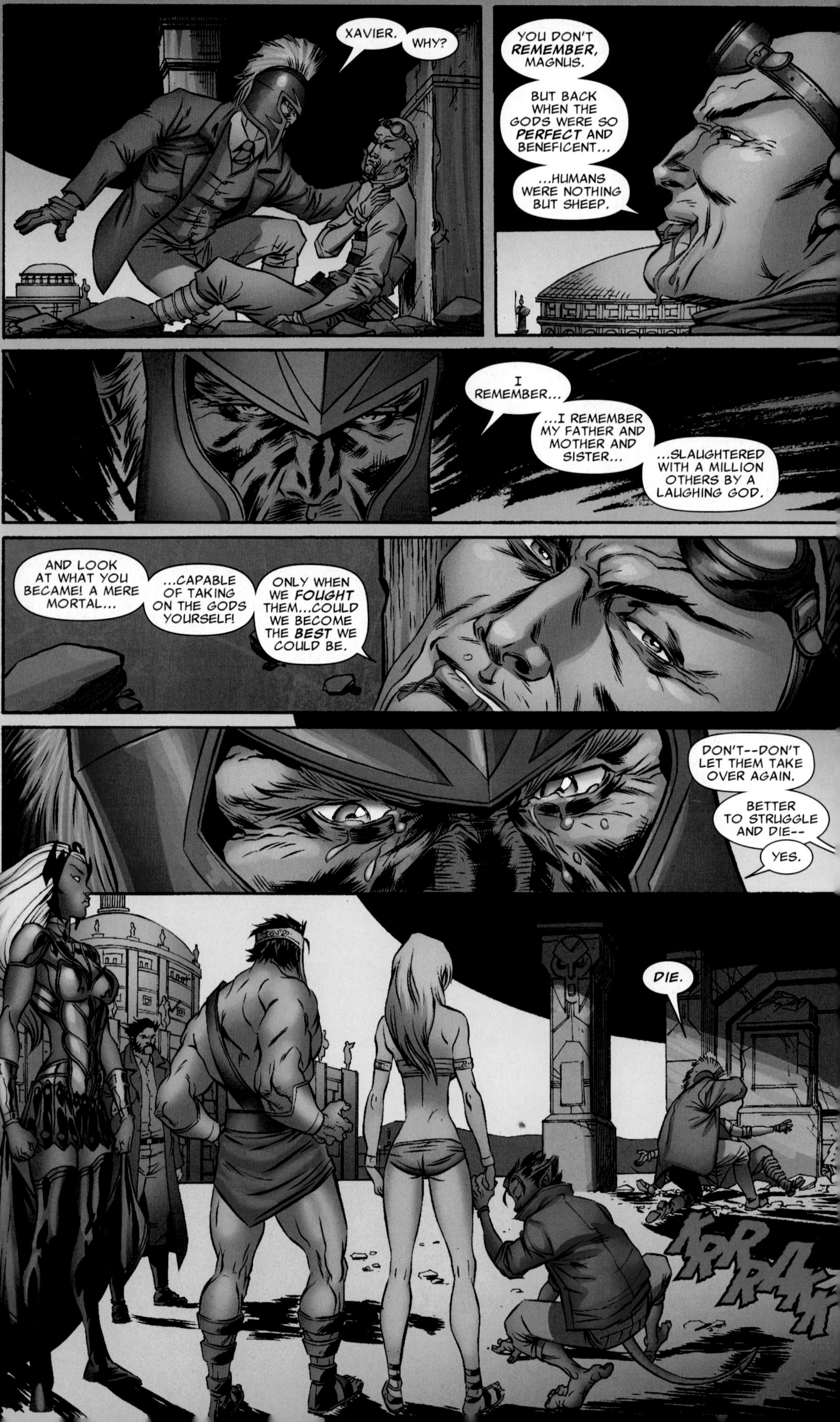
XAVIER.
WHY?
YOU DON'T *REMEMBER,* MAGNUS.
BUT BACK WHEN THE GODS WERE SO *PERFECT* AND BENEFICENT...
...HUMANS WERE NOTHING BUT SHEEP.
I REMEMBER...
...I REMEMBER MY FATHER AND MOTHER AND SISTER...
...SLAUGHTERED WITH A MILLION OTHERS BY A LAUGHING GOD.
AND LOOK AT WHAT YOU BECAME! A MERE MORTAL...
...CAPABLE OF TAKING ON THE GODS YOURSELF!
ONLY WHEN WE *FOUGHT* THEM...COULD WE BECOME THE *BEST* WE COULD BE.
DON'T--DON'T LET THEM TAKE OVER AGAIN.
BETTER TO STRUGGLE AND DIE--
YES.
DIE.

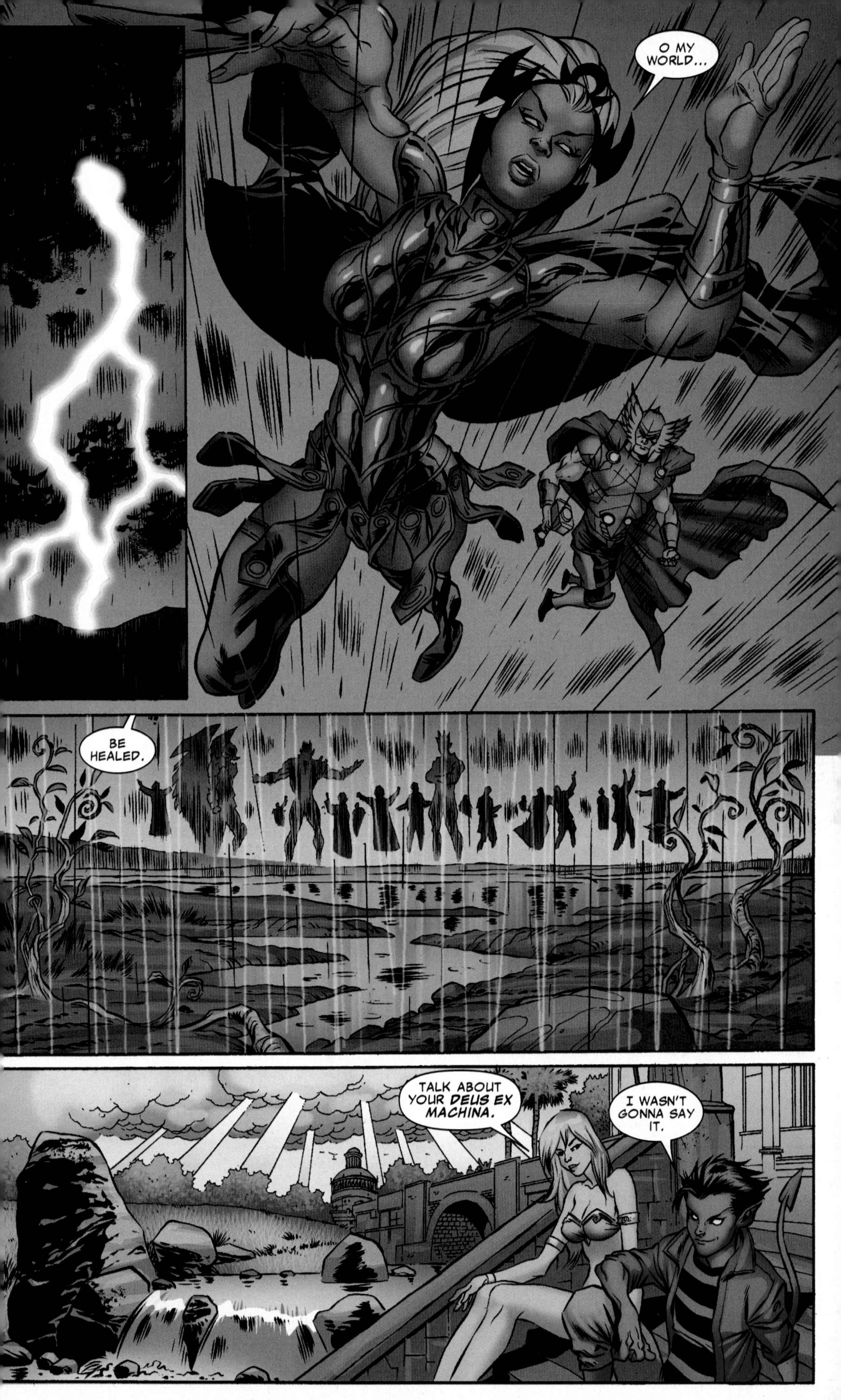
O MY WORLD...
BE HEALED.
TALK ABOUT YOUR DEUS EX MACHINA.
I WASN'T GONNA SAY IT.

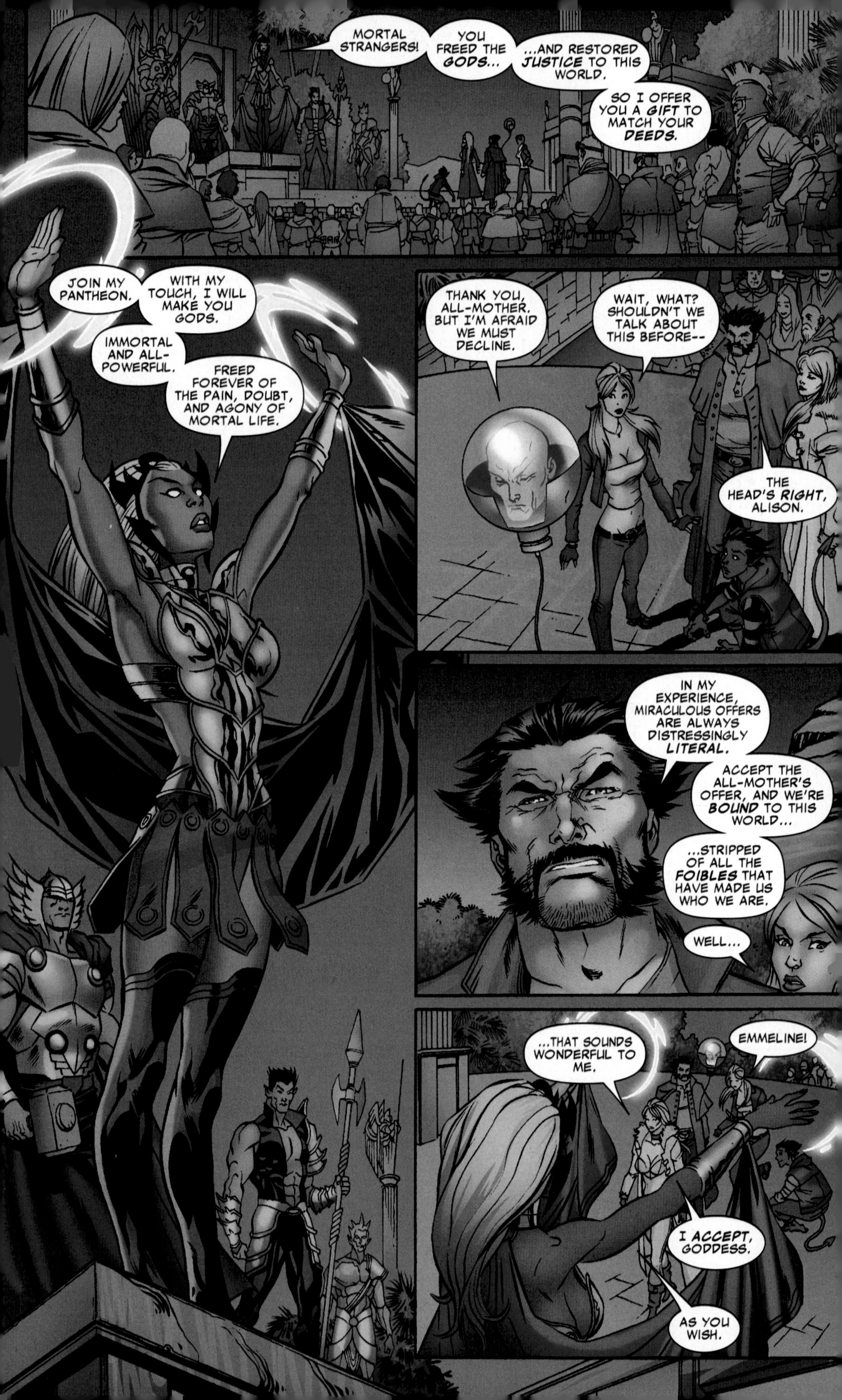
MORTAL STRANGERS!
YOU FREED THE GODS...
...AND RESTORED JUSTICE TO THIS WORLD.
SO I OFFER YOU A GIFT TO MATCH YOUR DEEDS.
JOIN MY PANTHEON.
WITH MY TOUCH, I WILL MAKE YOU GODS.
IMMORTAL AND ALL-POWERFUL.
FREED FOREVER OF THE PAIN, DOUBT, AND AGONY OF MORTAL LIFE.
THANK YOU, ALL-MOTHER. BUT I'M AFRAID WE MUST DECLINE.
WAIT, WHAT? SHOULDN'T WE TALK ABOUT THIS BEFORE--
THE HEAD'S RIGHT, ALISON.
IN MY EXPERIENCE, MIRACULOUS OFFERS ARE ALWAYS DISTRESSINGLY LITERAL.
ACCEPT THE ALL-MOTHER'S OFFER, AND WE'RE BOUND TO THIS WORLD...
...STRIPPED OF ALL THE FOIBLES THAT HAVE MADE US WHO WE ARE.
WELL...
...THAT SOUNDS WONDERFUL TO ME.
EMMELINE!
I ACCEPT, GODDESS.
AS YOU WISH.

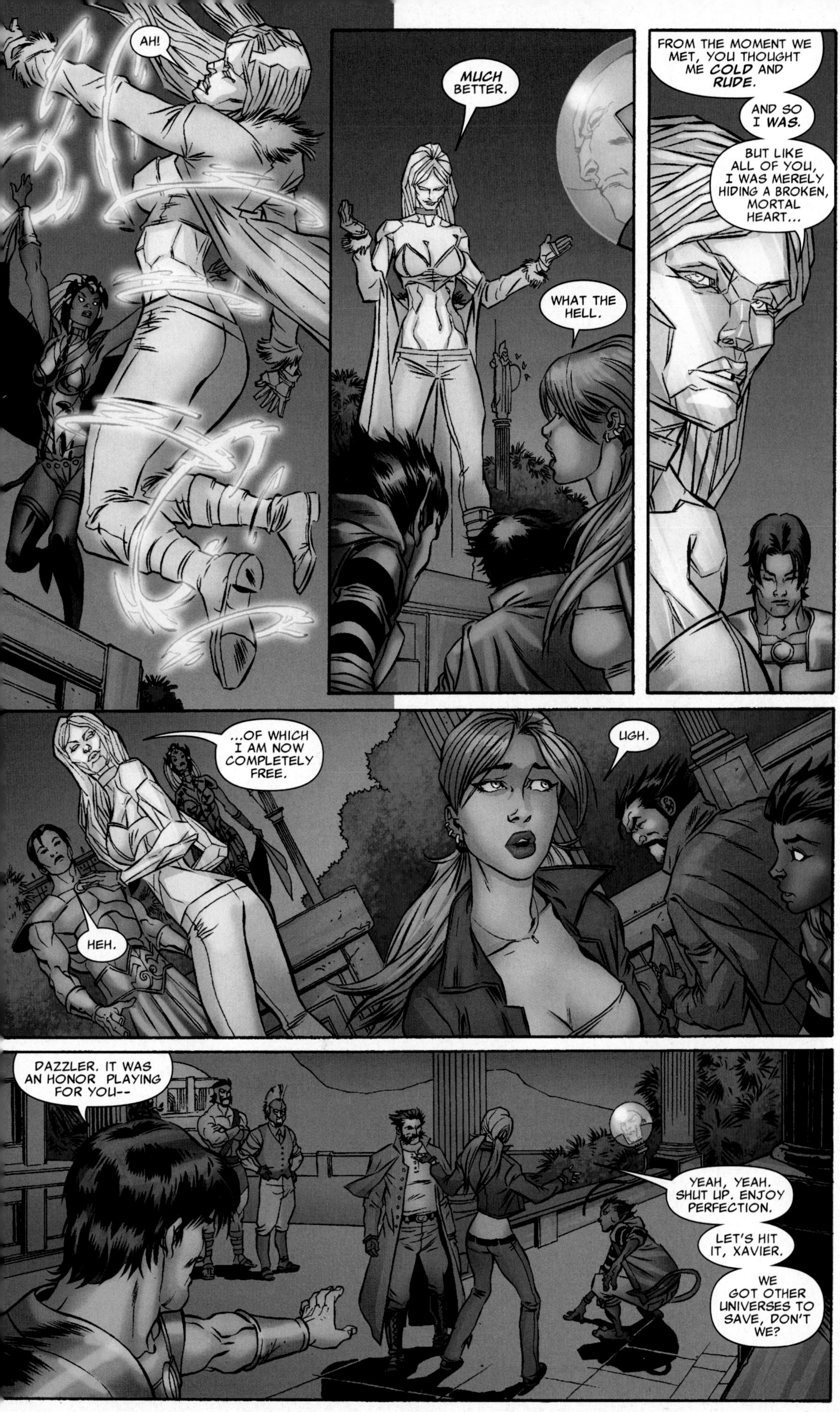
AH!
MUCH BETTER.
WHAT THE HELL.
FROM THE MOMENT WE MET, YOU THOUGHT ME COLD AND RUDE.
AND SO I WAS.
BUT LIKE ALL OF YOU, I WAS MERELY HIDING A BROKEN, MORTAL HEART...
...OF WHICH I AM NOW COMPLETELY FREE.
HEH.
UGH.
DAZZLER. IT WAS AN HONOR PLAYING FOR YOU--
YEAH, YEAH. SHUT UP. ENJOY PERFECTION.
LET'S HIT IT, XAVIER.
WE GOT OTHER UNIVERSES TO SAVE, DON'T WE?

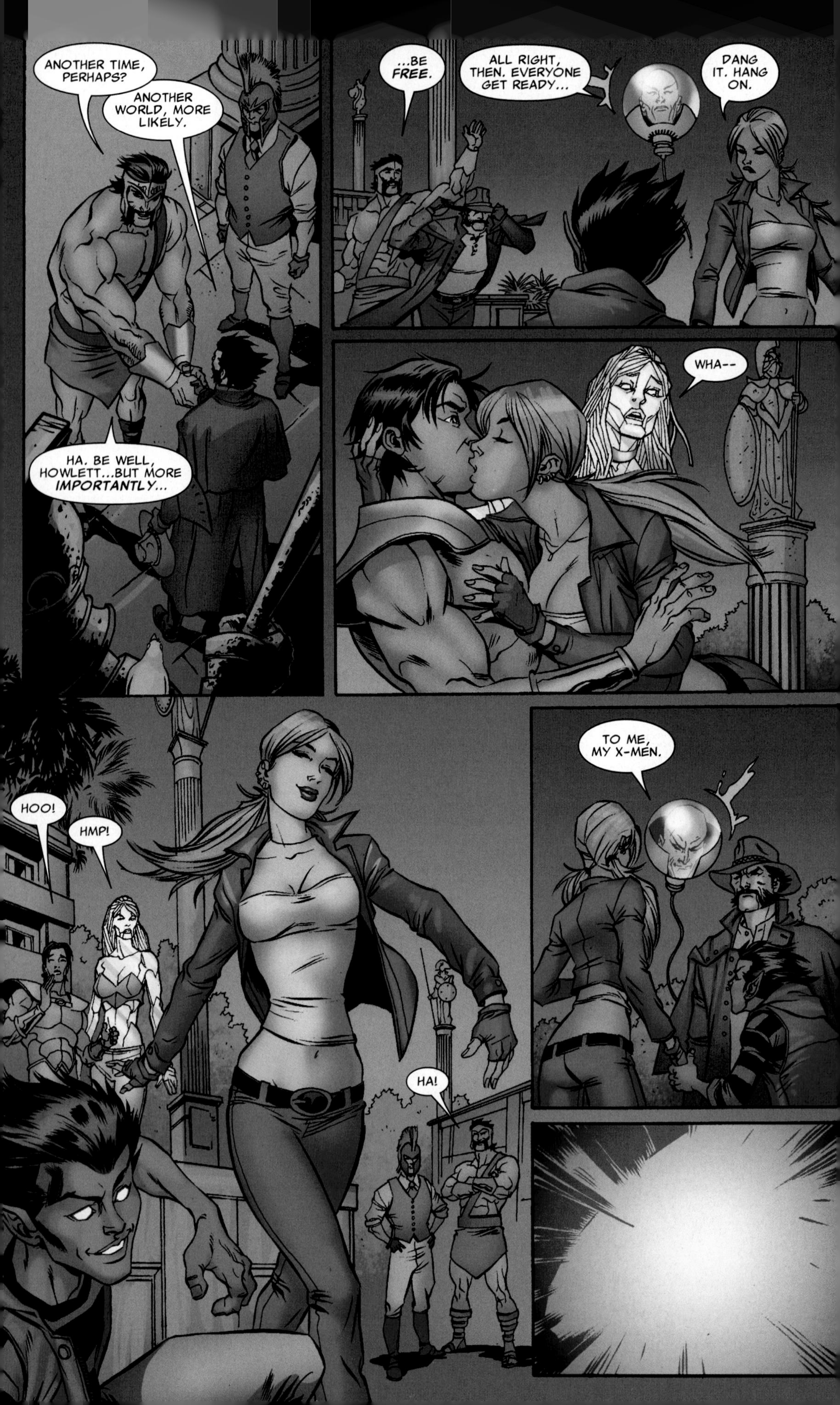

ANOTHER TIME, PERHAPS?
ANOTHER WORLD, MORE LIKELY.
HA. BE WELL, HOWLETT...BUT MORE IMPORTANTLY...
...BE FREE.
ALL RIGHT, THEN. EVERYONE GET READY...
DANG IT. HANG ON.
WHA--
HOO!
HMP!
HA!
TO ME, MY X-MEN.

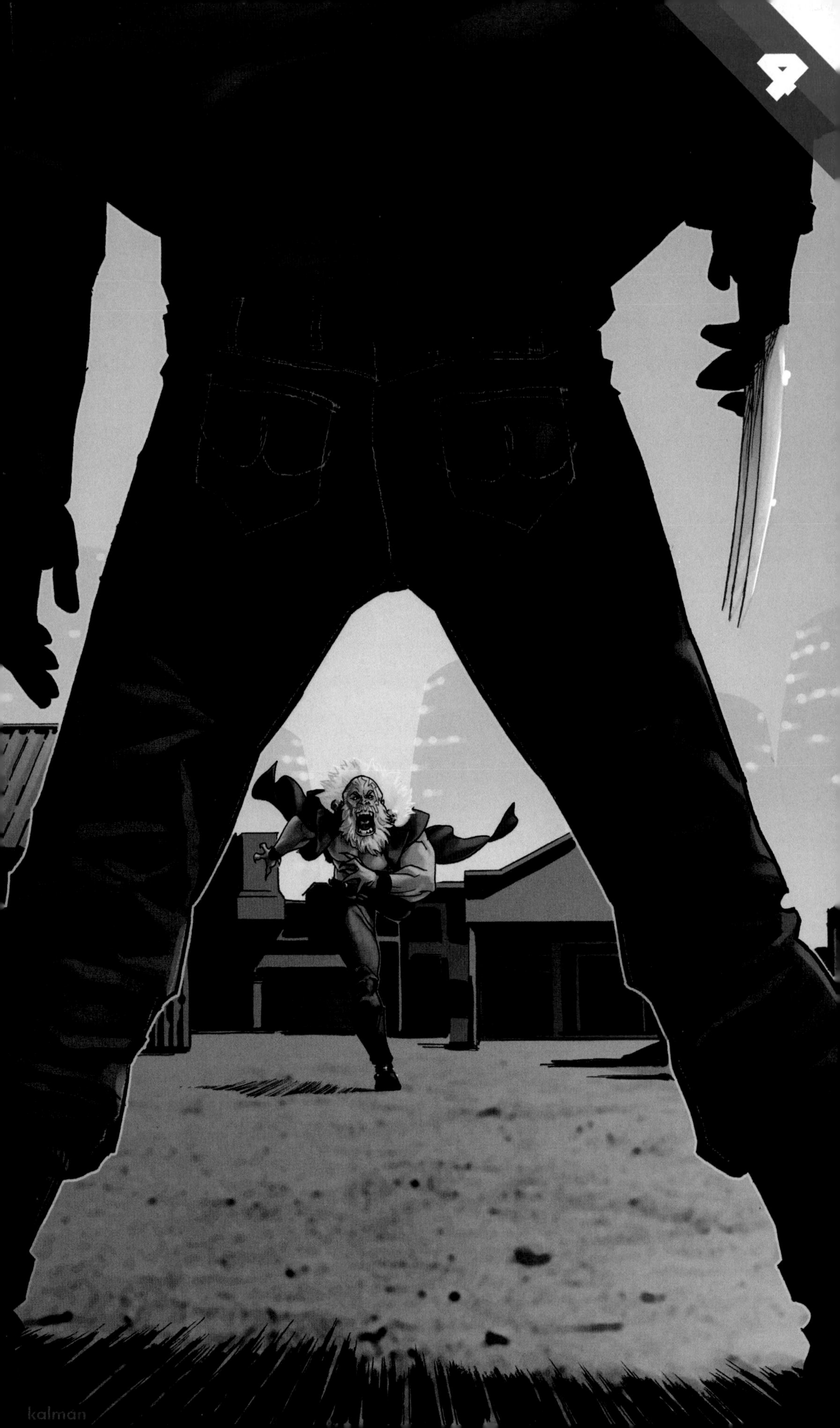
4
kalman

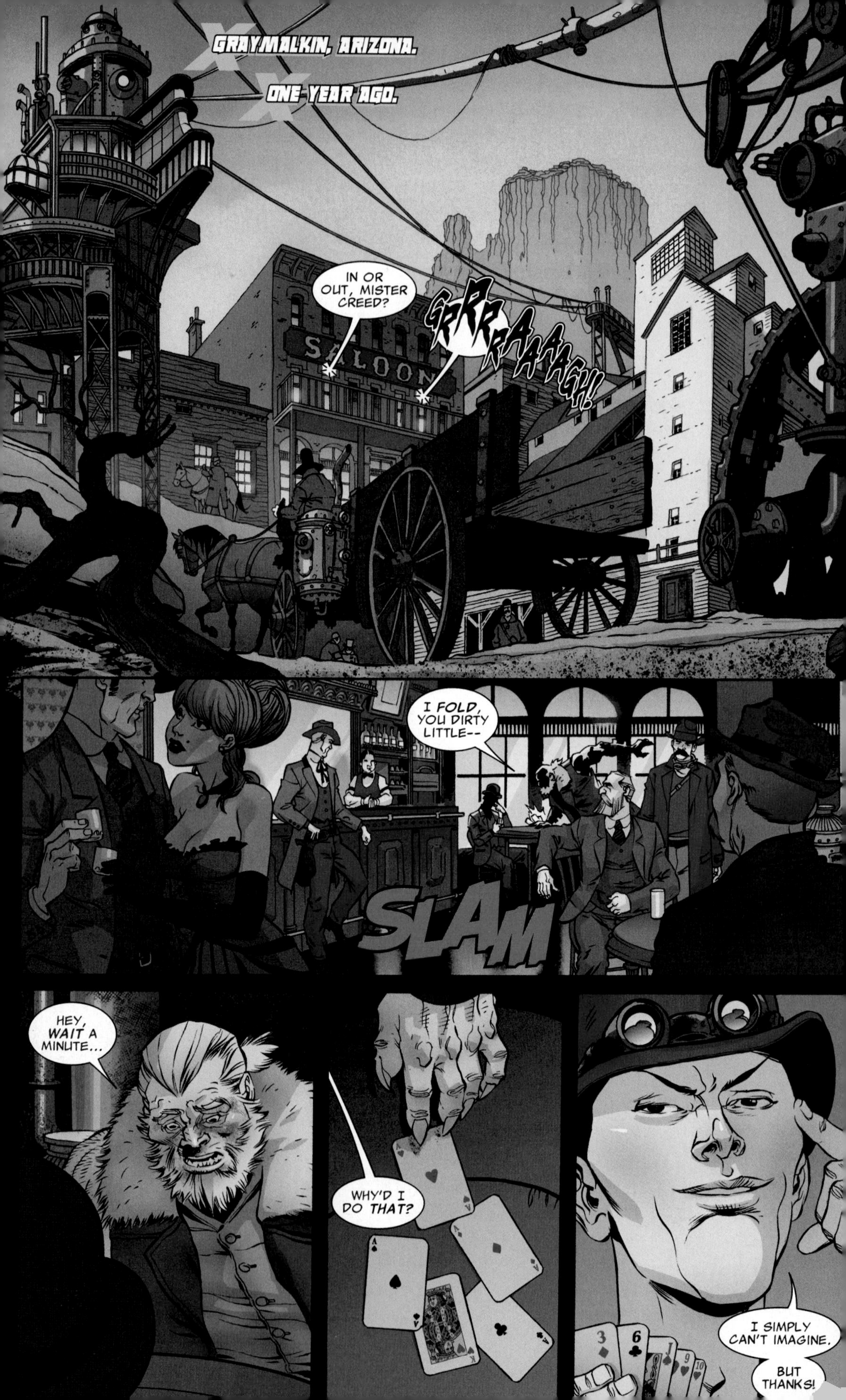
GRAYMALKIN, ARIZONA.
ONE YEAR AGO.
IN OR OUT, MISTER CREED?
GRRRRAAAAGH!!
I FOLD, YOU DIRTY LITTLE--
SLAM
HEY, WAIT A MINUTE...
WHY'D I DO THAT?
I SIMPLY CAN'T IMAGINE.
BUT THANKS!

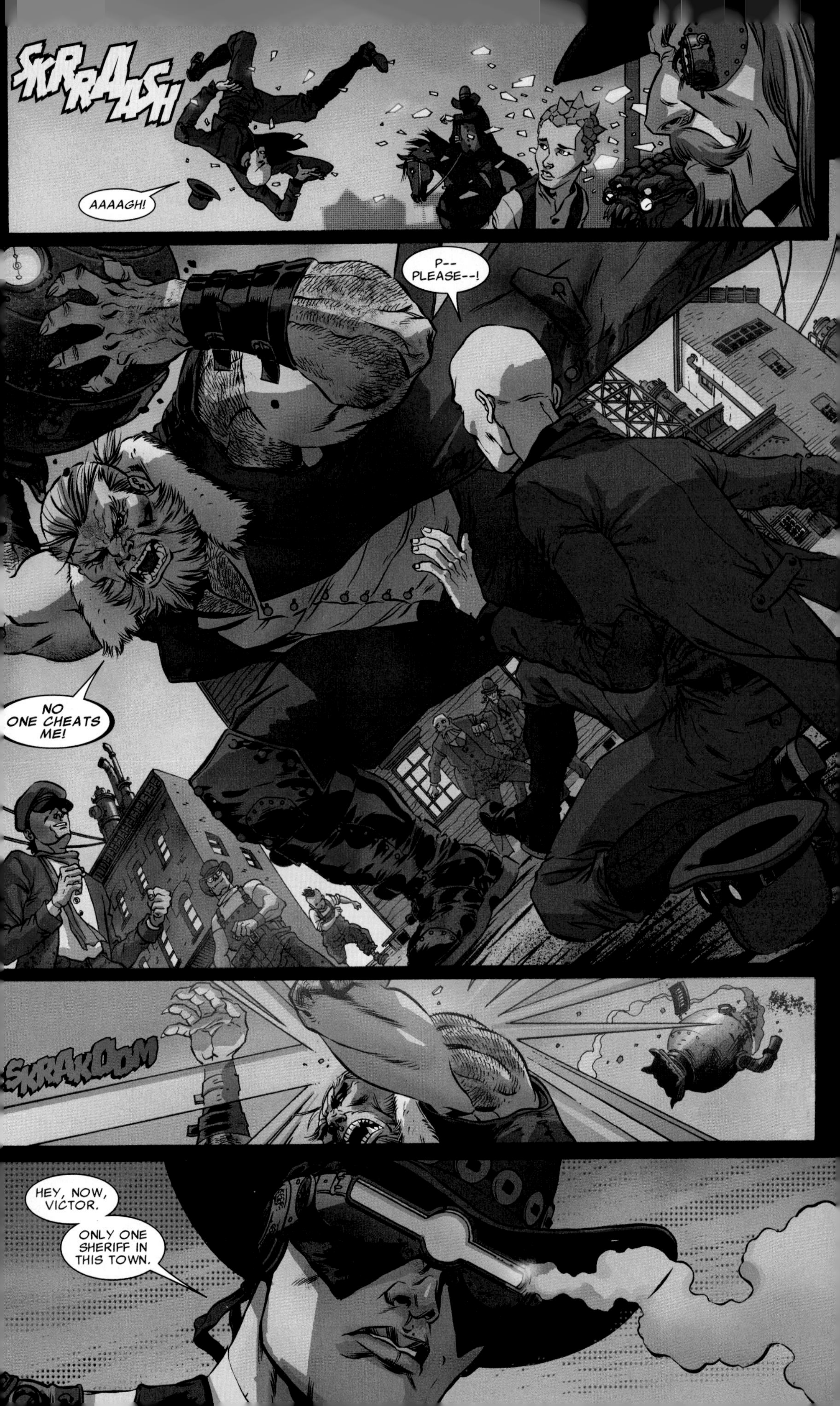
SKRRAASH
AAAAGH!
P-- PLEASE--!
NO ONE CHEATS ME!
SKRAKOOM
HEY, NOW, VICTOR.
ONLY ONE SHERIFF IN THIS TOWN.

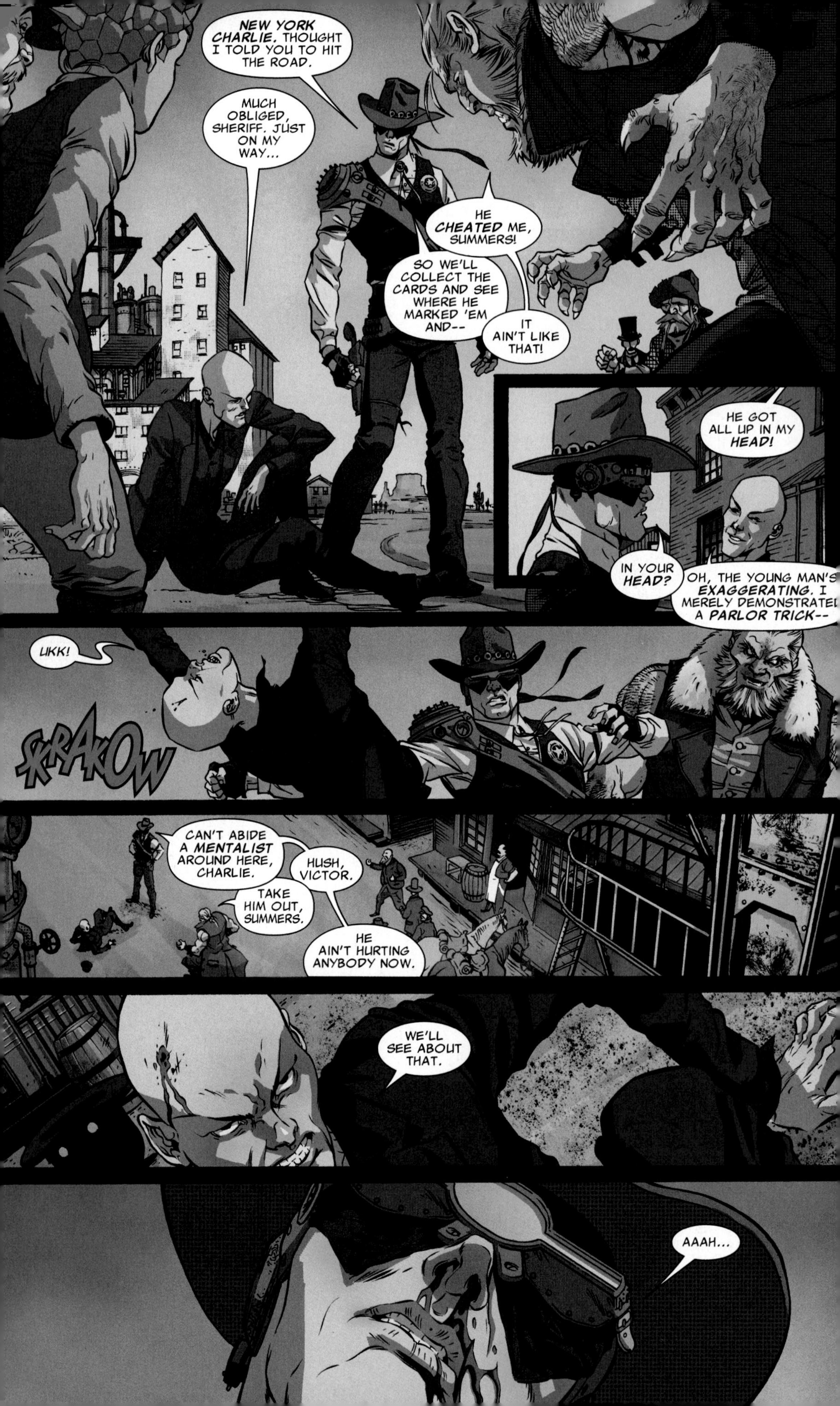

NEW YORK CHARLIE. THOUGHT I TOLD YOU TO HIT THE ROAD.
MUCH OBLIGED, SHERIFF. JUST ON MY WAY...
HE CHEATED ME, SUMMERS!
SO WE'LL COLLECT THE CARDS AND SEE WHERE HE MARKED 'EM AND--
IT AIN'T LIKE THAT!
HE GOT ALL UP IN MY HEAD!
IN YOUR HEAD?
OH, THE YOUNG MAN'S EXAGGERATING. I MERELY DEMONSTRATED A PARLOR TRICK--
UKK!
SKRAKOW
CAN'T ABIDE A MENTALIST AROUND HERE, CHARLIE.
HUSH, VICTOR.
TAKE HIM OUT, SUMMERS.
HE AIN'T HURTING ANYBODY NOW.
WE'LL SEE ABOUT THAT.
AAAH...

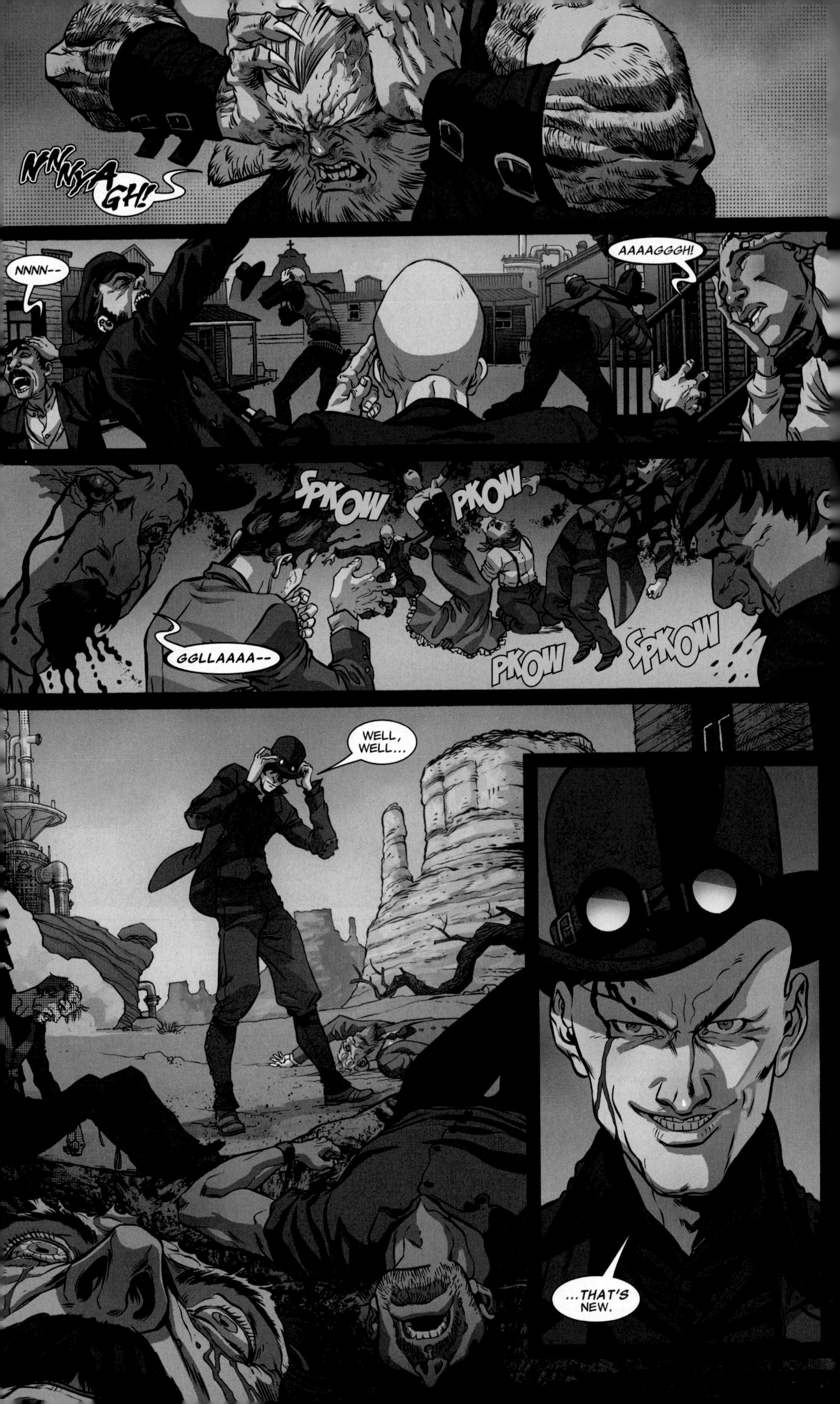
NNNNYAGH!
NNNN--
AAAAGGGH!
SPKOW
PKOW
GGLLAAAA--
PKOW
SPKOW
WELL, WELL...
...THAT'S NEW.

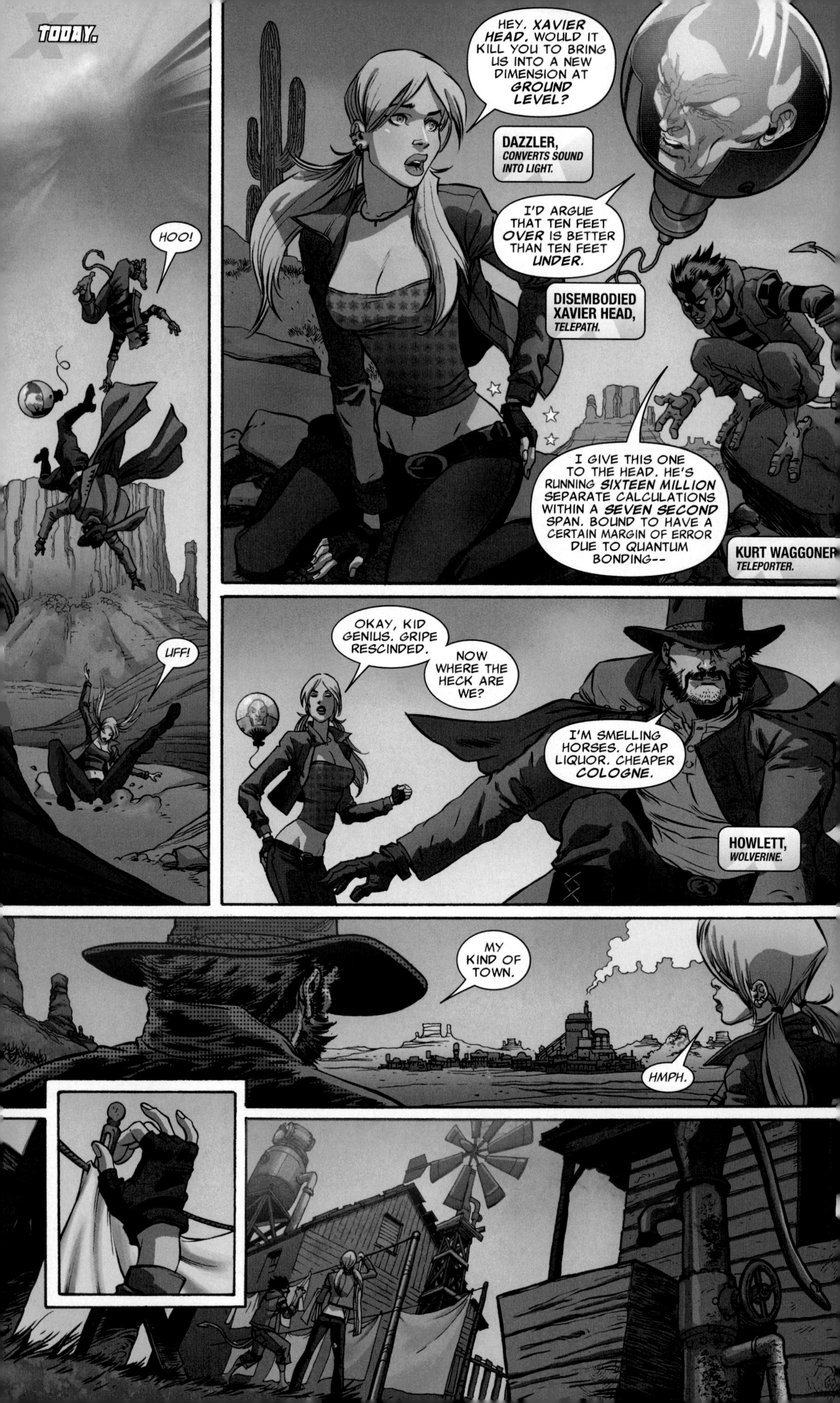
TODAY.
HOO!
UFF!
HEY. XAVIER HEAD. WOULD IT KILL YOU TO BRING US INTO A NEW DIMENSION AT GROUND LEVEL?
DAZZLER, CONVERTS SOUND INTO LIGHT.
I'D ARGUE THAT TEN FEET OVER IS BETTER THAN TEN FEET UNDER.
DISEMBODIED XAVIER HEAD, TELEPATH.
I GIVE THIS ONE TO THE HEAD. HE'S RUNNING SIXTEEN MILLION SEPARATE CALCULATIONS WITHIN A SEVEN SECOND SPAN. BOUND TO HAVE A CERTAIN MARGIN OF ERROR DUE TO QUANTUM BONDING--
KURT WAGGONER TELEPORTER.
OKAY, KID GENIUS. GRIPE RESCINDED.
NOW WHERE THE HECK ARE WE?
I'M SMELLING HORSES. CHEAP LIQUOR. CHEAPER COLOGNE.
HOWLETT, WOLVERINE.
MY KIND OF TOWN.
HMPH.

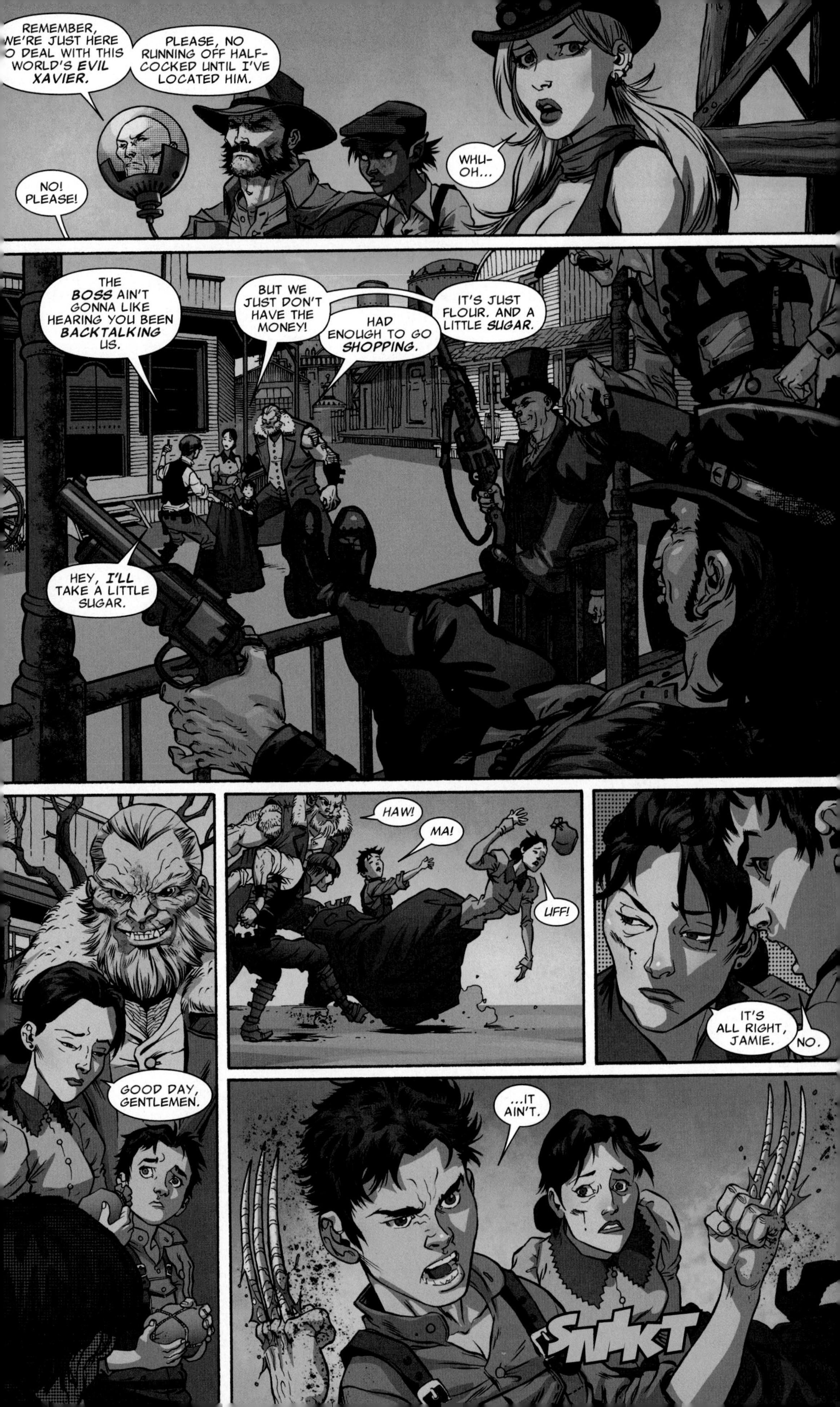

REMEMBER, WE'RE JUST HERE TO DEAL WITH THIS WORLD'S EVIL XAVIER.
PLEASE, NO RUNNING OFF HALF-COCKED UNTIL I'VE LOCATED HIM.
WHU-OH...
NO! PLEASE!
THE BOSS AIN'T GONNA LIKE HEARING YOU BEEN BACKTALKING US.
BUT WE JUST DON'T HAVE THE MONEY!
IT'S JUST FLOUR. AND A LITTLE SUGAR.
HAD ENOUGH TO GO SHOPPING.
HEY, I'LL TAKE A LITTLE SUGAR.
GOOD DAY, GENTLEMEN.
HAW!
MA!
UFF!
IT'S ALL RIGHT, JAMIE.
NO.
...IT AIN'T.
SNIKT

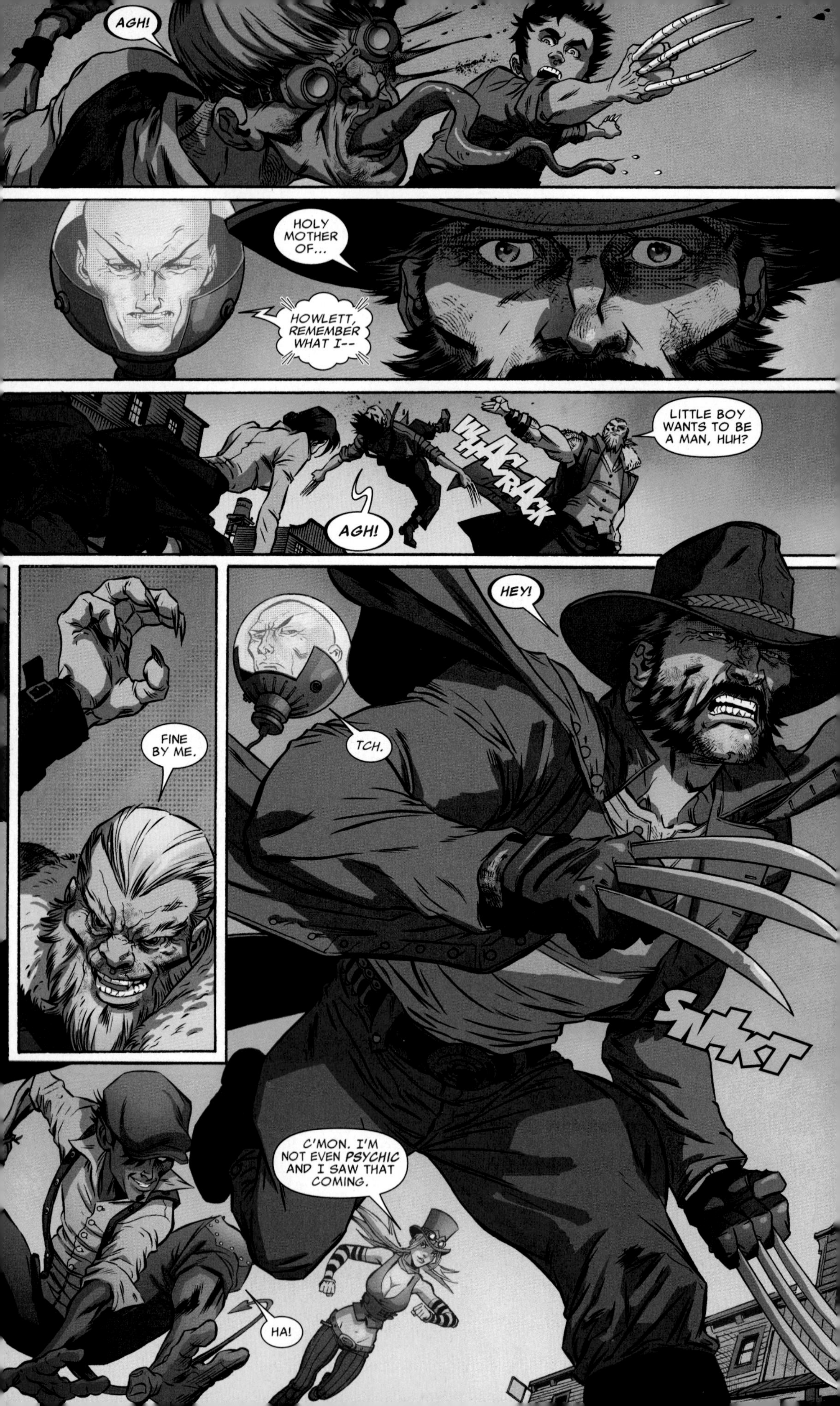
AGH!
HOLY MOTHER OF...
HOWLETT, REMEMBER WHAT I--
WHACRACK
LITTLE BOY WANTS TO BE A MAN, HUH?
AGH!
FINE BY ME.
HEY!
TCH.
SNIKT
C'MON. I'M NOT EVEN PSYCHIC AND I SAW THAT COMING.
HA!

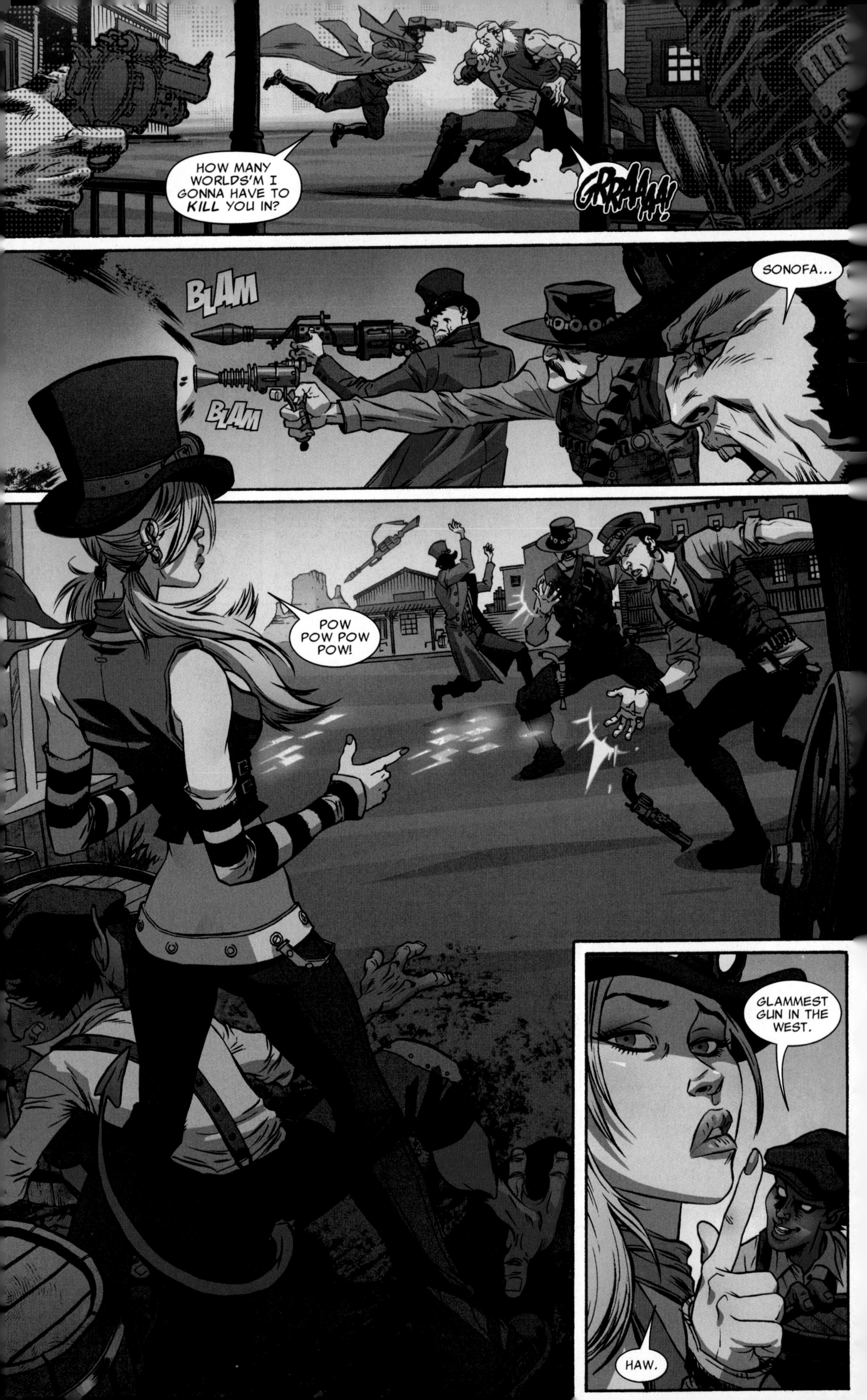
HOW MANY WORLDS'M I GONNA HAVE TO KILL YOU IN?
GRRAAAA!
BLAM
BLAM
SONOFA...
POW POW POW POW!
GLAMMEST GUN IN THE WEST.
HAW.

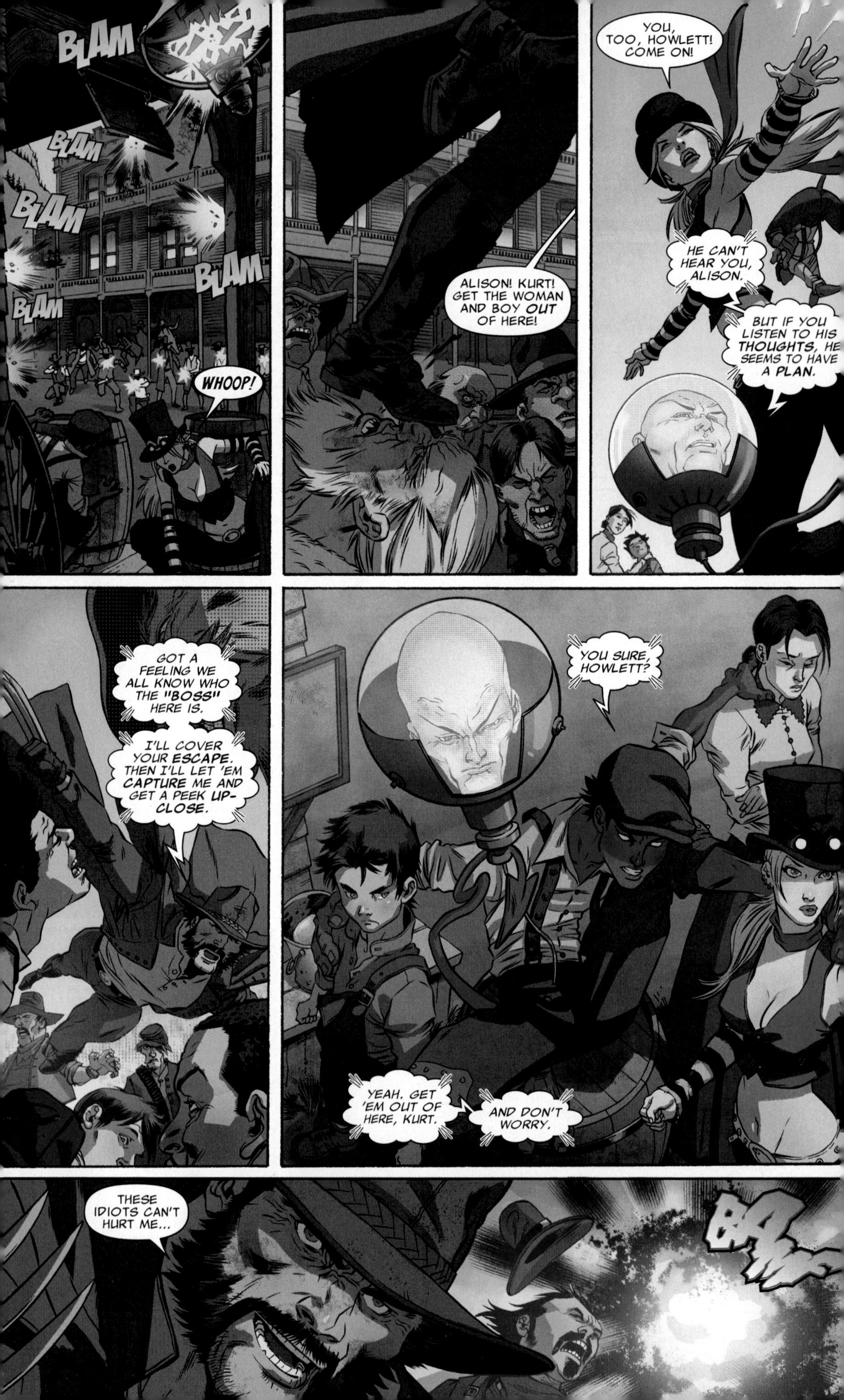
BLAM
BLAM
BLAM
BLAM
BLAM
WHOOP!
ALISON! KURT! GET THE WOMAN AND BOY OUT OF HERE!
YOU, TOO, HOWLETT! COME ON!
HE CAN'T HEAR YOU, ALISON.
BUT IF YOU LISTEN TO HIS THOUGHTS, HE SEEMS TO HAVE A PLAN.
GOT A FEELING WE ALL KNOW WHO THE "BOSS" HERE IS.
I'LL COVER YOUR ESCAPE. THEN I'LL LET 'EM CAPTURE ME AND GET A PEEK UP-CLOSE.
YOU SURE, HOWLETT?
YEAH. GET 'EM OUT OF HERE, KURT.
AND DON'T WORRY.
THESE IDIOTS CAN'T HURT ME...

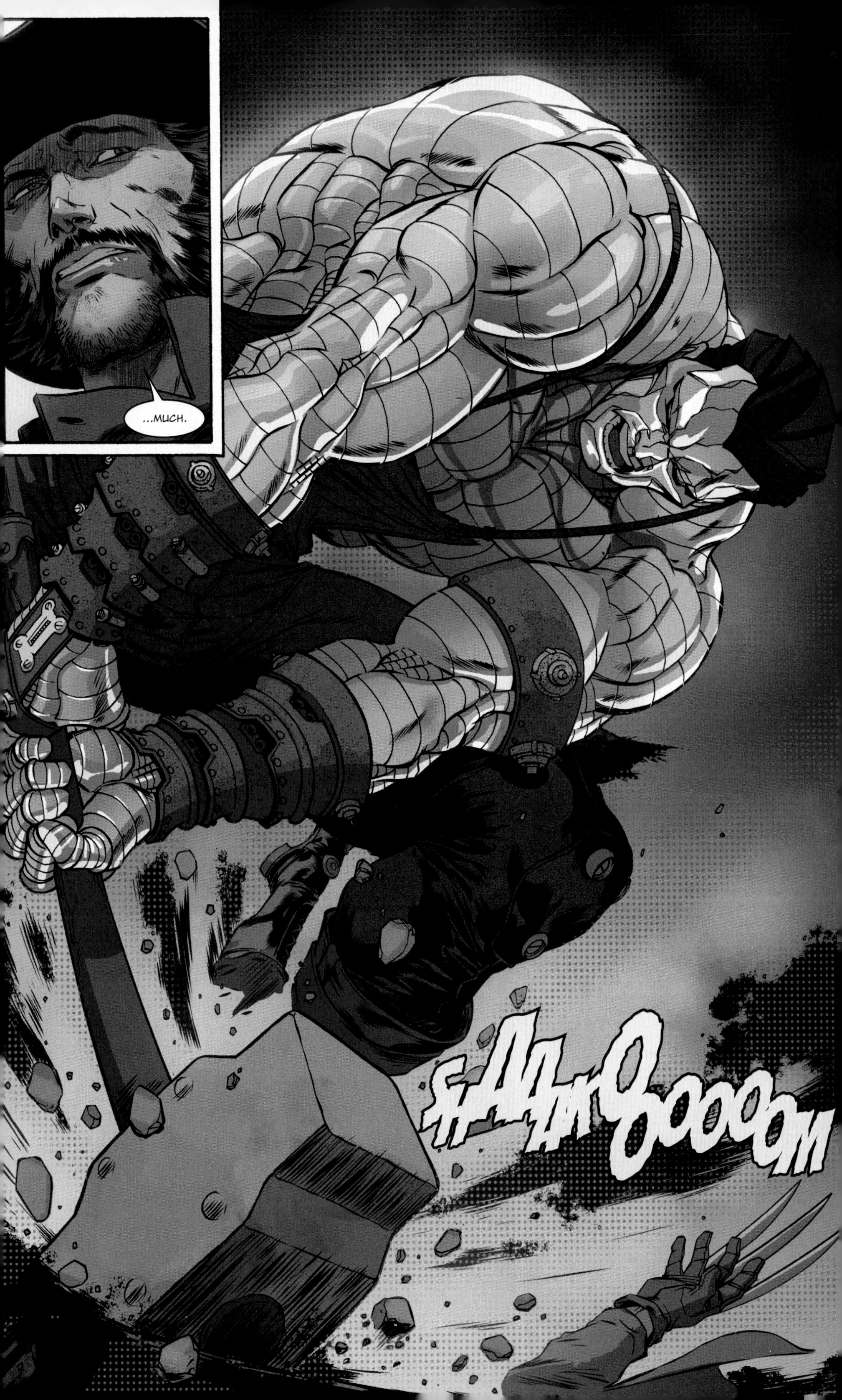

...MUCH.
SHHHBOOOOM

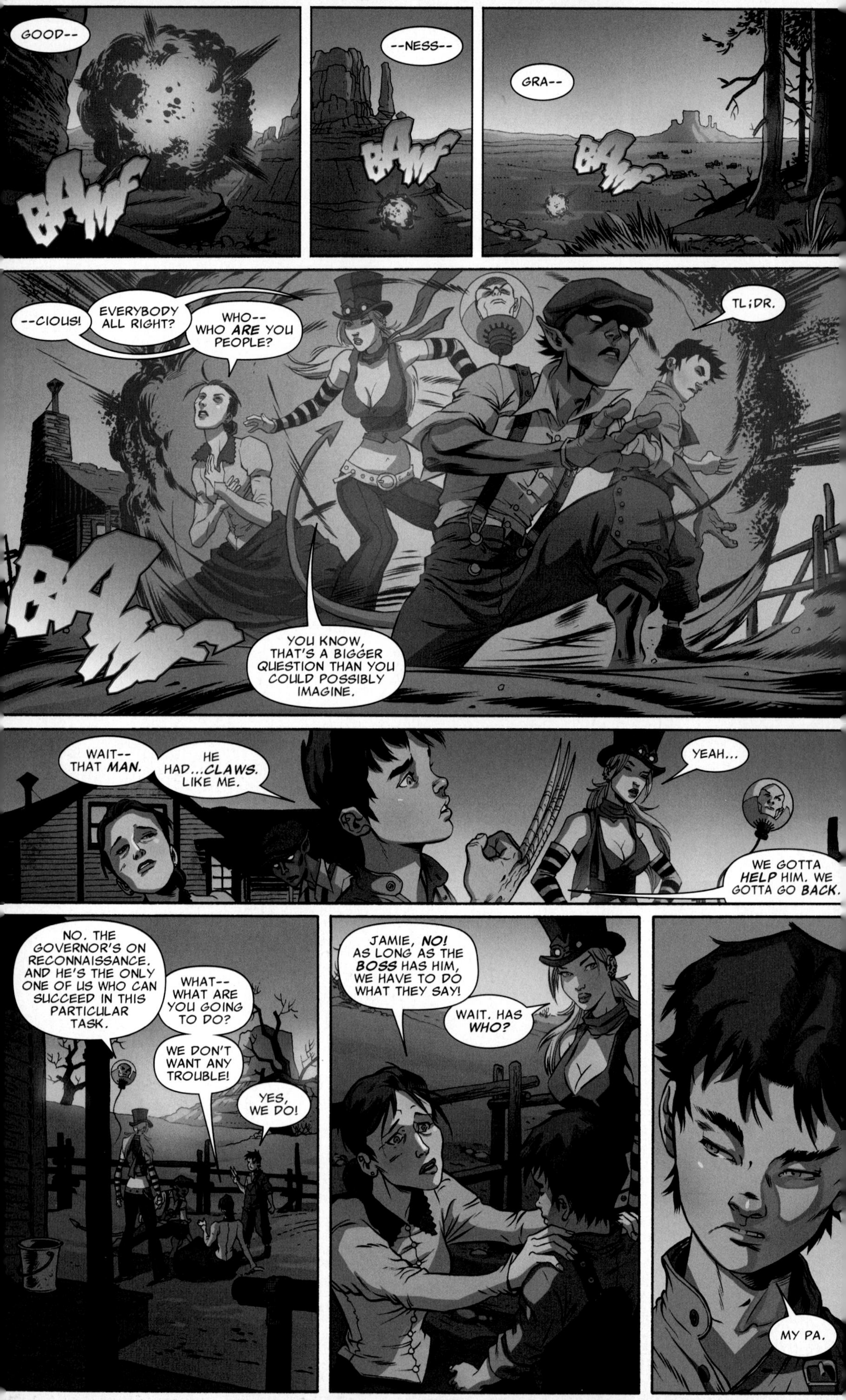
GOOD--
BAMF
--NESS--
BAMF
GRA--
BAMF
--CIOUS!
EVERYBODY ALL RIGHT?
WHO-- WHO ARE YOU PEOPLE?
TL;DR.
BAMF
YOU KNOW, THAT'S A BIGGER QUESTION THAN YOU COULD POSSIBLY IMAGINE.
WAIT-- THAT MAN.
HE HAD...CLAWS. LIKE ME.
YEAH...
WE GOTTA HELP HIM. WE GOTTA GO BACK.
NO. THE GOVERNOR'S ON RECONNAISSANCE. AND HE'S THE ONLY ONE OF US WHO CAN SUCCEED IN THIS PARTICULAR TASK.
WHAT-- WHAT ARE YOU GOING TO DO?
WE DON'T WANT ANY TROUBLE!
YES, WE DO!
JAMIE, NO! AS LONG AS THE BOSS HAS HIM, WE HAVE TO DO WHAT THEY SAY!
WAIT. HAS WHO?
MY PA.

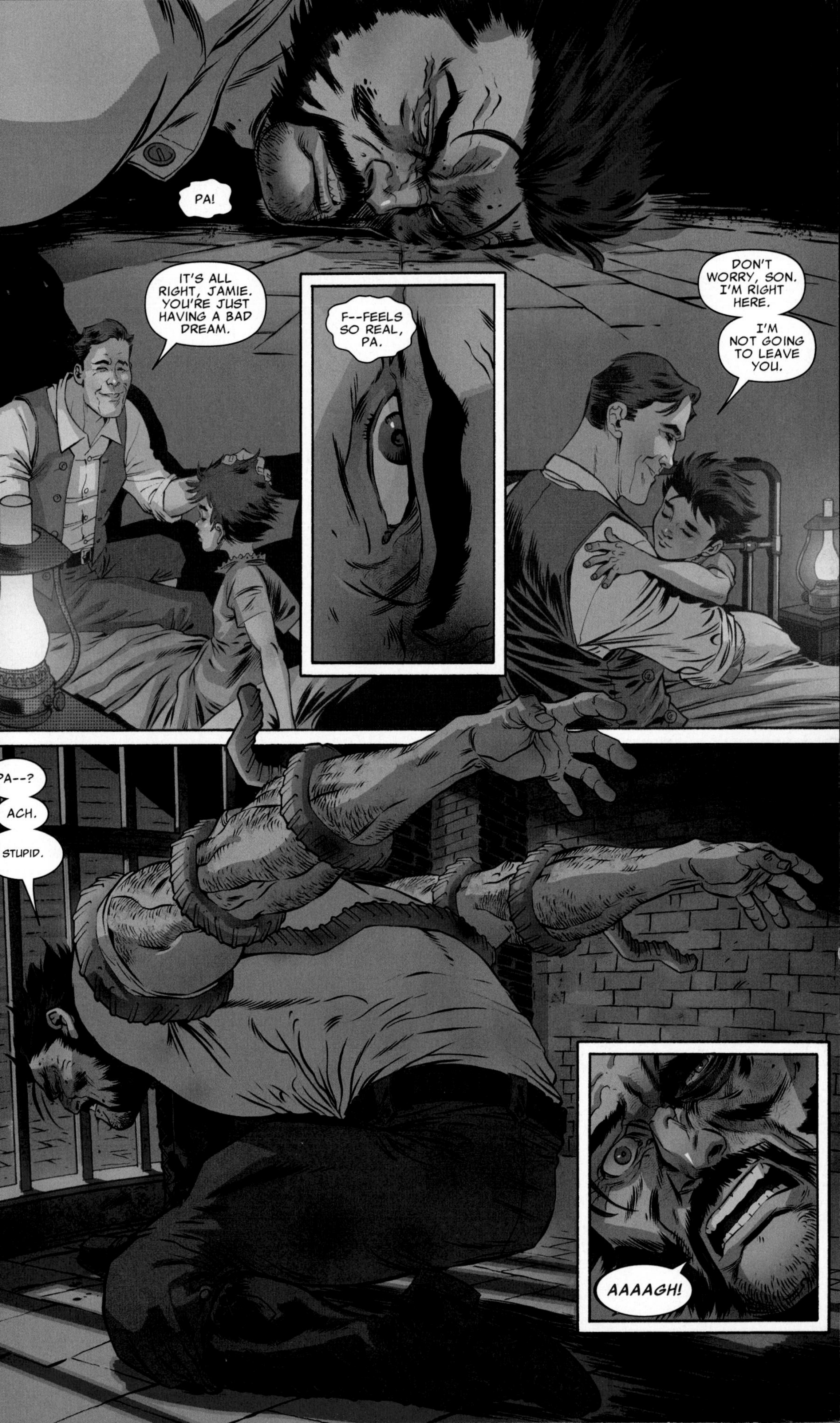
PA!
IT'S ALL RIGHT, JAMIE. YOU'RE JUST HAVING A BAD DREAM.
F--FEELS SO REAL, PA.
DON'T WORRY, SON. I'M RIGHT HERE.
I'M NOT GOING TO LEAVE YOU.
PA--?
ACH.
STUPID.
AAAAGH!

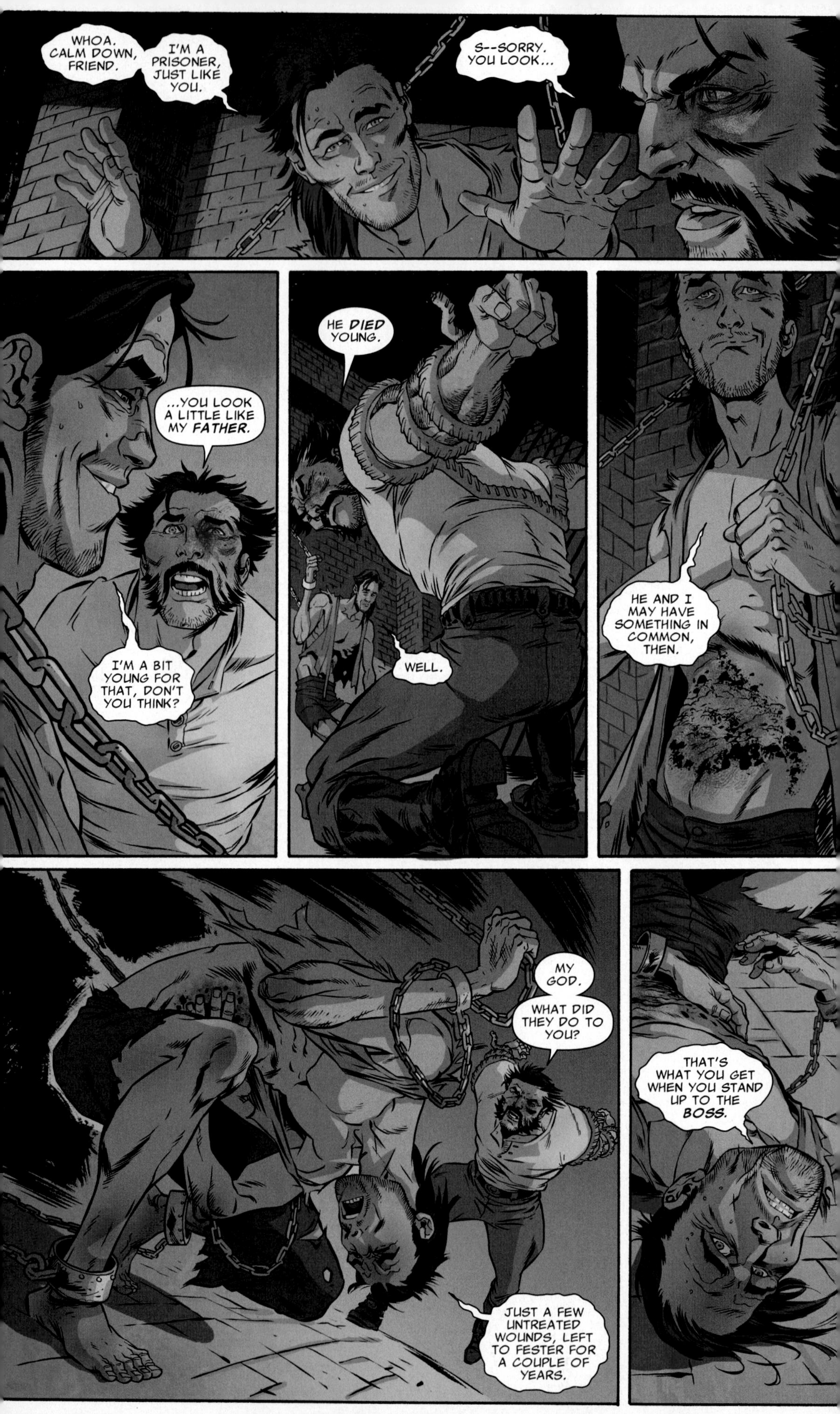
WHOA. CALM DOWN, FRIEND.
I'M A PRISONER, JUST LIKE YOU.
S--SORRY. YOU LOOK...
...YOU LOOK A LITTLE LIKE MY FATHER.
I'M A BIT YOUNG FOR THAT, DON'T YOU THINK?
HE DIED YOUNG.
WELL.
HE AND I MAY HAVE SOMETHING IN COMMON, THEN.
MY GOD.
WHAT DID THEY DO TO YOU?
JUST A FEW UNTREATED WOUNDS, LEFT TO FESTER FOR A COUPLE OF YEARS.
THAT'S WHAT YOU GET WHEN YOU STAND UP TO THE BOSS.

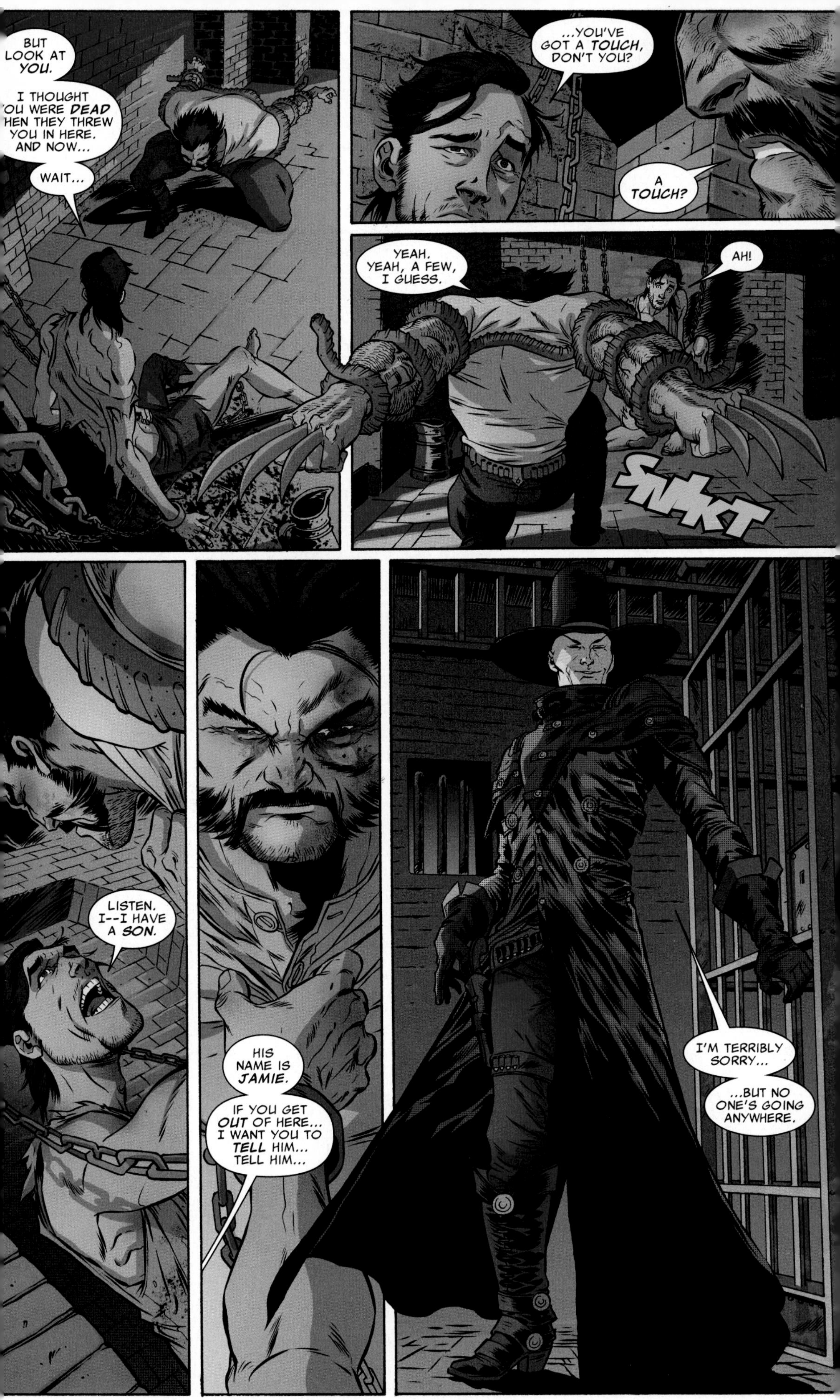
BUT LOOK AT YOU.
I THOUGHT YOU WERE DEAD WHEN THEY THREW YOU IN HERE. AND NOW...
WAIT...
...YOU'VE GOT A TOUCH, DON'T YOU?
A TOUCH?
YEAH. YEAH, A FEW, I GUESS.
AH!
SNIKT
LISTEN. I--I HAVE A SON.
HIS NAME IS JAMIE.
IF YOU GET OUT OF HERE... I WANT YOU TO TELL HIM... TELL HIM...
I'M TERRIBLY SORRY...
...BUT NO ONE'S GOING ANYWHERE.

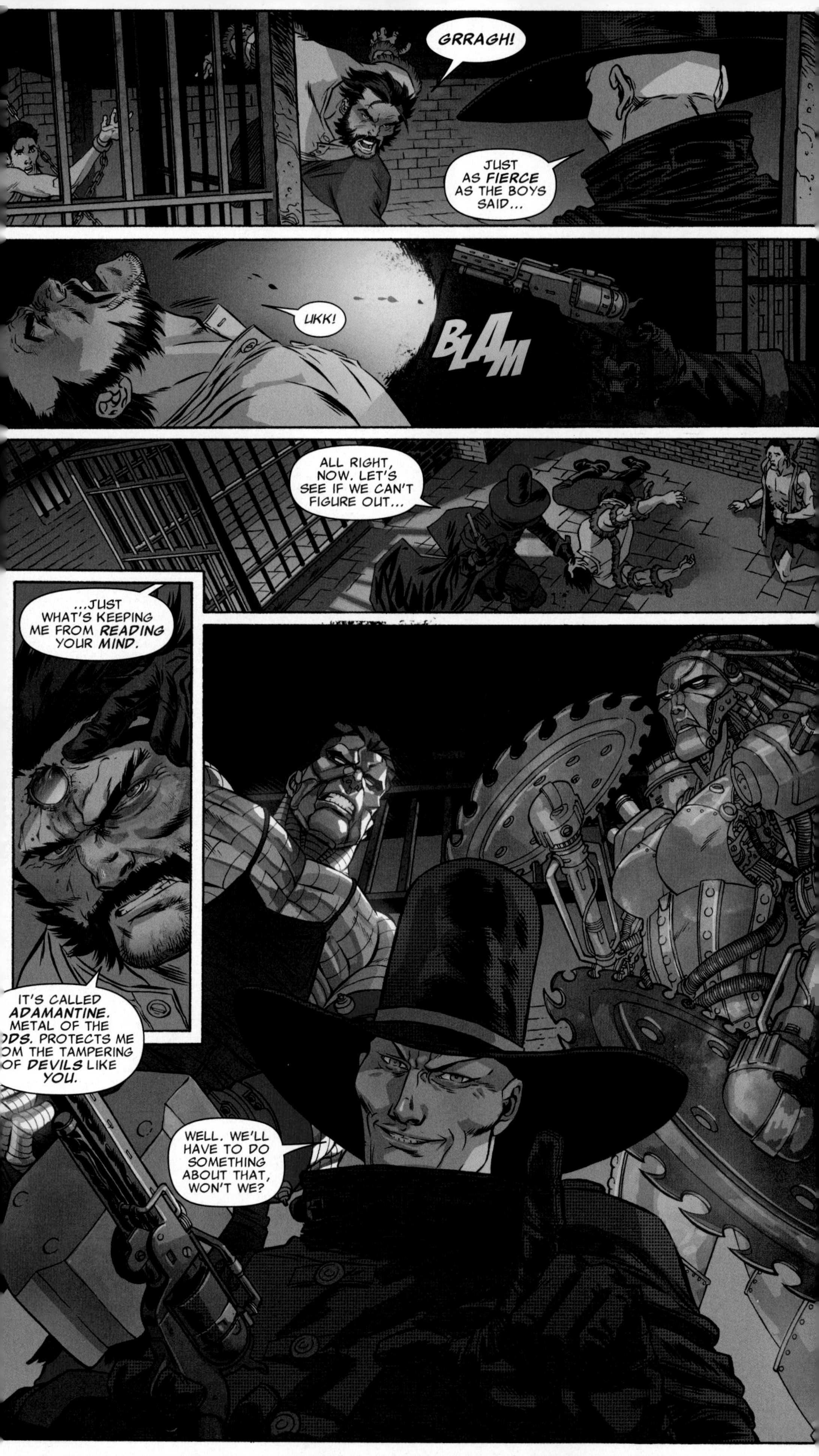
GRRAGH!
JUST AS FIERCE AS THE BOYS SAID...
UKK!
BLAM
ALL RIGHT, NOW. LET'S SEE IF WE CAN'T FIGURE OUT...
...JUST WHAT'S KEEPING ME FROM READING YOUR MIND.
IT'S CALLED ADAMANTINE. METAL OF THE ODS. PROTECTS ME OM THE TAMPERING OF DEVILS LIKE YOU.
WELL. WE'LL HAVE TO DO SOMETHING ABOUT THAT, WON'T WE?

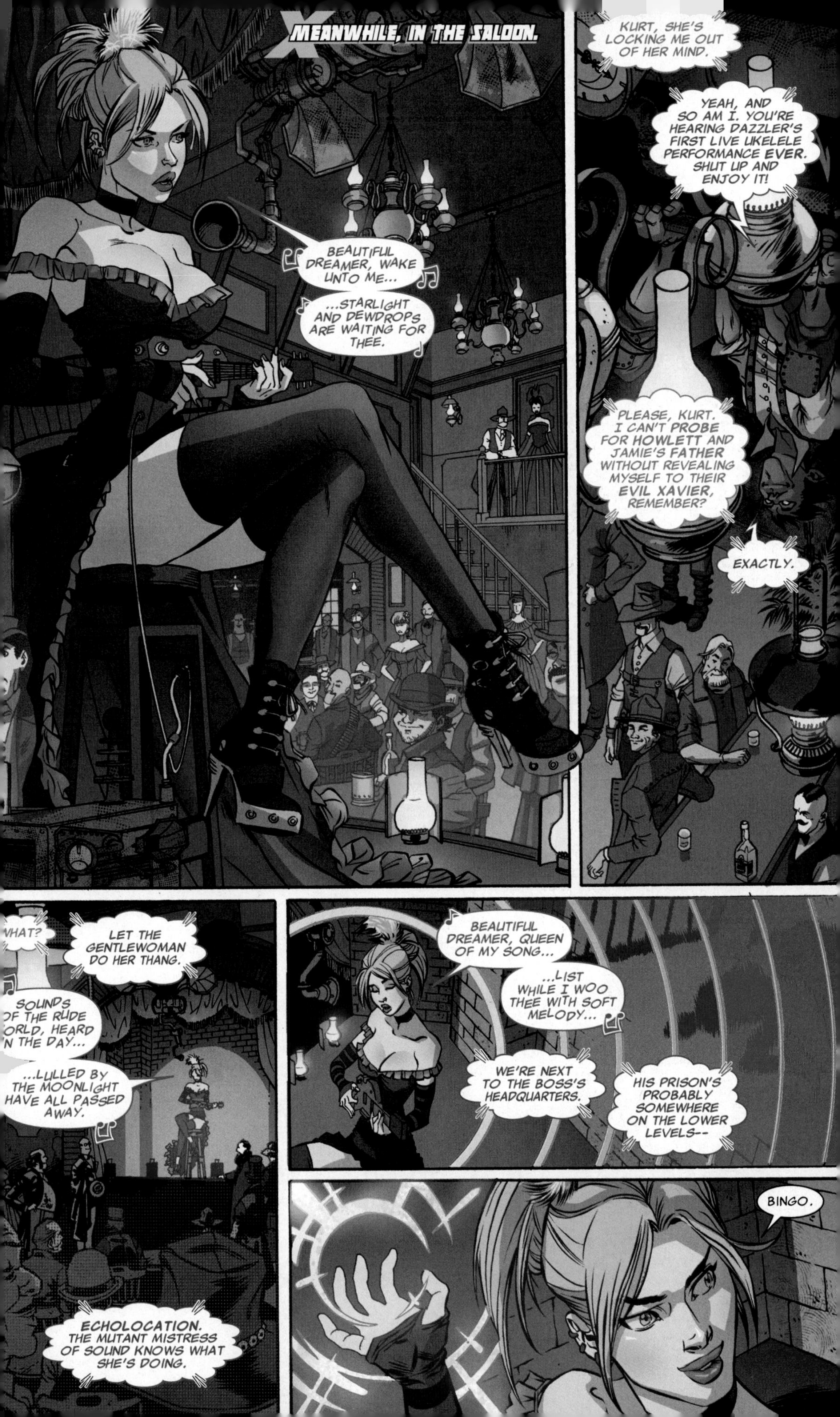
MEANWHILE, IN THE SALOON.
BEAUTIFUL DREAMER, WAKE UNTO ME...
...STARLIGHT AND DEWDROPS ARE WAITING FOR THEE.
KURT, SHE'S LOCKING ME OUT OF HER MIND.
YEAH, AND SO AM I. YOU'RE HEARING DAZZLER'S FIRST LIVE UKELELE PERFORMANCE EVER. SHUT UP AND ENJOY IT!
PLEASE, KURT. I CAN'T PROBE FOR HOWLETT AND JAMIE'S FATHER WITHOUT REVEALING MYSELF TO THEIR EVIL XAVIER, REMEMBER?
EXACTLY.
WHAT?
LET THE GENTLEWOMAN DO HER THANG.
SOUNDS OF THE RUDE WORLD, HEARD IN THE DAY...
...LULLED BY THE MOONLIGHT HAVE ALL PASSED AWAY.
ECHOLOCATION. THE MUTANT MISTRESS OF SOUND KNOWS WHAT SHE'S DOING.
BEAUTIFUL DREAMER, QUEEN OF MY SONG...
...LIST WHILE I WOO THEE WITH SOFT MELODY...
WE'RE NEXT TO THE BOSS'S HEADQUARTERS.
HIS PRISON'S PROBABLY SOMEWHERE ON THE LOWER LEVELS--
BINGO.

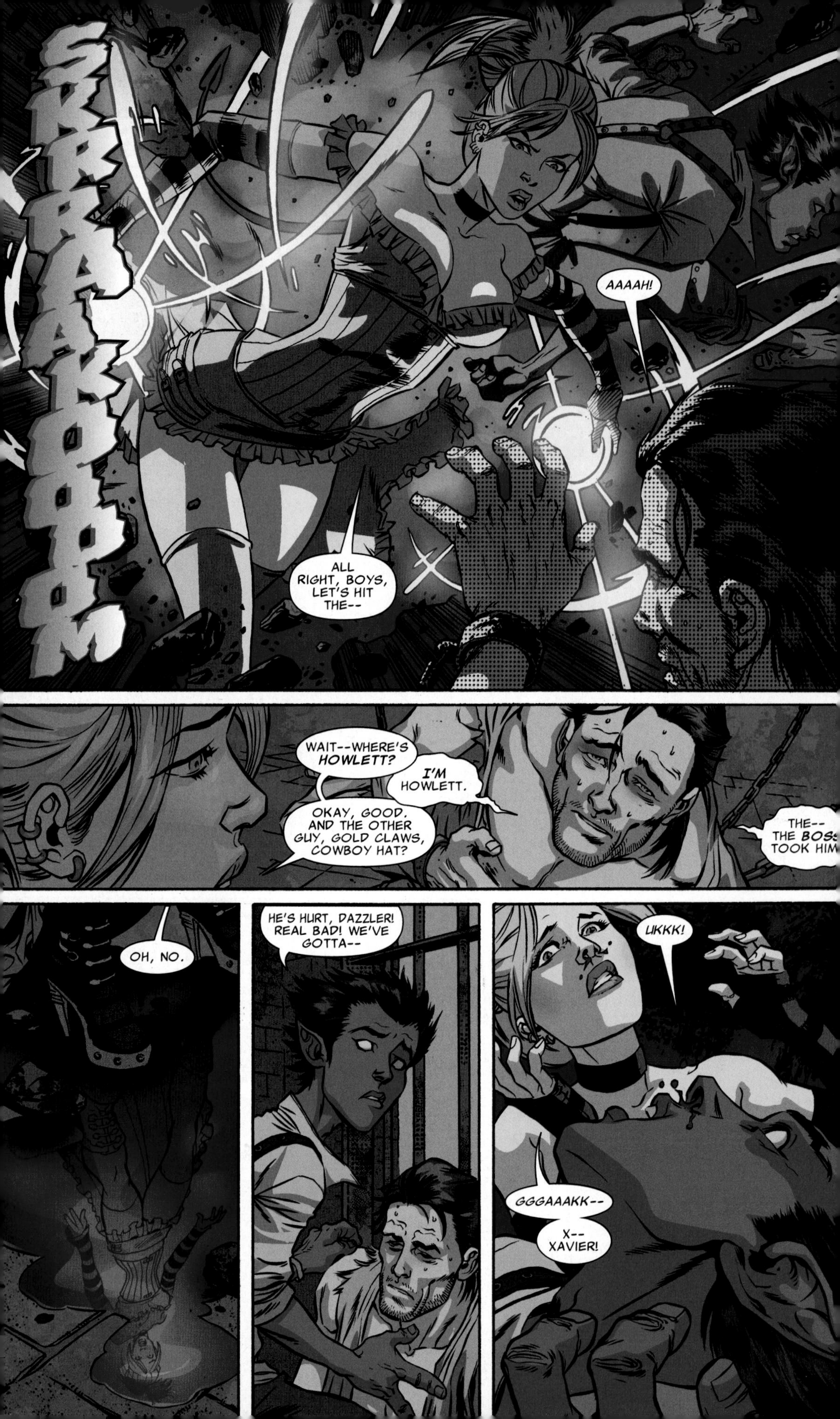

SPRAKOOOM
AAAAH!
ALL RIGHT, BOYS, LET'S HIT THE--
WAIT--WHERE'S HOWLETT?
I'M HOWLETT.
OKAY, GOOD. AND THE OTHER GUY, GOLD CLAWS, COWBOY HAT?
THE-- THE BOS TOOK HIM
OH, NO.
HE'S HURT, DAZZLER! REAL BAD! WE'VE GOTTA--
UKKK!
GGGAAAKK--
X-- XAVIER!

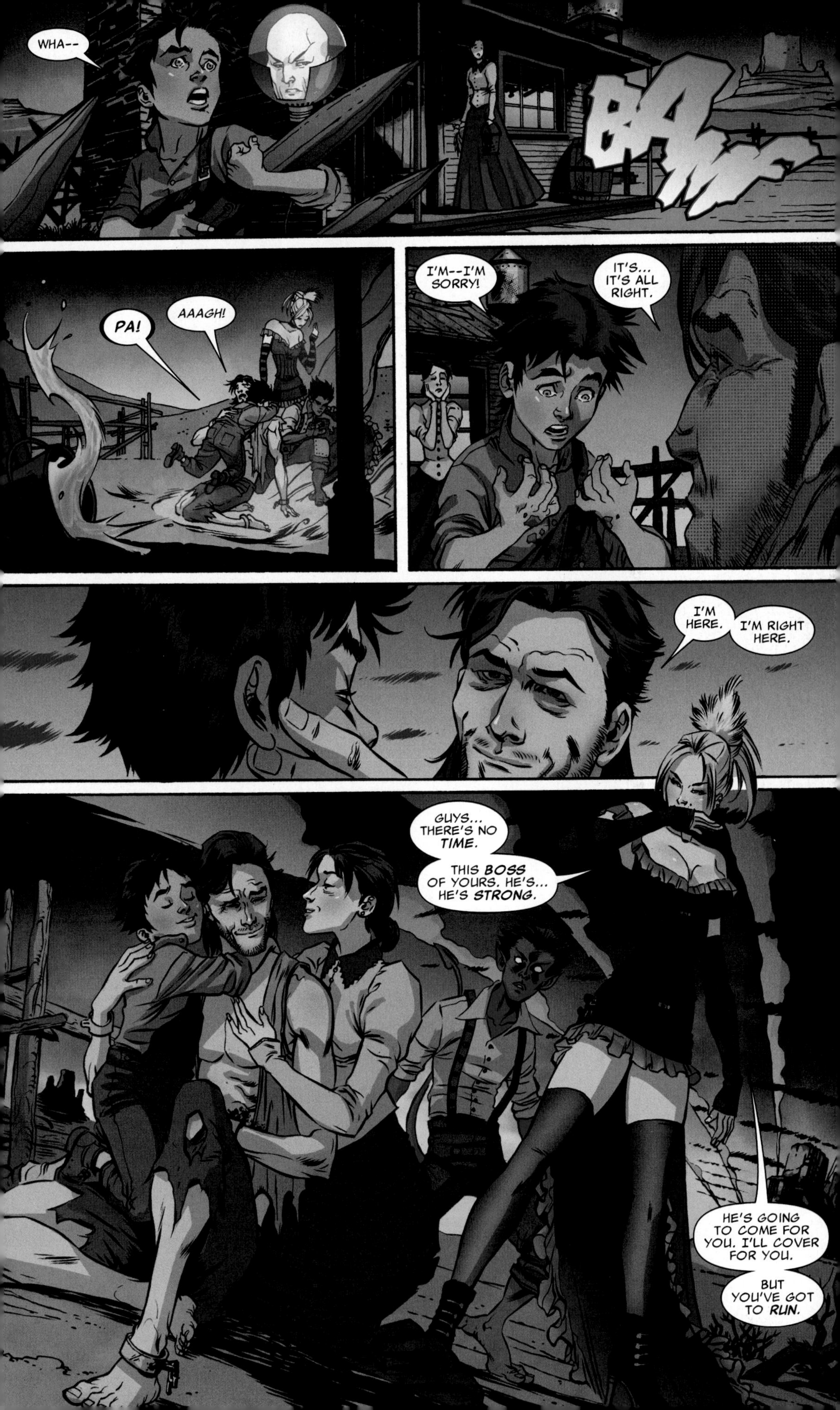
WHA--
BAM
PA!
AAAGH!
I'M--I'M SORRY!
IT'S... IT'S ALL RIGHT.
I'M HERE.
I'M RIGHT HERE.
GUYS... THERE'S NO TIME.
THIS BOSS OF YOURS. HE'S... HE'S STRONG.
HE'S GOING TO COME FOR YOU. I'LL COVER FOR YOU.
BUT YOU'VE GOT TO RUN.

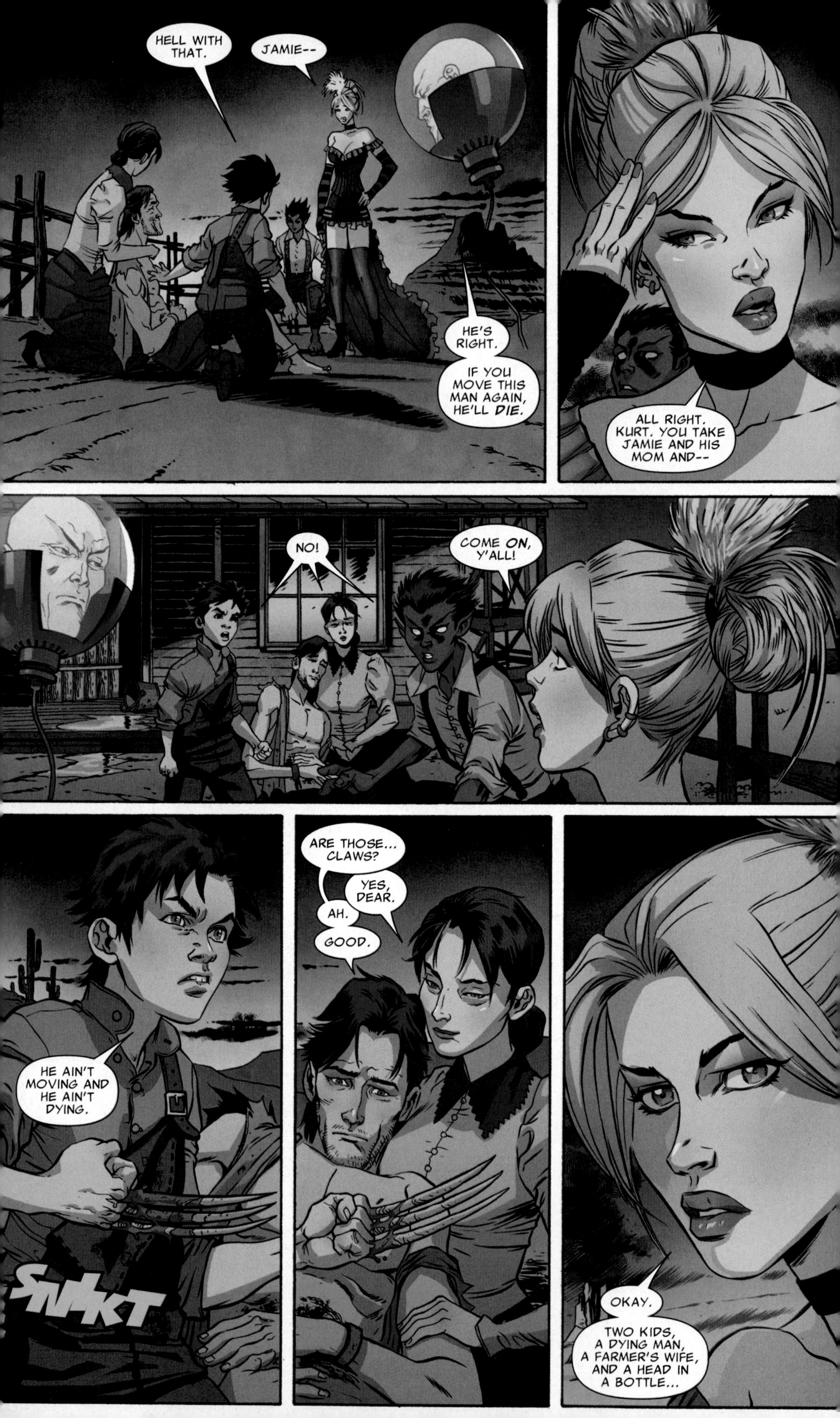
HELL WITH THAT.
JAMIE--
HE'S RIGHT.
IF YOU MOVE THIS MAN AGAIN, HE'LL DIE.
ALL RIGHT. KURT. YOU TAKE JAMIE AND HIS MOM AND--
NO!
COME ON, Y'ALL!
HE AIN'T MOVING AND HE AIN'T DYING.
SNIKT
ARE THOSE... CLAWS?
YES, DEAR.
AH.
GOOD.
OKAY.
TWO KIDS, A DYING MAN, A FARMER'S WIFE, AND A HEAD IN A BOTTLE...

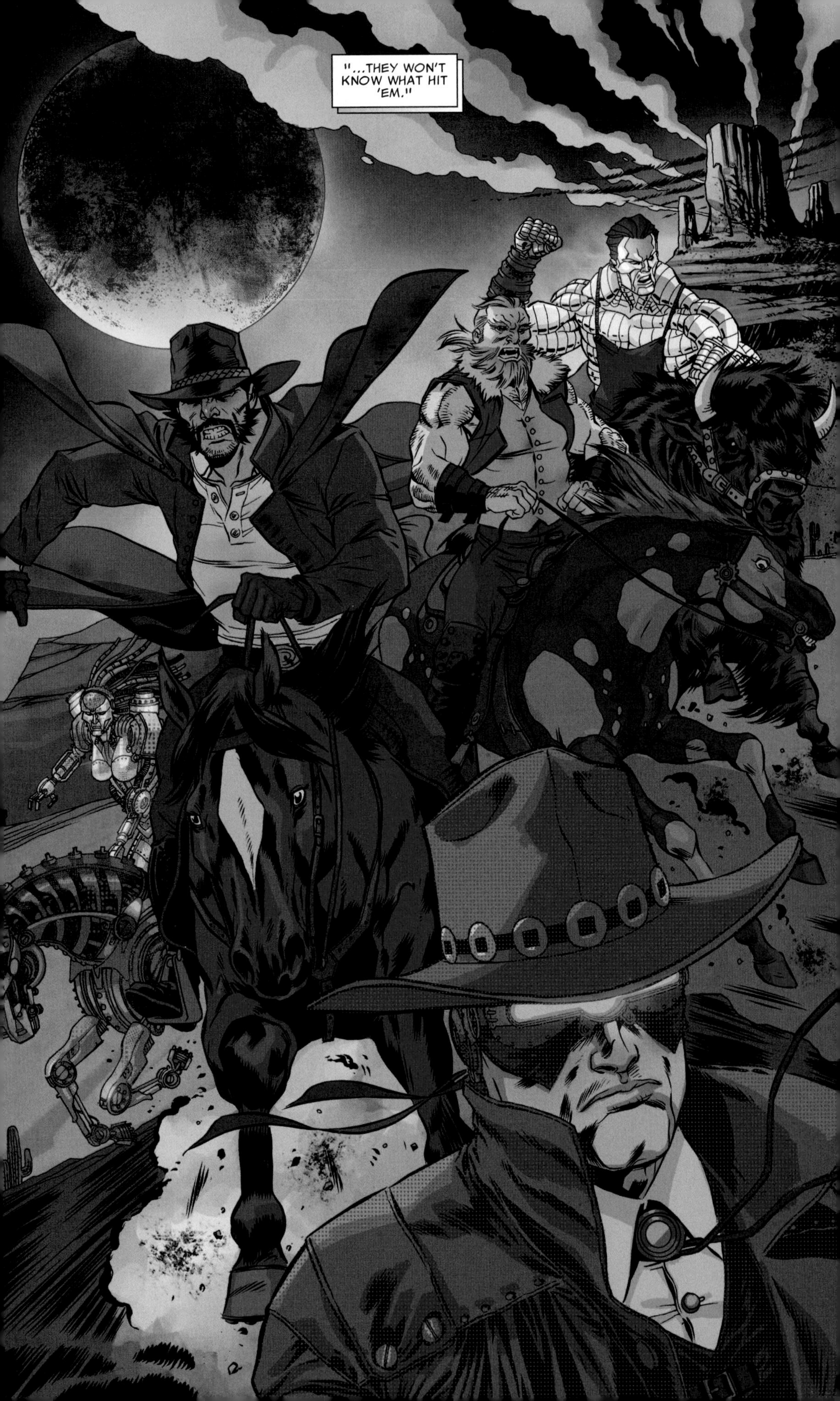
"...THEY WON'T KNOW WHAT HIT 'EM."

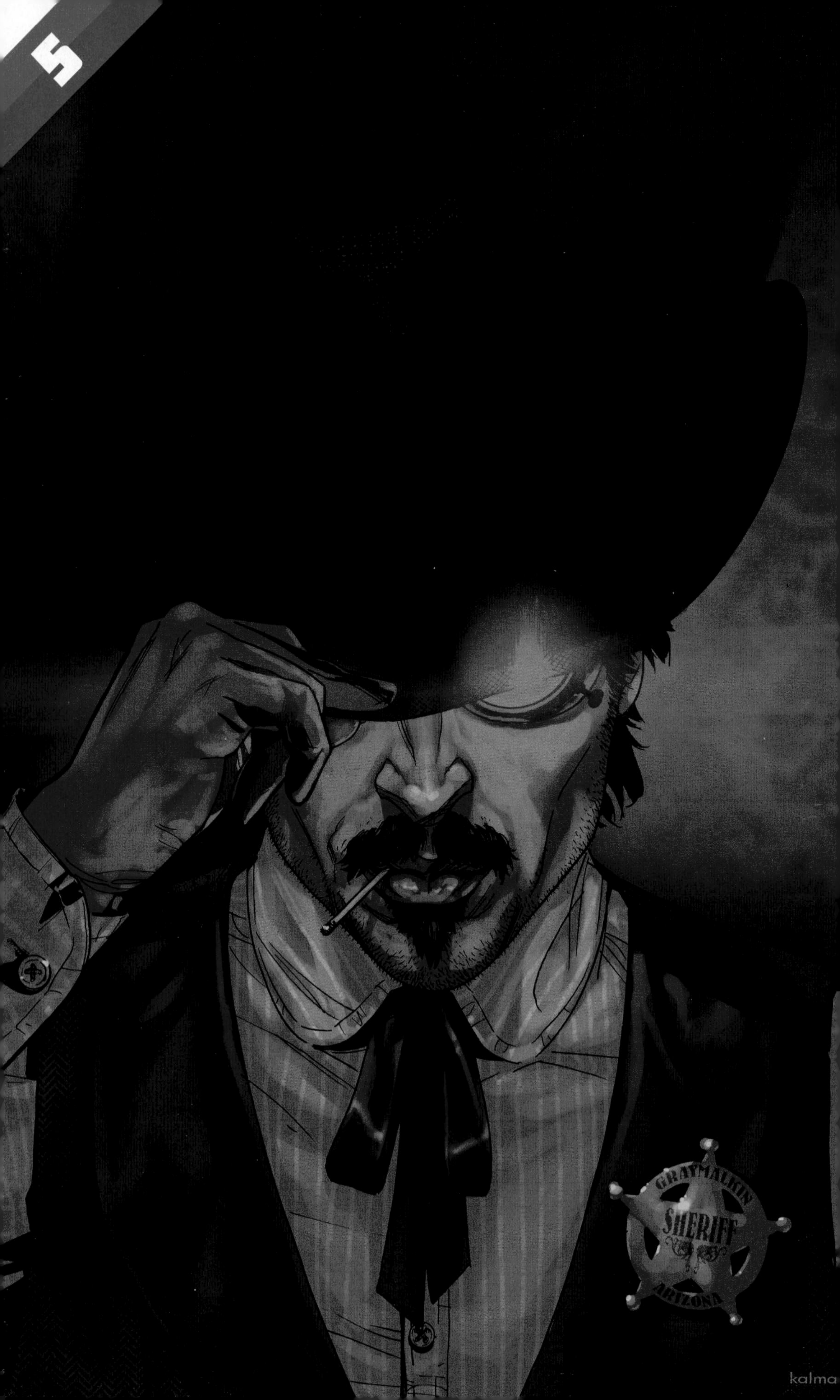
5
GRAYMALKIN
SHERIFF
ARIZONA
kalma

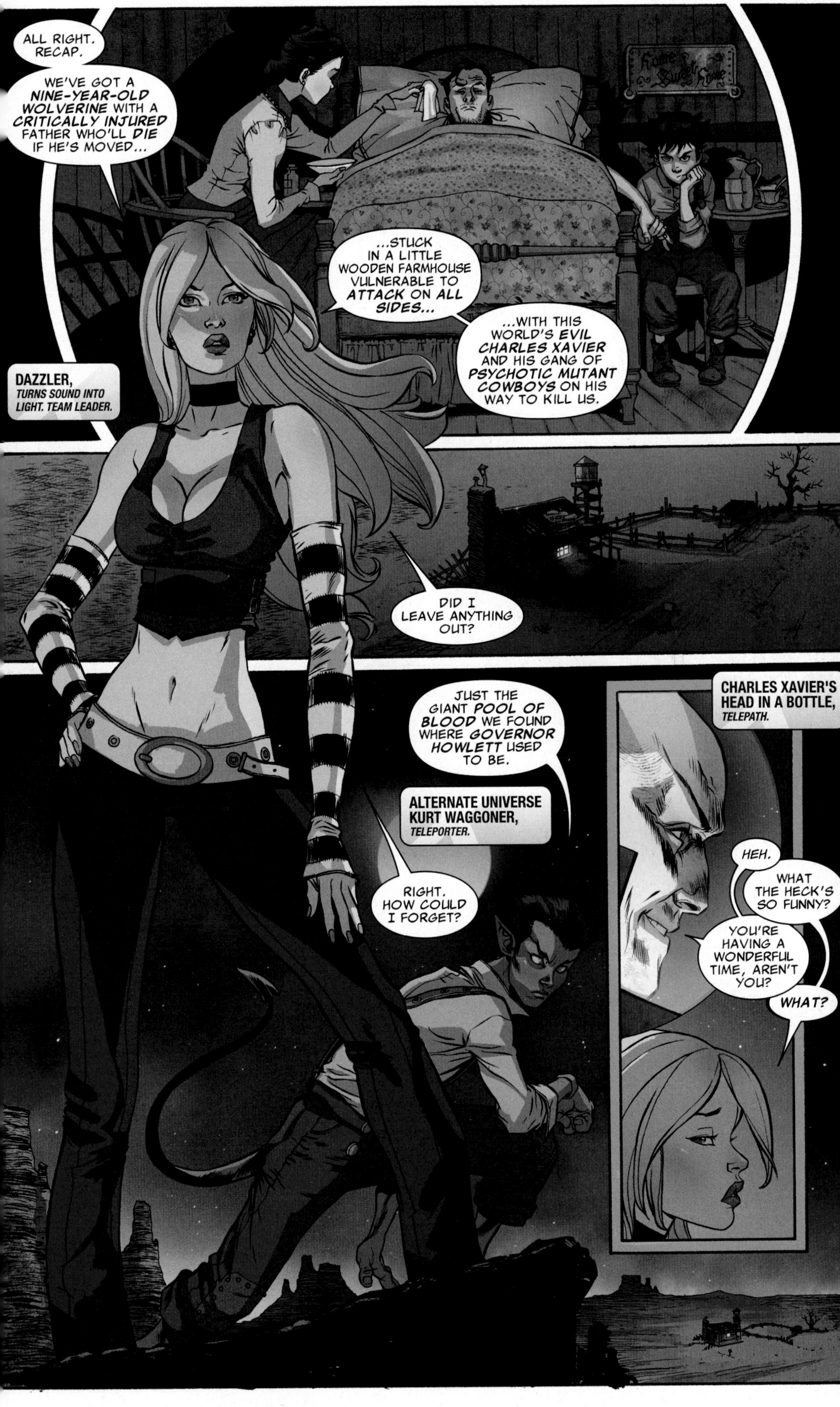
ALL RIGHT. RECAP.
WE'VE GOT A NINE-YEAR-OLD WOLVERINE WITH A CRITICALLY INJURED FATHER WHO'LL DIE IF HE'S MOVED...
...STUCK IN A LITTLE WOODEN FARMHOUSE VULNERABLE TO ATTACK ON ALL SIDES...
...WITH THIS WORLD'S EVIL CHARLES XAVIER AND HIS GANG OF PSYCHOTIC MUTANT COWBOYS ON HIS WAY TO KILL US.
DAZZLER, TURNS SOUND INTO LIGHT. TEAM LEADER.
DID I LEAVE ANYTHING OUT?
JUST THE GIANT POOL OF BLOOD WE FOUND WHERE GOVERNOR HOWLETT USED TO BE.
ALTERNATE UNIVERSE KURT WAGGONER, TELEPORTER.
RIGHT. HOW COULD I FORGET?
CHARLES XAVIER'S HEAD IN A BOTTLE, TELEPATH.
HEH.
WHAT THE HECK'S SO FUNNY?
YOU'RE HAVING A WONDERFUL TIME, AREN'T YOU?
WHAT?

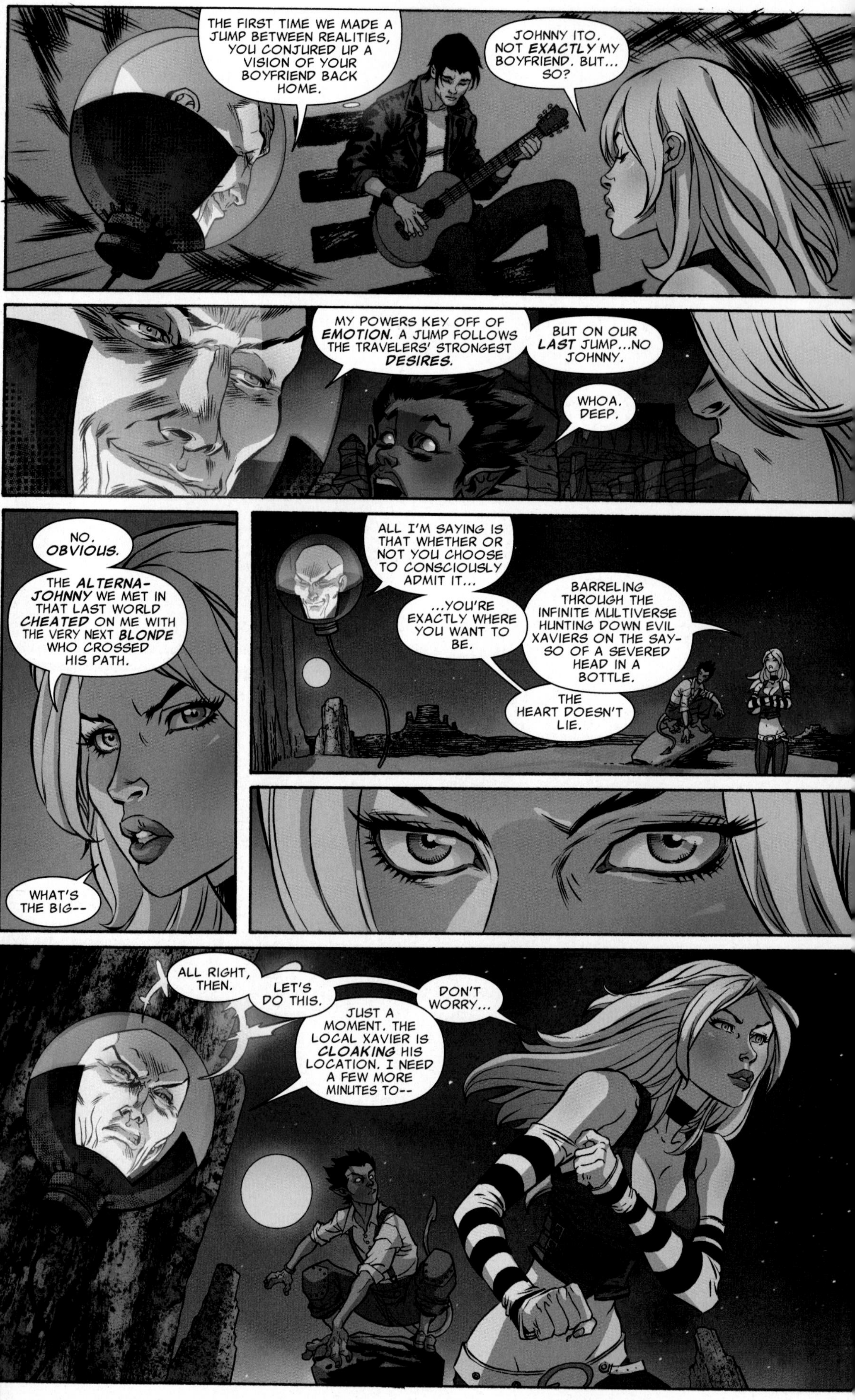
THE FIRST TIME WE MADE A JUMP BETWEEN REALITIES, YOU CONJURED UP A VISION OF YOUR BOYFRIEND BACK HOME.
JOHNNY ITO. NOT EXACTLY MY BOYFRIEND. BUT... SO?
MY POWERS KEY OFF OF EMOTION. A JUMP FOLLOWS THE TRAVELERS' STRONGEST DESIRES.
BUT ON OUR LAST JUMP...NO JOHNNY.
WHOA. DEEP.
NO. OBVIOUS.
THE ALTERNA-JOHNNY WE MET IN THAT LAST WORLD CHEATED ON ME WITH THE VERY NEXT BLONDE WHO CROSSED HIS PATH.
WHAT'S THE BIG--
ALL I'M SAYING IS THAT WHETHER OR NOT YOU CHOOSE TO CONSCIOUSLY ADMIT IT...
...YOU'RE EXACTLY WHERE YOU WANT TO BE.
BARRELING THROUGH THE INFINITE MULTIVERSE HUNTING DOWN EVIL XAVIERS ON THE SAY-SO OF A SEVERED HEAD IN A BOTTLE.
THE HEART DOESN'T LIE.
ALL RIGHT, THEN.
LET'S DO THIS.
DON'T WORRY...
JUST A MOMENT. THE LOCAL XAVIER IS CLOAKING HIS LOCATION. I NEED A FEW MORE MINUTES TO--

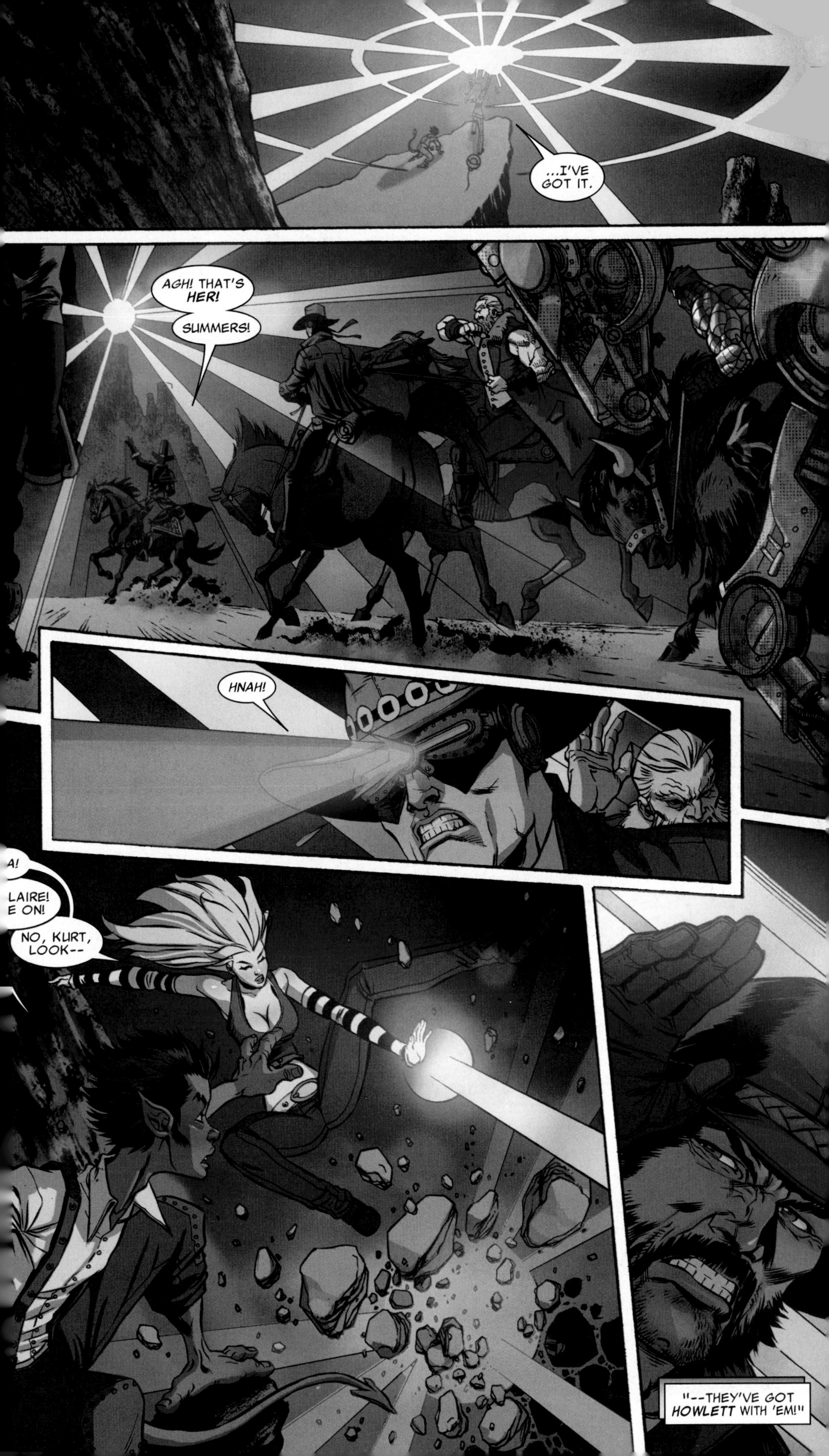
...I'VE GOT IT.
AGH! THAT'S HER!
SUMMERS!
HNAH!
NO, KURT, LOOK--
"--THEY'VE GOT HOWLETT WITH 'EM!"

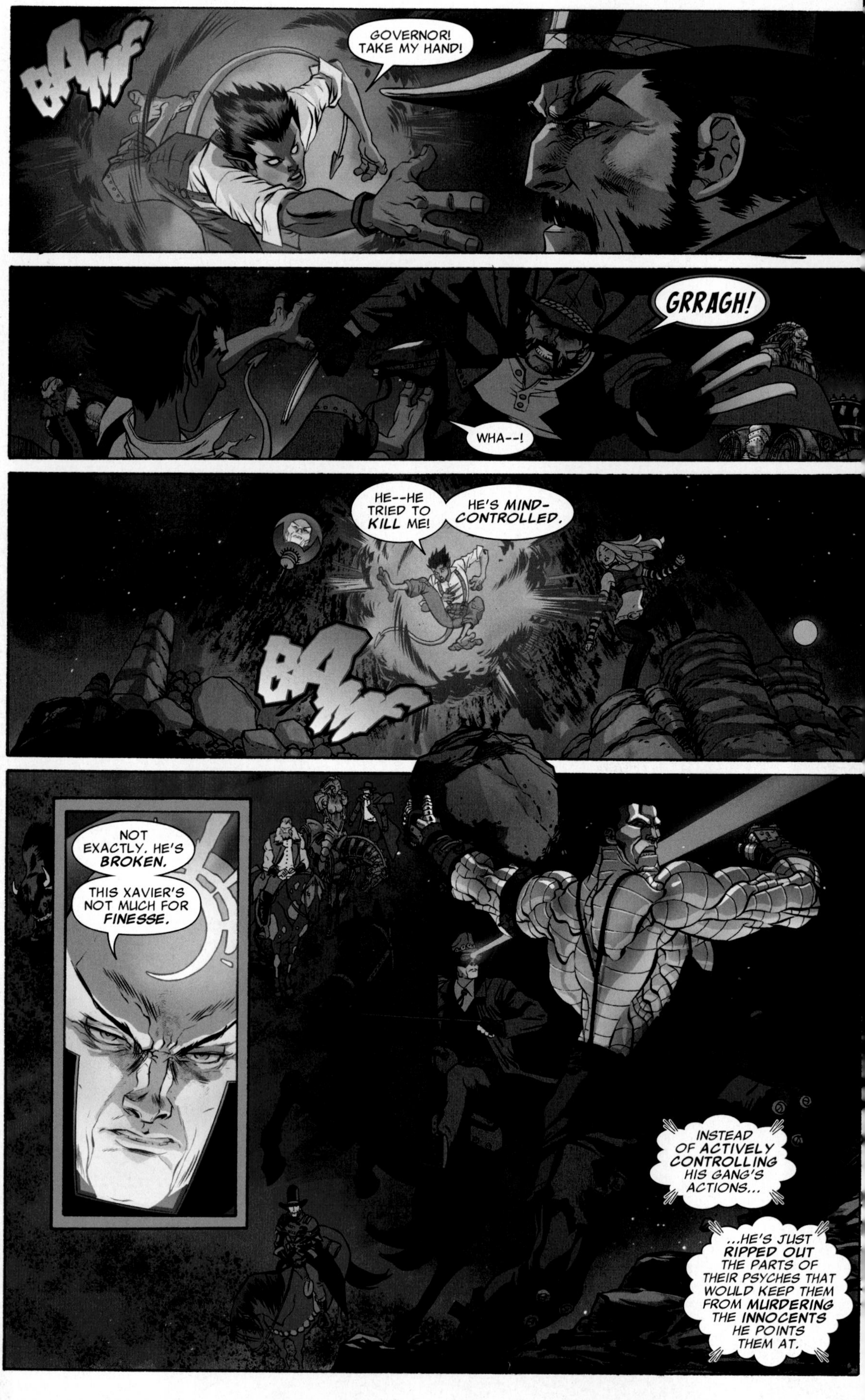
BAMF
GOVERNOR! TAKE MY HAND!
GRRAGH!
WHA--!
HE--HE TRIED TO KILL ME!
HE'S MIND-CONTROLLED.
BAMF
NOT EXACTLY. HE'S BROKEN.
THIS XAVIER'S NOT MUCH FOR FINESSE.
INSTEAD OF ACTIVELY CONTROLLING HIS GANG'S ACTIONS...
...HE'S JUST RIPPED OUT THE PARTS OF THEIR PSYCHES THAT WOULD KEEP THEM FROM MURDERING THE INNOCENTS HE POINTS THEM AT.

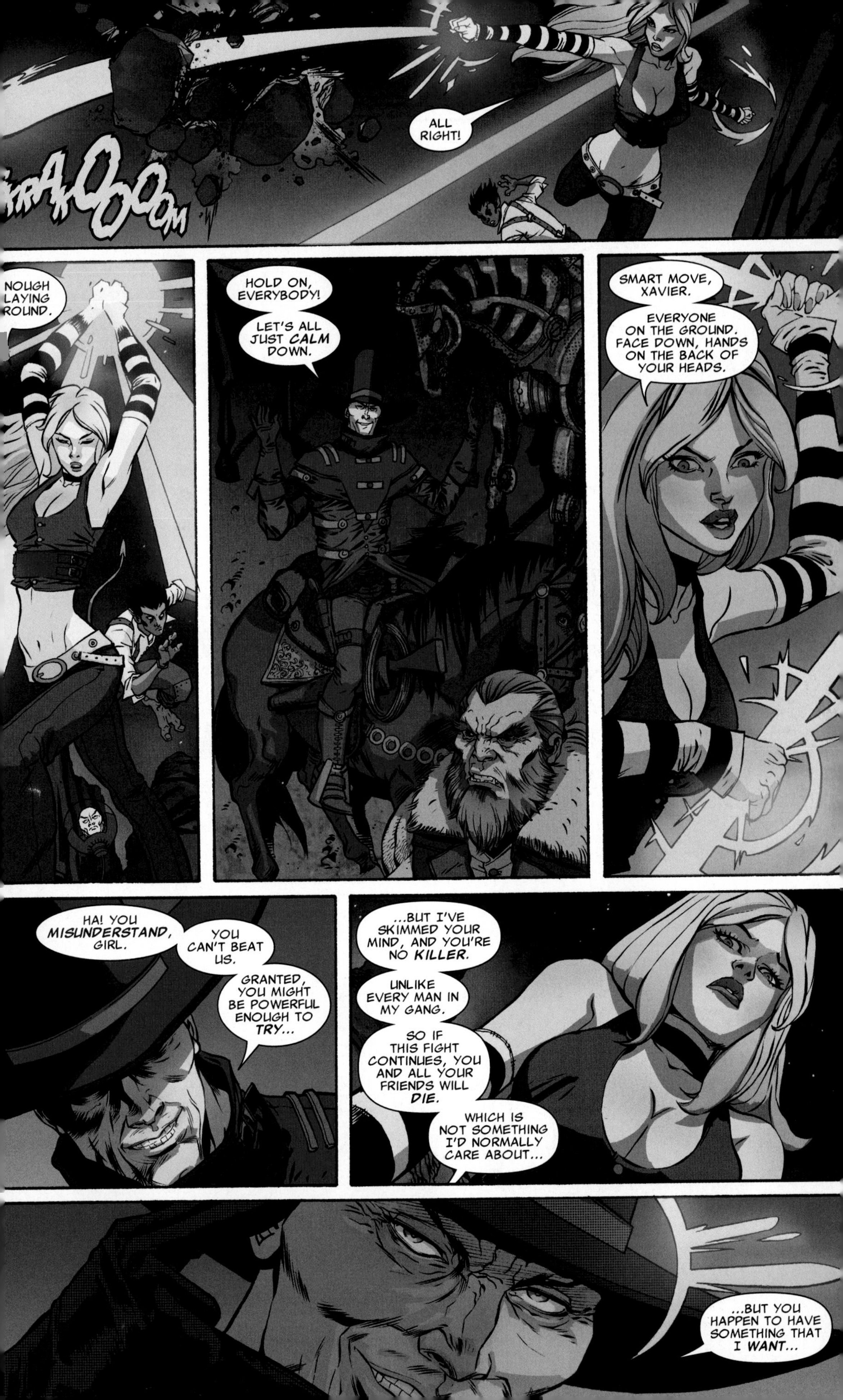

KRAKOOOOOM
ALL RIGHT!
NOUGH LAYING ROUND.
HOLD ON, EVERYBODY!
LET'S ALL JUST CALM DOWN.
SMART MOVE, XAVIER.
EVERYONE ON THE GROUND. FACE DOWN, HANDS ON THE BACK OF YOUR HEADS.
HA! YOU MISUNDERSTAND, GIRL.
YOU CAN'T BEAT US.
GRANTED, YOU MIGHT BE POWERFUL ENOUGH TO TRY...
...BUT I'VE SKIMMED YOUR MIND, AND YOU'RE NO KILLER.
UNLIKE EVERY MAN IN MY GANG.
SO IF THIS FIGHT CONTINUES, YOU AND ALL YOUR FRIENDS WILL DIE.
WHICH IS NOT SOMETHING I'D NORMALLY CARE ABOUT...
...BUT YOU HAPPEN TO HAVE SOMETHING THAT I WANT...

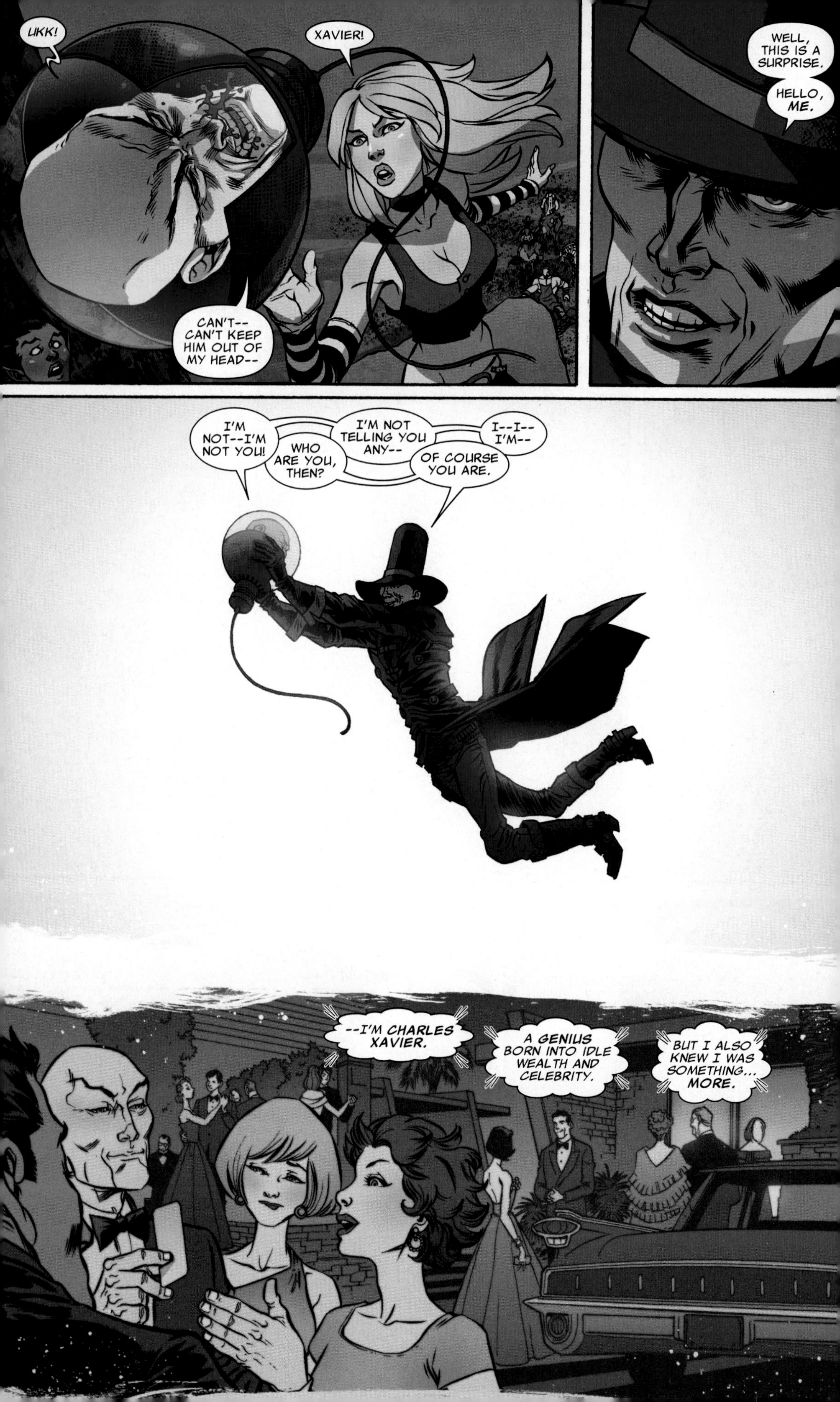
UKK!
XAVIER!
CAN'T-- CAN'T KEEP HIM OUT OF MY HEAD--
WELL, THIS IS A SURPRISE.
HELLO, ME.
I'M NOT--I'M NOT YOU!
WHO ARE YOU, THEN?
I'M NOT TELLING YOU ANY--
OF COURSE YOU ARE.
I--I-- I'M--
--I'M CHARLES XAVIER.
A GENIUS BORN INTO IDLE WEALTH AND CELEBRITY.
BUT I ALSO KNEW I WAS SOMETHING... MORE.

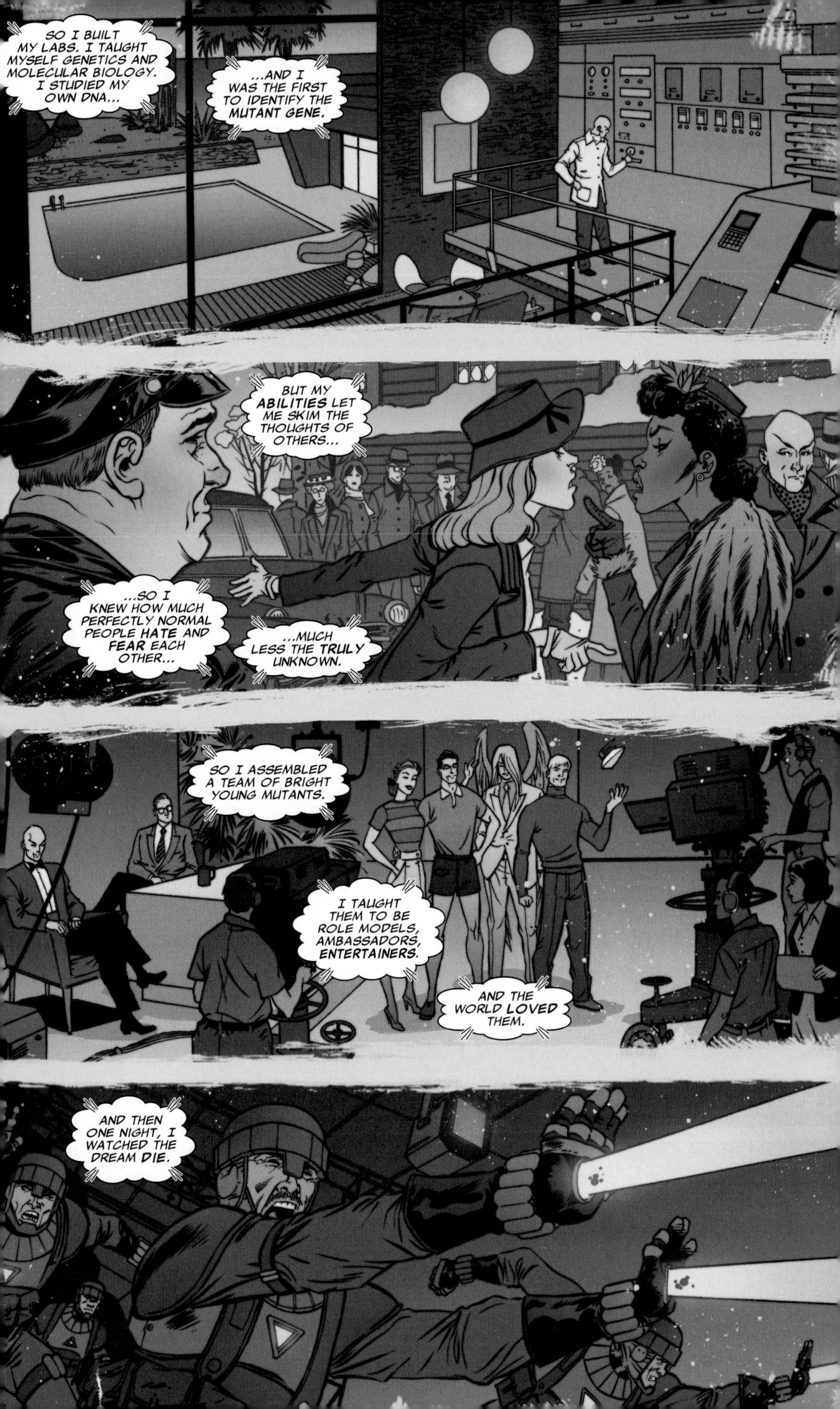
SO I BUILT MY LABS. I TAUGHT MYSELF GENETICS AND MOLECULAR BIOLOGY. I STUDIED MY OWN DNA...
...AND I WAS THE FIRST TO IDENTIFY THE MUTANT GENE.
BUT MY ABILITIES LET ME SKIM THE THOUGHTS OF OTHERS...
...SO I KNEW HOW MUCH PERFECTLY NORMAL PEOPLE HATE AND FEAR EACH OTHER...
...MUCH LESS THE TRULY UNKNOWN.
SO I ASSEMBLED A TEAM OF BRIGHT YOUNG MUTANTS.
I TAUGHT THEM TO BE ROLE MODELS, AMBASSADORS, ENTERTAINERS.
AND THE WORLD LOVED THEM.
AND THEN ONE NIGHT, I WATCHED THE DREAM DIE.

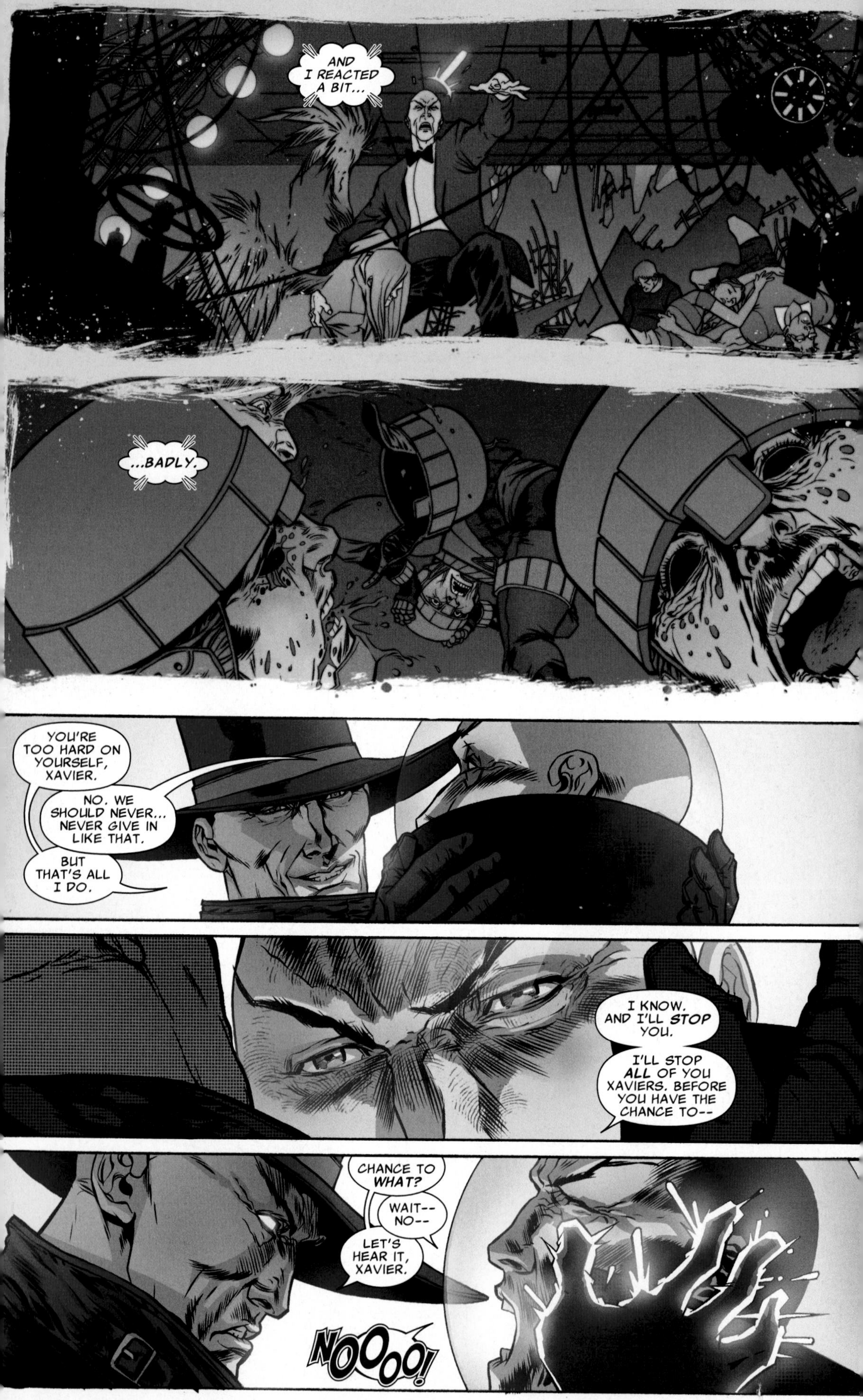
AND I REACTED A BIT...
...BADLY.
YOU'RE TOO HARD ON YOURSELF, XAVIER.
NO. WE SHOULD NEVER... NEVER GIVE IN LIKE THAT.
BUT THAT'S ALL I DO.
I KNOW. AND I'LL STOP YOU.
I'LL STOP ALL OF YOU XAVIERS. BEFORE YOU HAVE THE CHANCE TO--
CHANCE TO WHAT?
WAIT-- NO--
LET'S HEAR IT, XAVIER.
NOOOO!

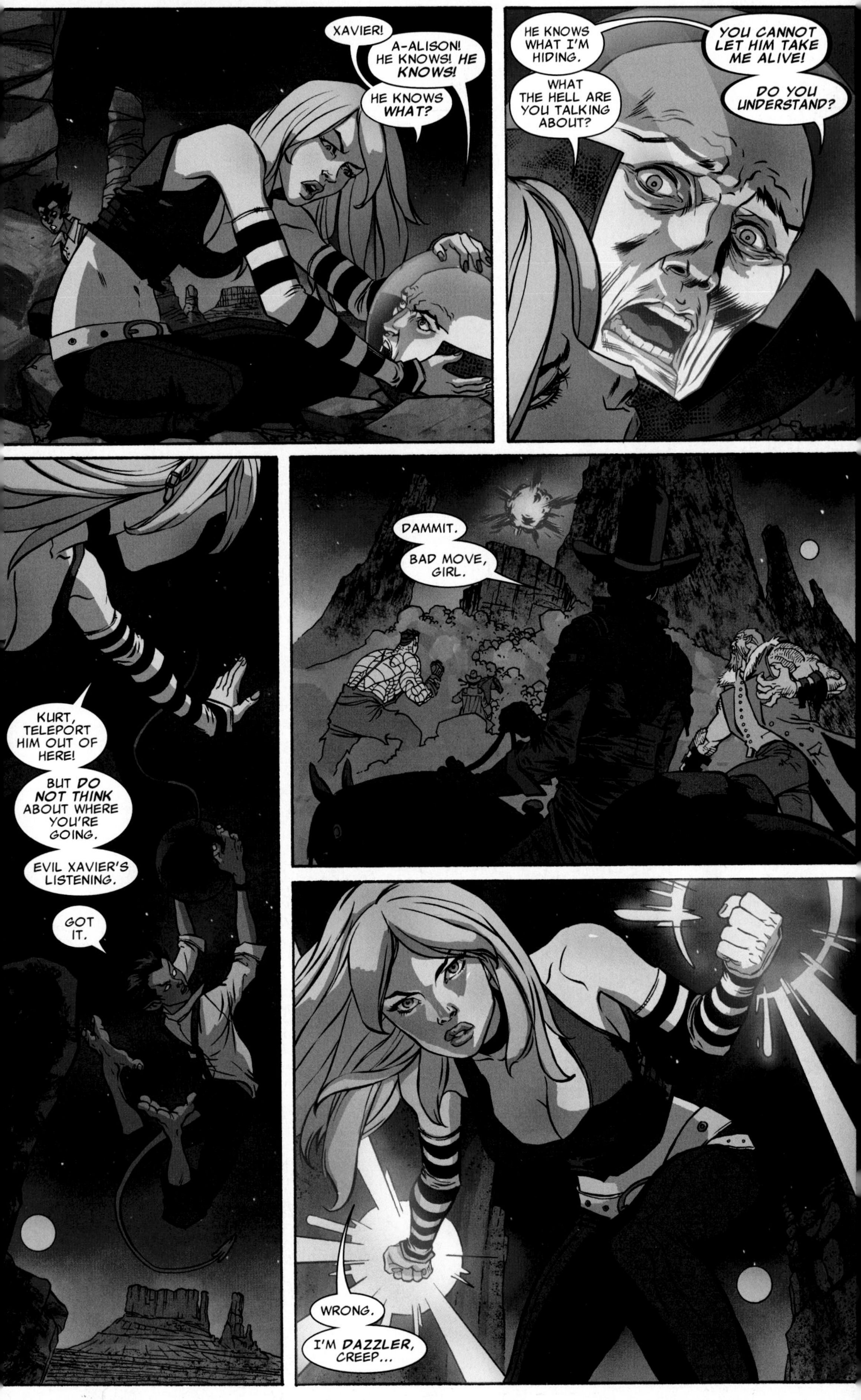
XAVIER!
A-ALISON! HE KNOWS! *HE KNOWS!*
HE KNOWS *WHAT?*
HE KNOWS WHAT I'M HIDING.
WHAT THE HELL ARE YOU TALKING ABOUT?
YOU CANNOT LET HIM TAKE ME ALIVE!
DO YOU UNDERSTAND?
KURT, TELEPORT HIM OUT OF HERE!
BUT *DO NOT THINK* ABOUT WHERE YOU'RE GOING.
EVIL XAVIER'S LISTENING.
GOT IT.
DAMMIT.
BAD MOVE, GIRL.
WRONG.
I'M *DAZZLER*, CREEP...

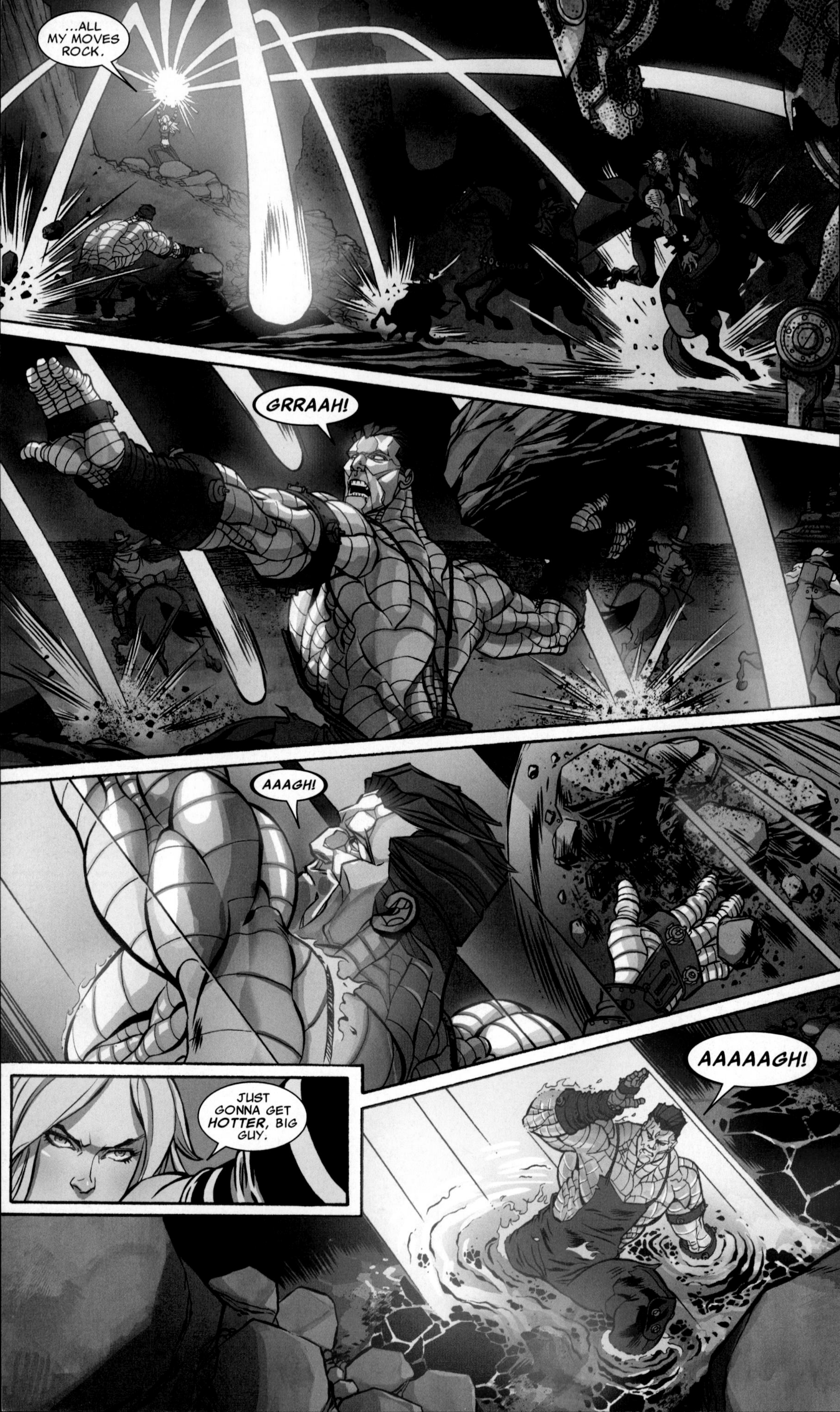
...ALL MY MOVES ROCK.
GRRAAH!
AAAGH!
JUST GONNA GET HOTTER, BIG GUY.
AAAAAGH!

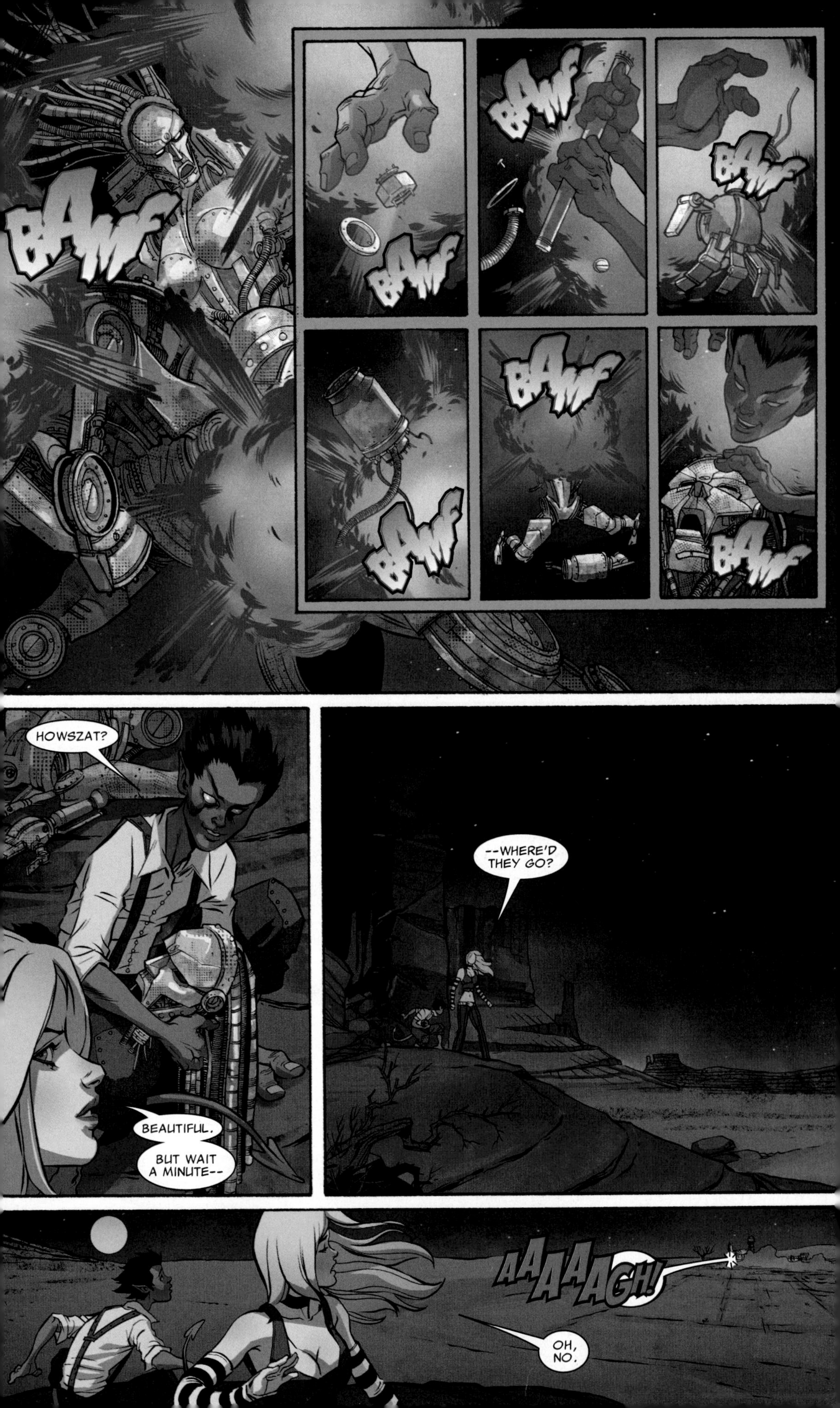
BAMF
BAMF
BAMF
BAMF
BAMF
BAMF
BAMF
HOWSZAT?
BEAUTIFUL.
BUT WAIT A MINUTE--
--WHERE'D THEY GO?
AAAAAGH!
OH, NO.

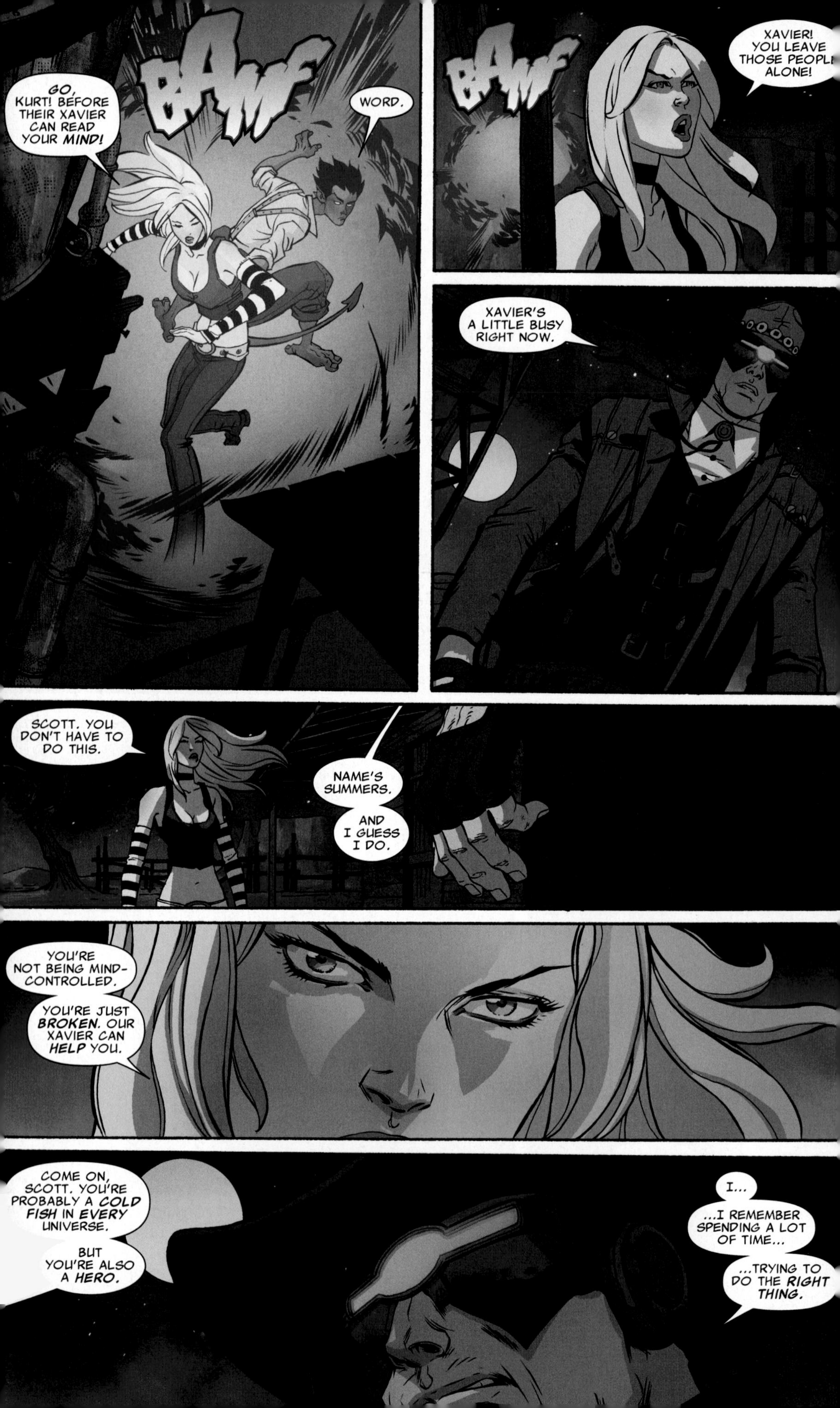
BAMF
GO, KURT! BEFORE THEIR XAVIER CAN READ YOUR MIND!
WORD.
BAMF
XAVIER! YOU LEAVE THOSE PEOPLE ALONE!
XAVIER'S A LITTLE BUSY RIGHT NOW.
SCOTT. YOU DON'T HAVE TO DO THIS.
NAME'S SUMMERS.
AND I GUESS I DO.
YOU'RE NOT BEING MIND-CONTROLLED.
YOU'RE JUST BROKEN. OUR XAVIER CAN HELP YOU.
COME ON, SCOTT. YOU'RE PROBABLY A COLD FISH IN EVERY UNIVERSE.
BUT YOU'RE ALSO A HERO.
I...
...I REMEMBER SPENDING A LOT OF TIME...
...TRYING TO DO THE RIGHT THING.

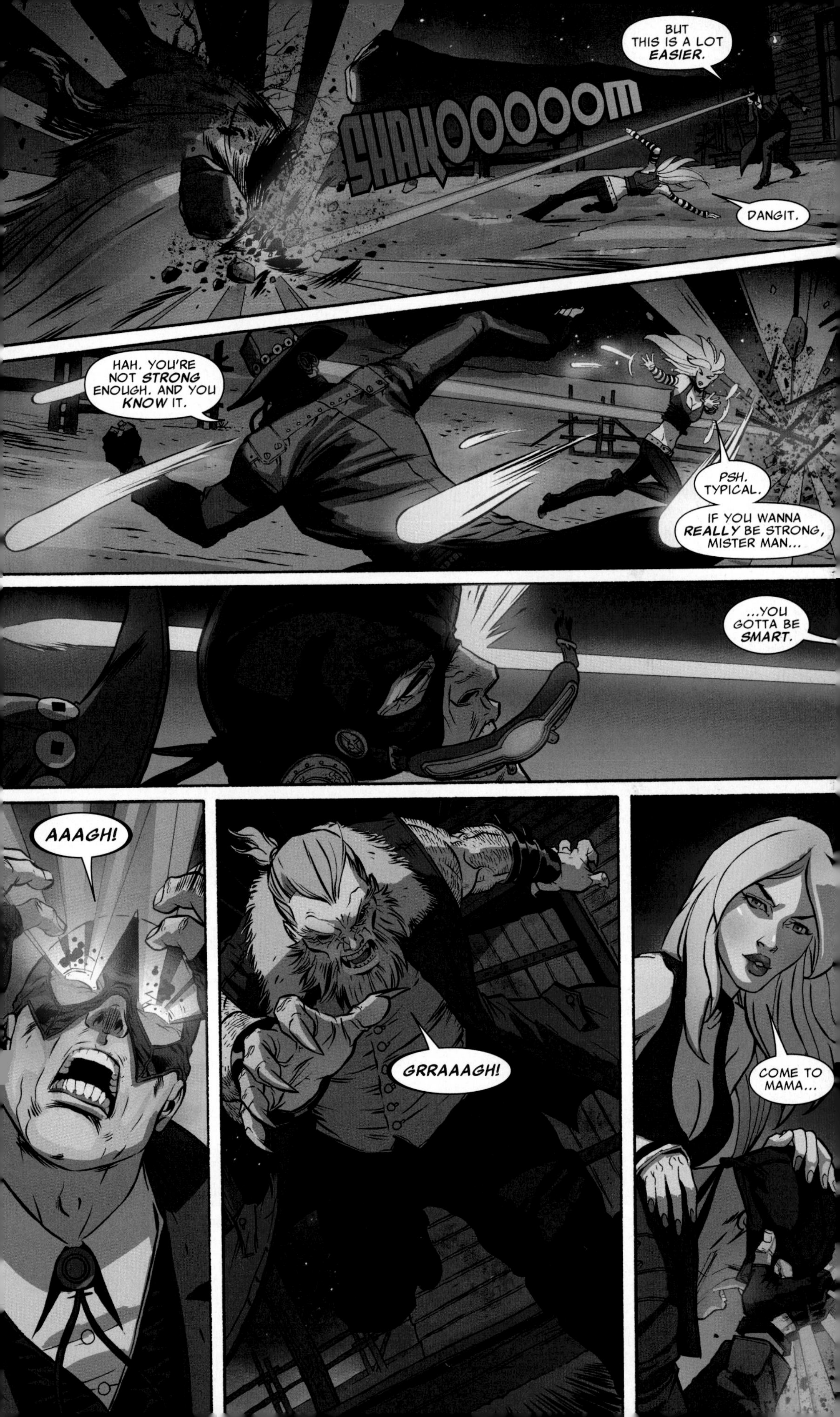
BUT THIS IS A LOT EASIER.
SHAKOOOOOM
DANGIT.
HAH. YOU'RE NOT STRONG ENOUGH. AND YOU KNOW IT.
PSH. TYPICAL.
IF YOU WANNA REALLY BE STRONG, MISTER MAN...
...YOU GOTTA BE SMART.
AAAGH!
GRRAAAGH!
COME TO MAMA...

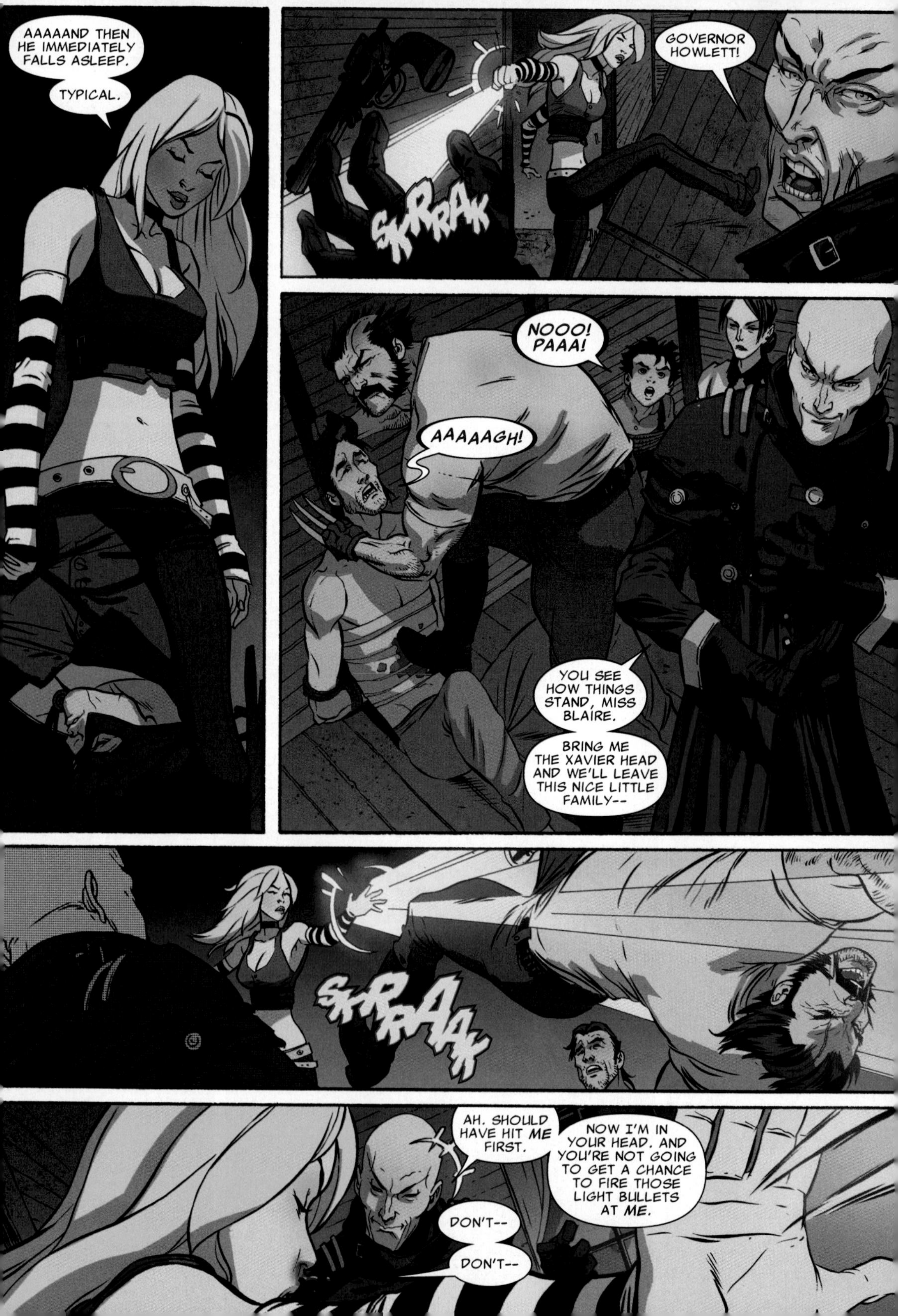
AAAAAND THEN HE IMMEDIATELY FALLS ASLEEP.
TYPICAL.
SKRRAK
GOVERNOR HOWLETT!
NOOO! PAAA!
AAAAAGH!
YOU SEE HOW THINGS STAND, MISS BLAIRE.
BRING ME THE XAVIER HEAD AND WE'LL LEAVE THIS NICE LITTLE FAMILY--
SKRRAAK
AH. SHOULD HAVE HIT ME FIRST.
NOW I'M IN YOUR HEAD. AND YOU'RE NOT GOING TO GET A CHANCE TO FIRE THOSE LIGHT BULLETS AT ME.
DON'T--
DON'T--

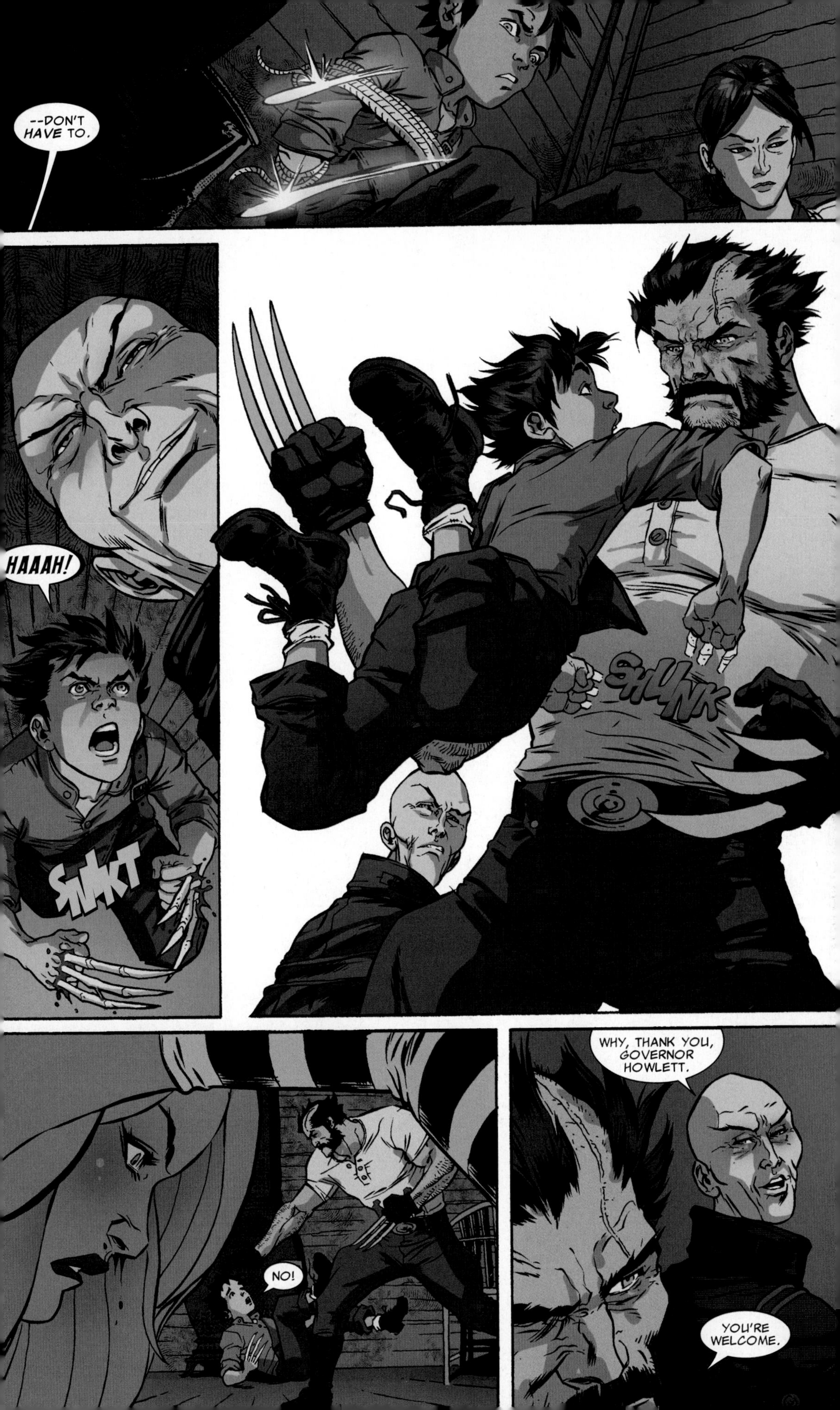
--DON'T HAVE TO.
HAAAH!
SNIKT
SHUNK
NO!
WHY, THANK YOU, GOVERNOR HOWLETT.
YOU'RE WELCOME.

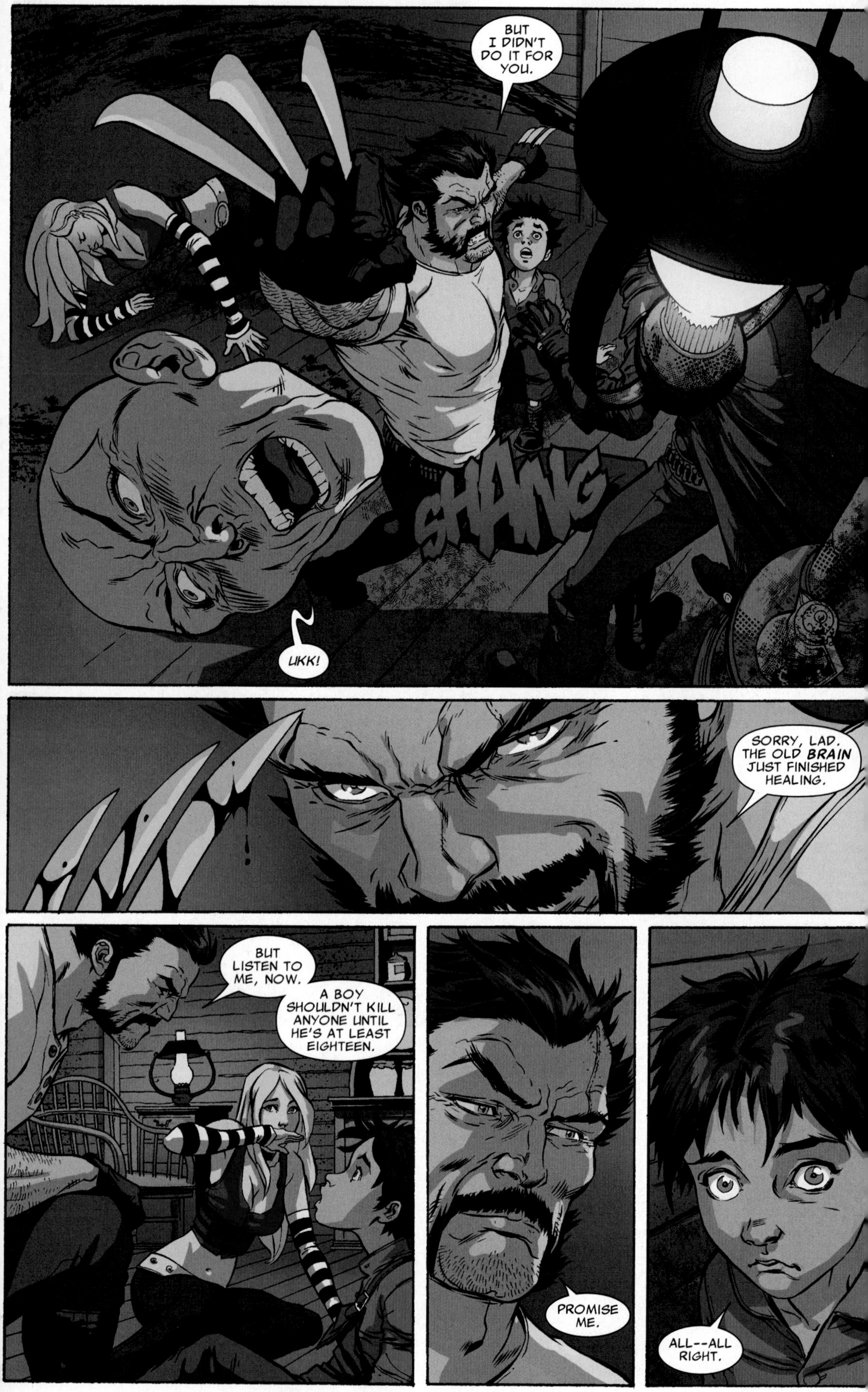
BUT I DIDN'T DO IT FOR YOU.
SHANG
UKK!
SORRY, LAD. THE OLD BRAIN JUST FINISHED HEALING.
BUT LISTEN TO ME, NOW.
A BOY SHOULDN'T KILL ANYONE UNTIL HE'S AT LEAST EIGHTEEN.
PROMISE ME.
ALL--ALL RIGHT.

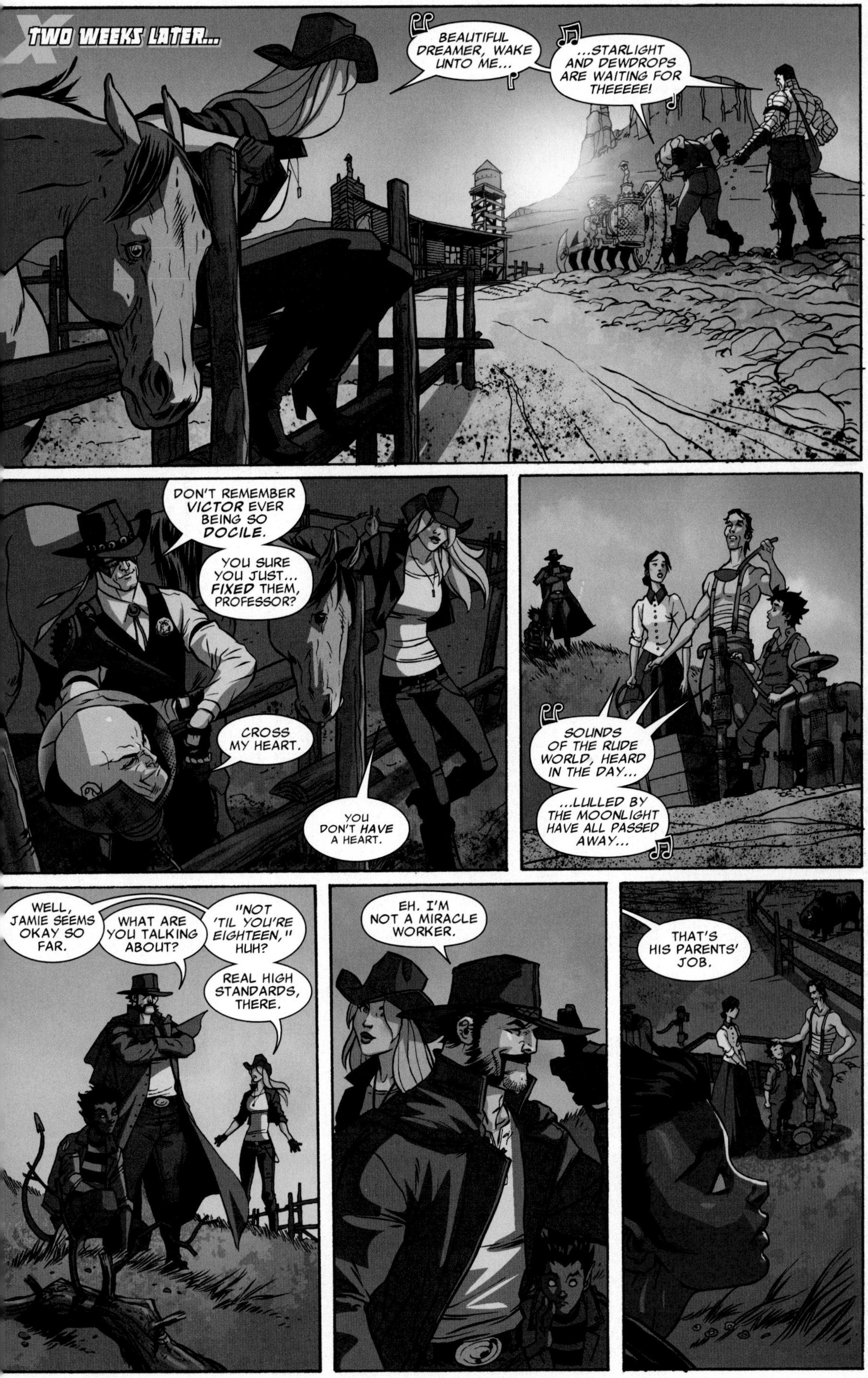
TWO WEEKS LATER...
BEAUTIFUL DREAMER, WAKE UNTO ME...
...STARLIGHT AND DEWDROPS ARE WAITING FOR THEEEEE!
DON'T REMEMBER VICTOR EVER BEING SO DOCILE.
YOU SURE YOU JUST... FIXED THEM, PROFESSOR?
CROSS MY HEART.
YOU DON'T HAVE A HEART.
SOUNDS OF THE RUDE WORLD, HEARD IN THE DAY...
...LULLED BY THE MOONLIGHT HAVE ALL PASSED AWAY...
WELL, JAMIE SEEMS OKAY SO FAR.
WHAT ARE YOU TALKING ABOUT?
"NOT 'TIL YOU'RE EIGHTEEN," HUH?
REAL HIGH STANDARDS, THERE.
EH. I'M NOT A MIRACLE WORKER.
THAT'S HIS PARENTS' JOB.

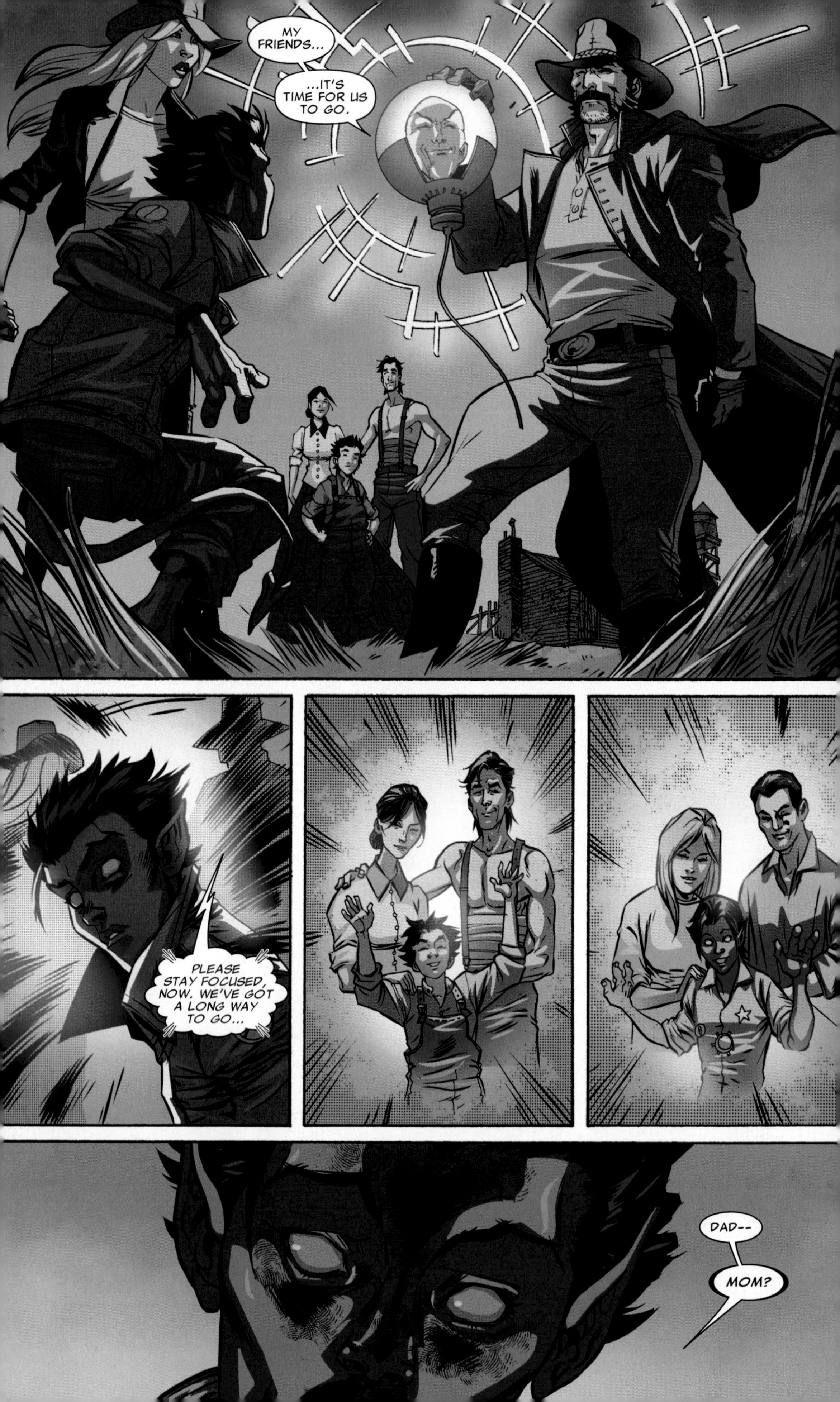
MY FRIENDS...
...IT'S TIME FOR US TO GO.
PLEASE STAY FOCUSED, NOW. WE'VE GOT A LONG WAY TO GO...
DAD--
MOM?

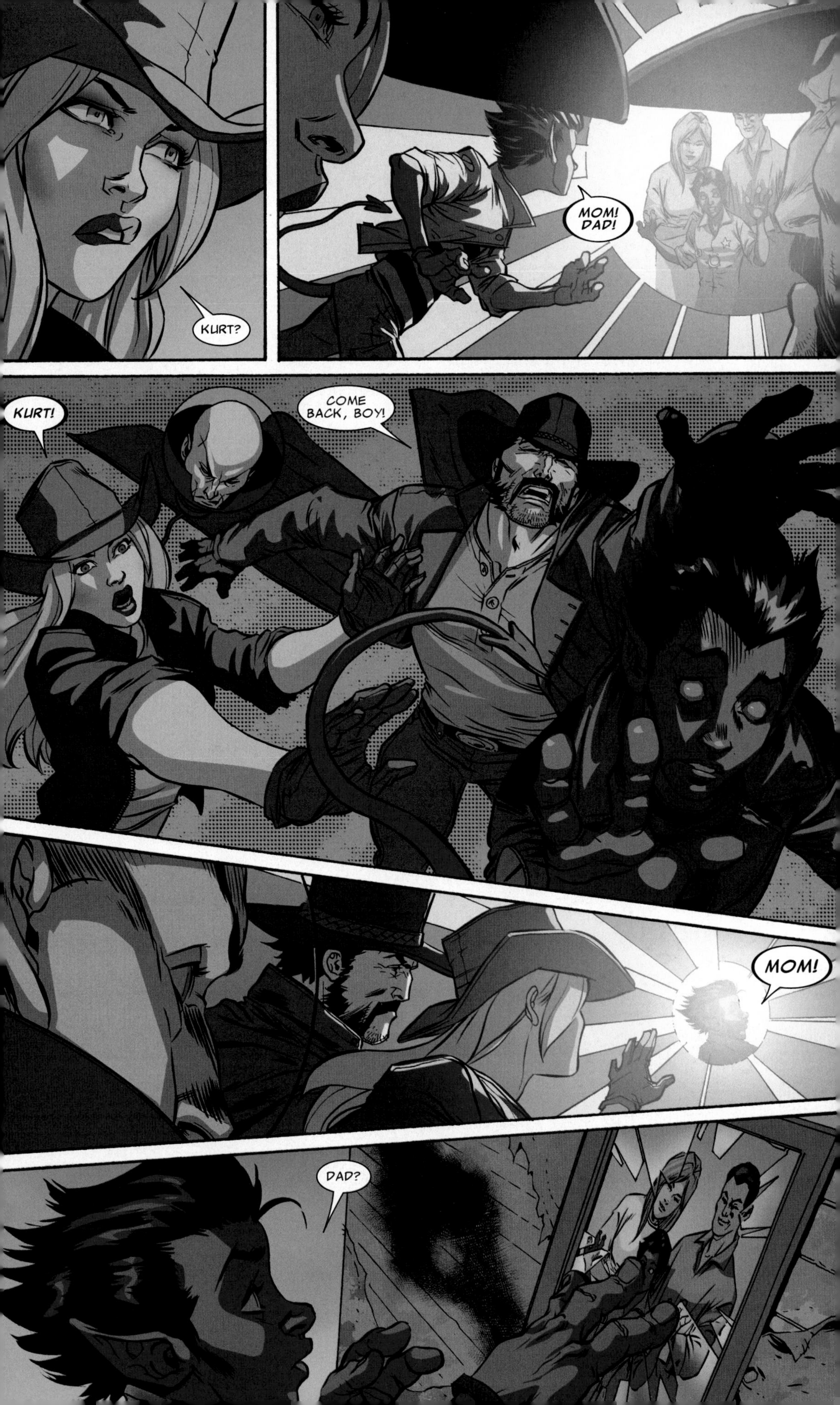
KURT?
MOM! DAD!
KURT!
COME BACK, BOY!
MOM!
DAD?

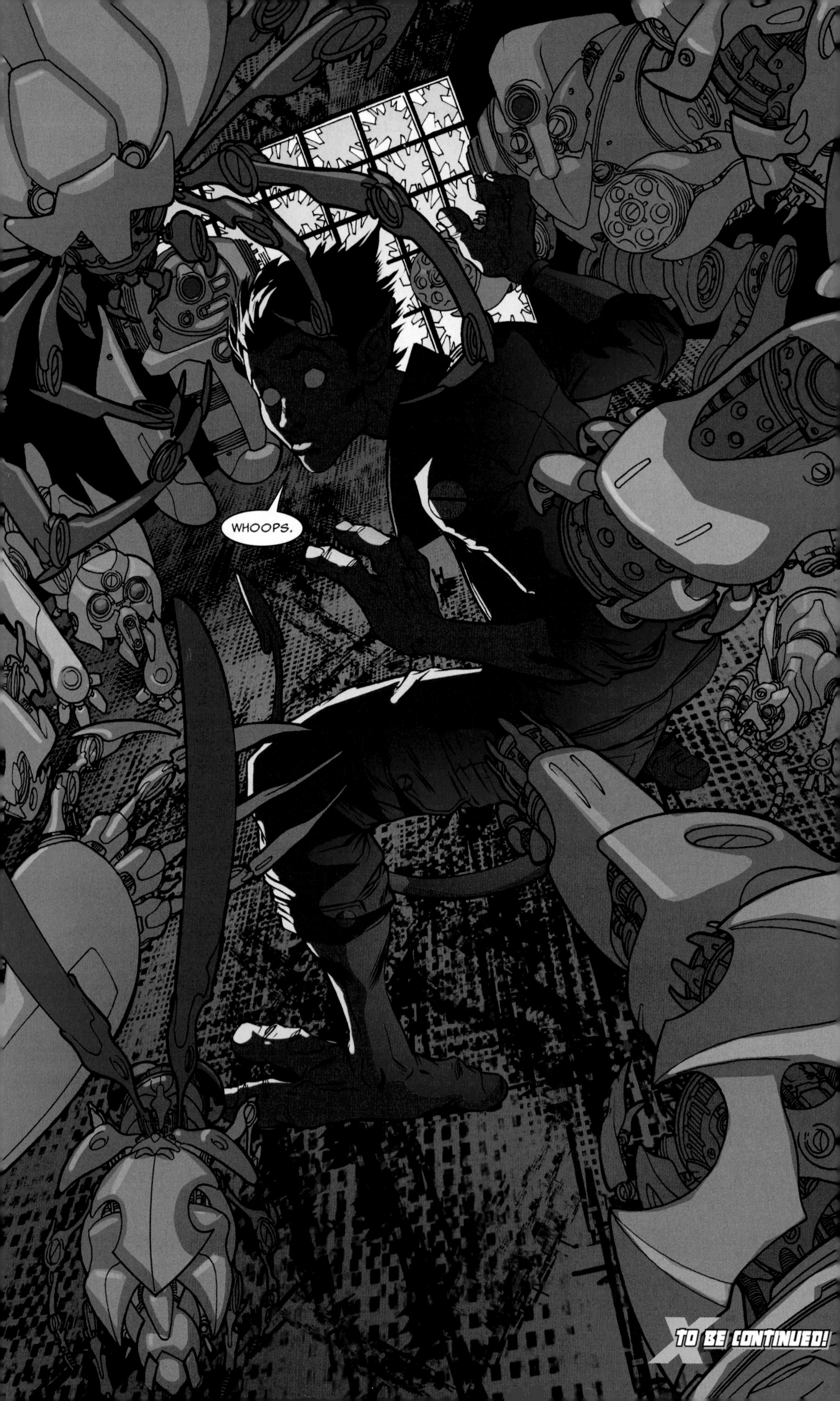
WHOOPS.
TO BE CONTINUED!

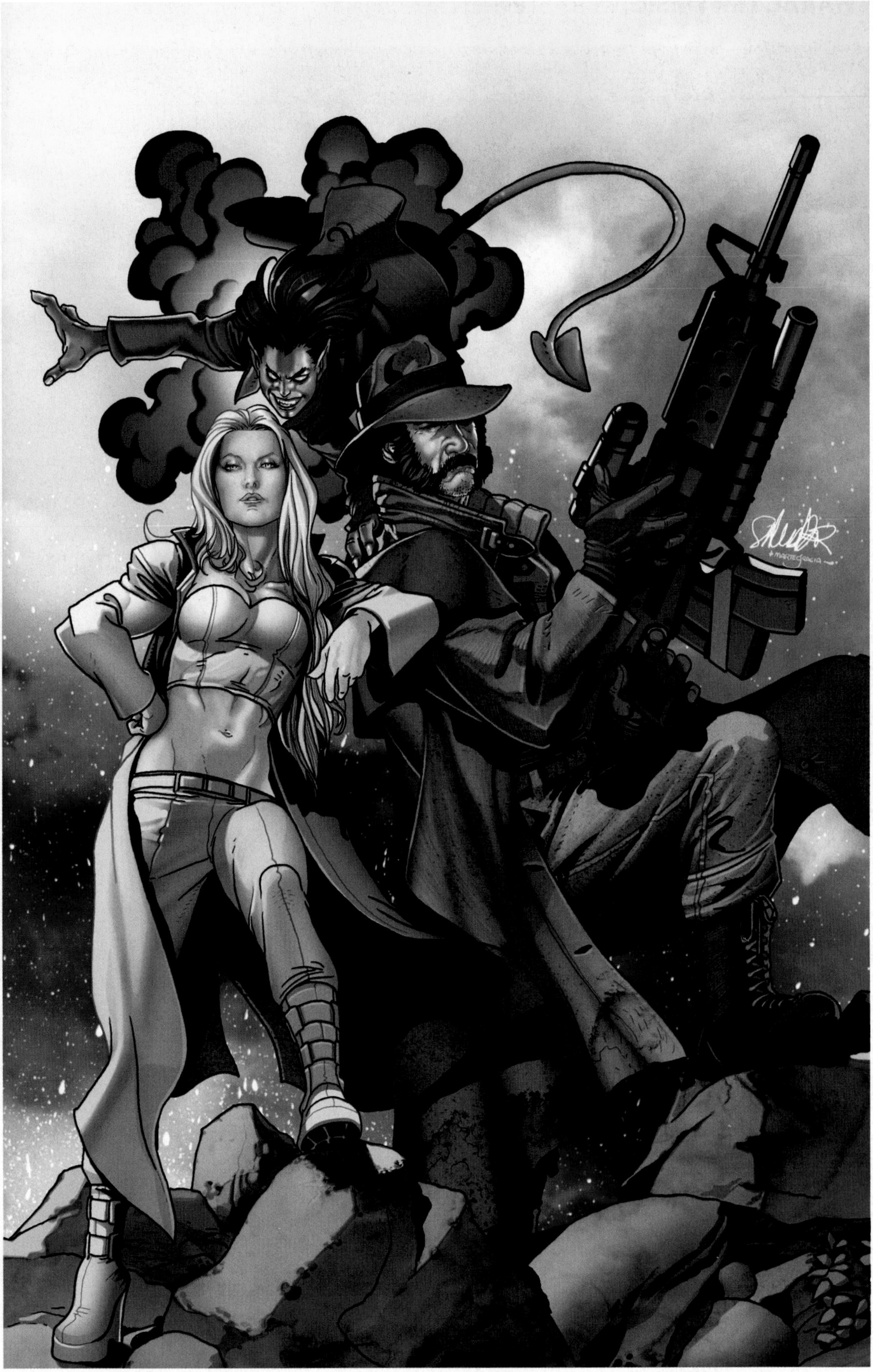

***X-TREME X-MEN #1* VARIANT** BY SALVADOR LARROCA & MARTE GRACIA

CHARACTER DESIGNS BY STEPHEN SEGOVIA

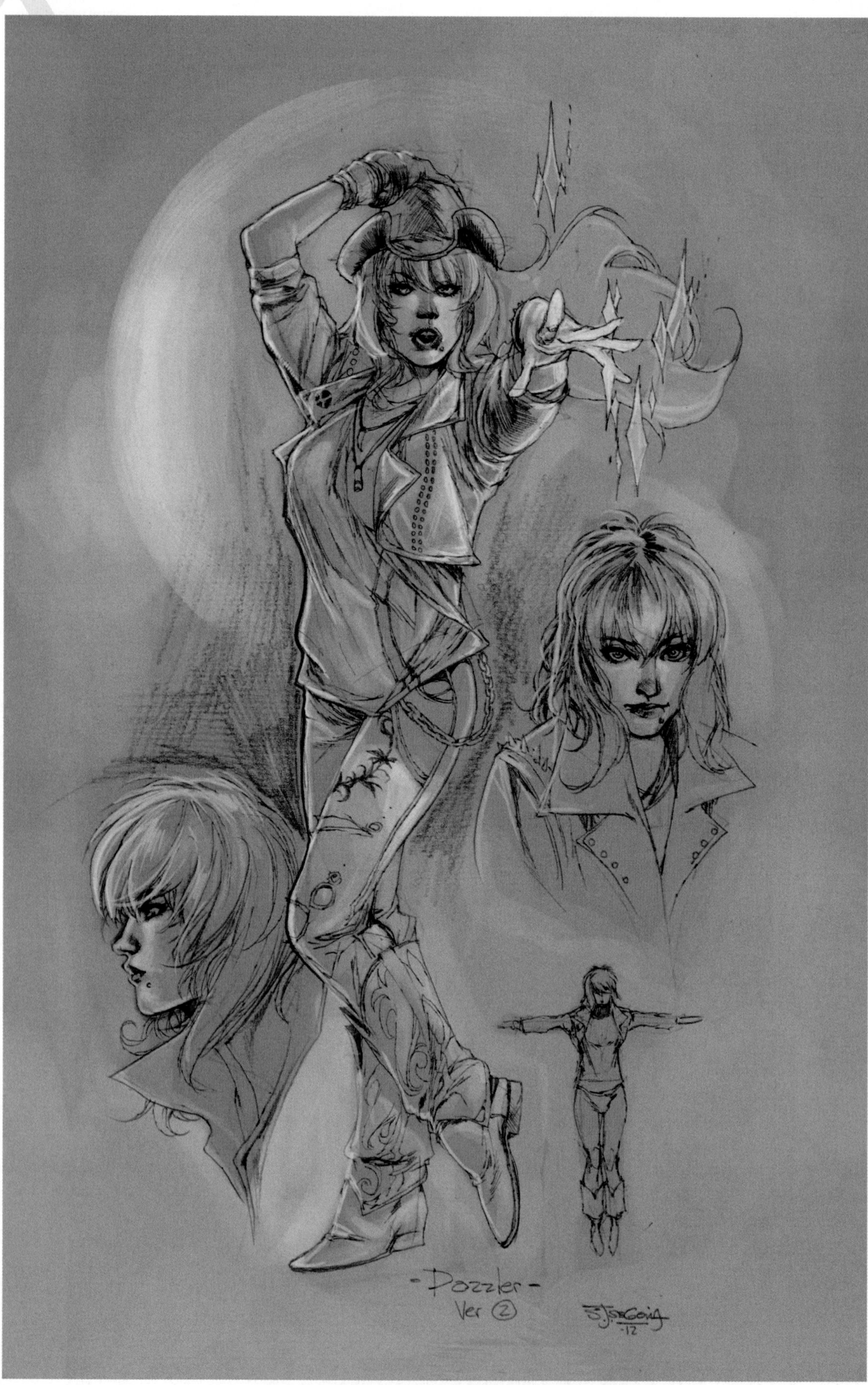

-Dazzler-
Ver 2
S.J. SEGOVIA '12

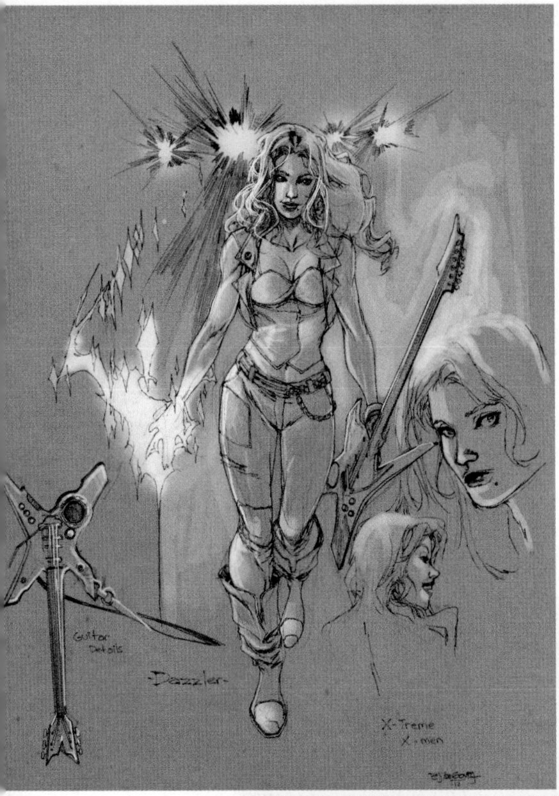
Guitar Details
-Dazzler-
X-Treme X-men

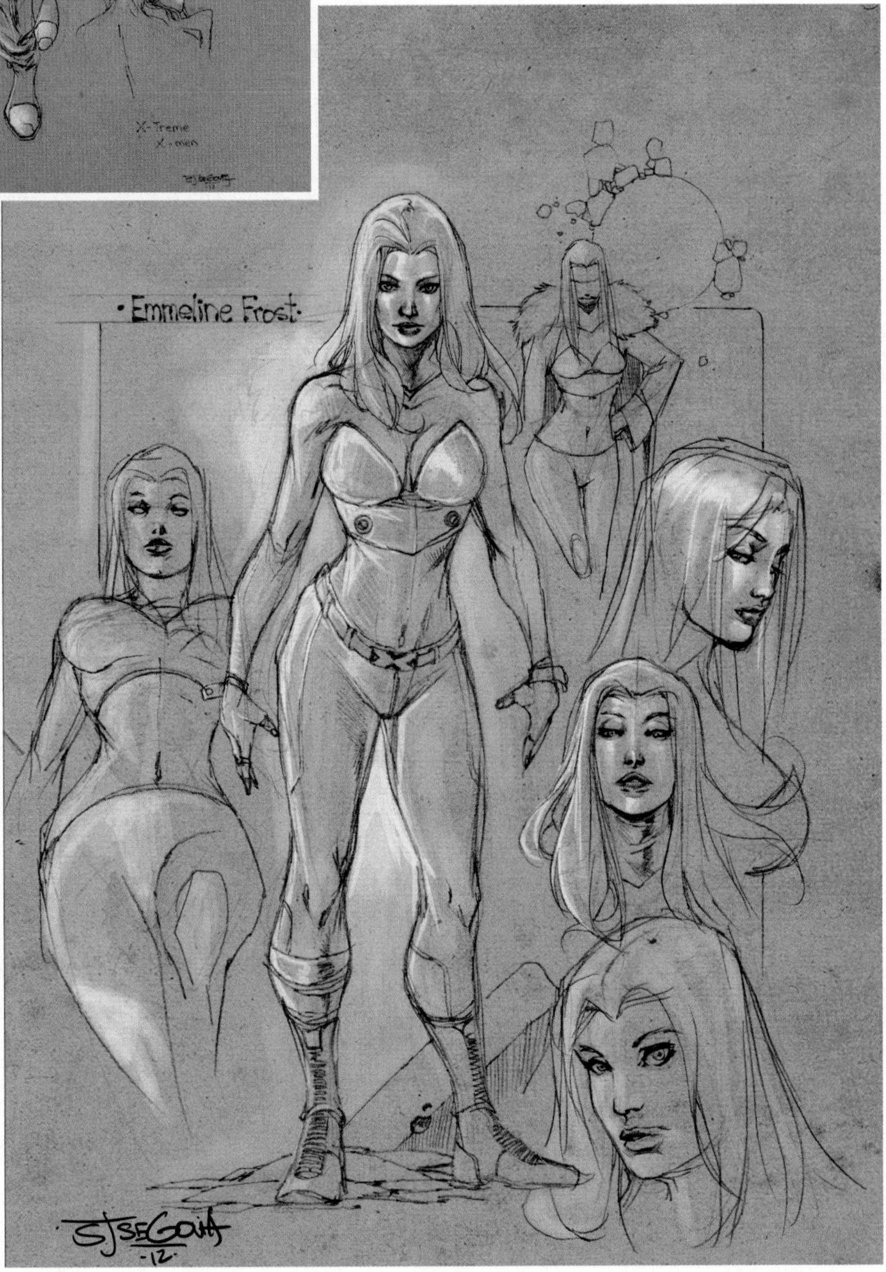
·Emmeline Frost·
SJ SEGOVIA
·12·

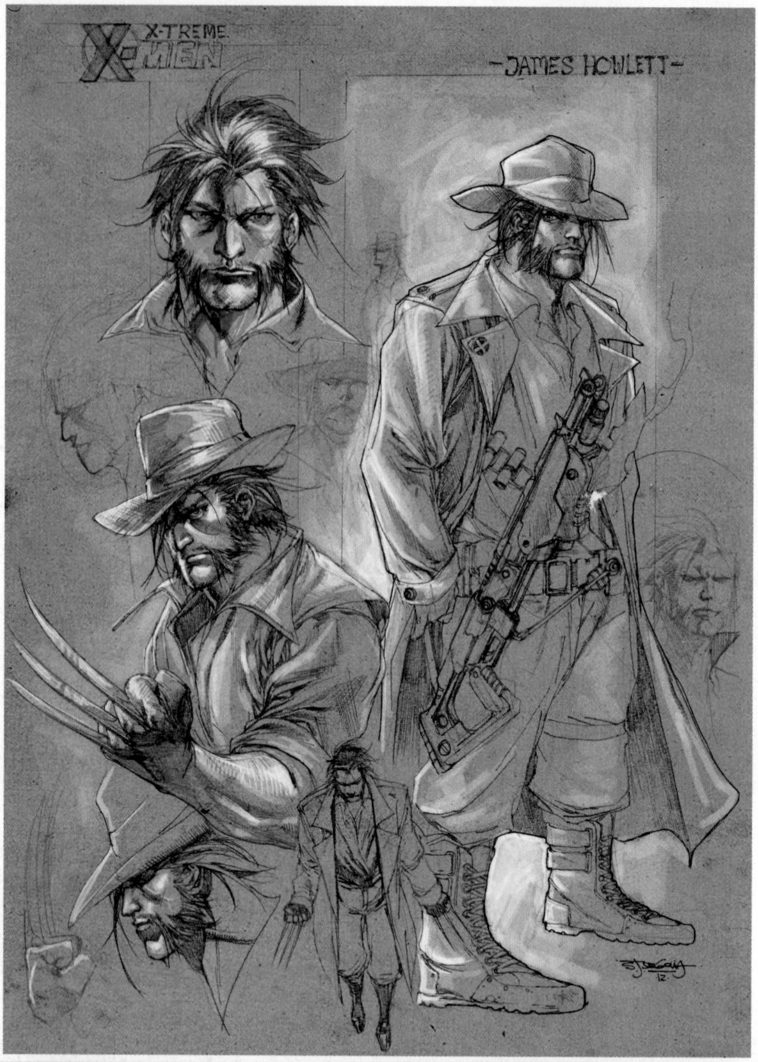
X-TREME X-MEN
-JAMES HOWLETT-

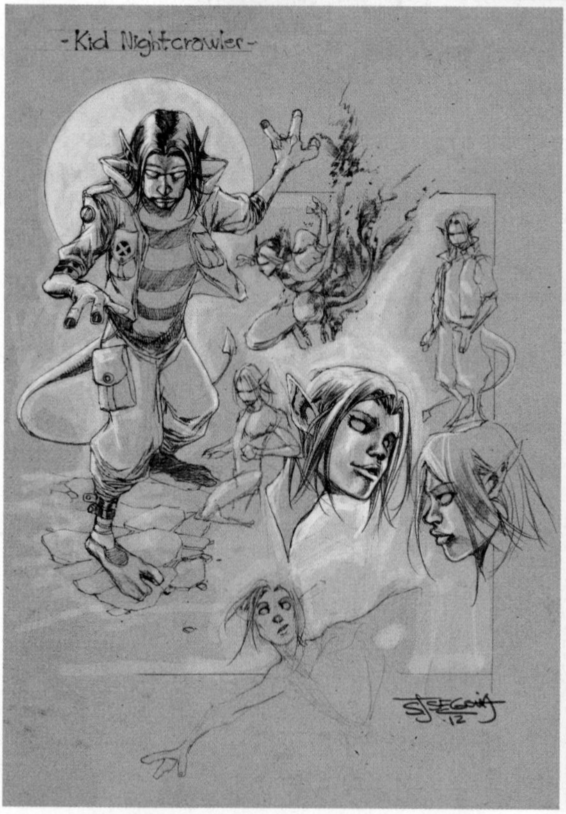
-Kid Nightcrawler-

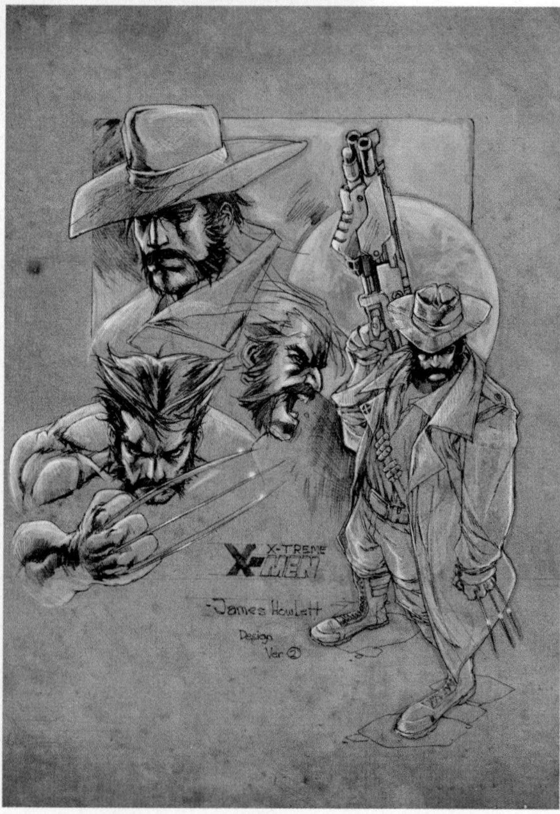
X-TREME X-MEN
-James Howlett
Design
Ver 2